TeenCoder™ Series

TeenCoder™: Java Programming

Student Textbook

Second Edition

Copyright 2013

Homeschool Programming, Inc.

TeenCoder™: Java Programming

Second Edition

ISBN: 978-0-9830749-7-7

Terms of Use

This course is copyright protected. Copyright 2013 © Homeschool Programming, Inc. Purchase of this course constitutes your agreement to the Terms of Use. You are not allowed to distribute any part of the course materials by any means to anyone else. You are not allowed to make it available for free (or fee) on any other source of distribution media, including the Internet, by means of posting the file, or a link to the file on newsgroups, forums, blogs or any other location. You may reproduce (print or copy) course materials as needed for your personal use only.

Disclaimer

Homeschool Programming, Inc, and their officers and shareholders, assume no liability for damage to personal computers or loss of data residing on personal computers arising due to the use or misuse of this course material. Always follow instructions provided by the manufacturer of 3rd party programs that may be included or referenced by this course.

Contact Us

You may contact Homeschool Programming, Inc. through the information and links provided on our website: http://www.HomeschoolProgramming.com. We welcome your comments and questions regarding this course or other related programming courses you would like to study!

Other Courses

Homeschool Programming, Inc. currently has two product lines for students: KidCoder™ and TeenCoder™. Our KidCoder™ Series provides easy, step-by-step programming curriculum for 4th through 12th graders. The Visual Basic series teaches introductory programming concepts in a fun, graphical manner. The Web Design series lets students create their own websites in HTML. Our TeenCoder™ Series provides introductory programming curriculum for high-school students. These courses are college-preparatory material designed for the student who may wish to pursue a career in Computer Science or enhance their transcript with a technical elective. Students can learn C#, Java, game programming, and Android application development.

3rd Party Copyrights

This course teaches Java™ as the programming language using the Eclipse™ Integrated Development Environment. Sun, the Sun logo, Sun Microsystems, Java, and all Java-related trademarks are trademarks or registered trademarks of Sun Microsystems, Inc. and Oracle Corporation. Eclipse, Eclipse logos, and related trademarks are properties of the Eclipse Foundation.

Instructional Videos

This course may be accompanied by optional Instructional Videos. These Flash-based videos will play directly from a DVD drive on the student's computer. Instructional Videos are supplements to the Student Textbook, covering every chapter and lesson with fun, animated re-enforcement of the main topics.

Instructional Videos are intended for students who enjoy a more audio-visual style of learning. They are not replacements for the Student Textbook, which is still required to complete this course! However by watching the Instructional Videos first, students may begin each textbook chapter and lesson already having some grasp of the material to be read. Where applicable, the videos will also show "Screencasts" of a real programmer demonstrating some concept or activity within the software development environment.

This Student Textbook and accompanying material are entirely sufficient to complete the course successfully! Instructional Videos are optional for students who would benefit from the alternate presentation of the material. For more information or to purchase the videos separately, please refer to the product descriptions on our website: http://www.HomeschoolProgramming.com.

Table of Contents

Terms of Use 3

Disclaimer 3

Contact Us 3

Other Courses 3

3rd Party Copyrights 3

Instructional Videos 4

Table of Contents 5

Before You Begin 9

Minimum Hardware and Software Requirements 9

Conventions Used in This Text 10

What You Will Learn and Do In This Course 11

What You Need to Know Before Starting 11

Getting Help 11

Course Errata 12

Chapter One: Introduction to Java Programming 13

Lesson One: Overview of Computer Programming and Java 13

Lesson Two: Parts of a Programming Language 18

Lesson Three: The Java Platform 21

Lesson Four: The Java Integrated Development Environments 26

Activity: Install Course Software and JDK 28

Chapter Two: Getting Started with Java 31

Lesson One: Writing Your First Program 31

Lesson Two: Building and Running from the Command Line 37

Lesson Three: Java Classes and Packages 41

Activity: Show Time! 45

Chapter Three: The Eclipse IDE 47

Lesson One: The Eclipse Online Community 47

Activity: Install Eclipse 49

TeenCoder™: Java Programming

Lesson Two: Eclipse Java IDE 50

Lesson Three: Creating an Eclipse Project 54

Lesson Four: Help and Reference Documentation 62

Activity: Eclipse "ShowTime" Project 66

Chapter Four: Data Types and Variables 67

Lesson One: Primitive Data Types 67

Lesson Two: Variables 69

Lesson Three: Reference Data Types 77

Lesson Four: Printing Data 79

Activity: Your First Variables 82

Chapter Five: Working With Strings 83

Lesson One: Comparing Strings 83

Lesson Two: Common String Operations 85

Lesson Three: Formatting and Building Strings 88

Lesson Four: Converting Between Strings and Numbers 93

Activity: String Theory 95

Chapter Six: User Input 97

Lesson One: Using Command Line Parameters 97

Lesson Two: Interactive User Input 100

Lesson Three: Validating User Input 105

Activity: Conversation Piece 107

Chapter Seven: Basic Flow Control 109

Lesson One: Logical Expressions and Relational Operators 109

Lesson Two: Using the "if" Statement 117

Lesson Three: For Loops 121

Lesson Four: While Loops 124

Activity: Fun Factorials! 129

Chapter Eight: Writing Methods 131

Lesson One: Writing and Calling Methods 131

Lesson Two: Method Parameters and Return Values 134

Lesson Three: Calling Methods 137

Activity: Checkerboard 141

Chapter Nine: Debugging and Exceptions 143

Lesson One: Logic Errors, Runtime Errors and Exceptions 143

Lesson Two: Finding Runtime Errors 145

Lesson Three: The Eclipse Debugger 149

Activity: Bug Hunt 158

Chapter Ten: Object-Oriented Java Programming 159

Lesson One: Object-Oriented Concepts 159

Lesson Two: Defining a Class 161

Lesson Three: Public, Private and Protected Members 165

Lesson Four: Constructors 167

Lesson Five: Object Interfaces 169

Lesson Six: Static Members 172

Activity: Let's Go Racing! 174

Chapter Eleven: Graphical Java Programs 175

Lesson One: Java Swing 175

Lesson Two: Creating a Simple Window 177

Lesson Three: Event-Driven Programming 183

Lesson Four: Layout Managers 189

Activity: Phone Dialer 198

Chapter Twelve: Swing Input Controls 199

Lesson One: Text and Numeric Input 199

Lesson Two: List Input 207

Lesson Three: Option Input 212

Activity: Pizza Place 216

Chapter Thirteen: Arrays and Collections 217

Lesson One: Arrays 217

Lesson Two: Java Lists 222

Lesson Three: Iterators 228

Activity: Baseball Stats 231

Chapter Fourteen: Recursion, Sorting, and Searching 233

Lesson One: Recursion 233

Lesson Two: Sorting Algorithms 237

Lesson Three: Searching Algorithms 244

Activity: Recursive Binary Search 246

Chapter Fifteen: Inheritance and Polymorphism 247

Lesson One: Jail Break! 247

Lesson Two: Base Classes and Derived Classes 249

Lesson Three: Using References to Base and Derived Classes 253

Lesson Four: Overriding Base Methods 255

Lesson Five: The "Object" Base Class 257

Lesson Six: Using Base Features from Derived Classes 259

Activity: Game Pieces 262

Chapter Sixteen: Final Project 263

Lesson One: The Jail Break Activity Starter 263

Activity One: Exploring the Activity Starter 264

Activity Two: Completing JailBreak.reset() 265

Activity Three: Selecting Game Pieces 265

Activity Four: Moving Game Pieces 266

Activity Five: Capturing Game Pieces 266

Activity Six: Ending the Game 267

What's Next? 269

Index 271

Before You Begin

Please read the following topics before you begin the course.

Minimum Hardware and Software Requirements

This is a hands-on programming course! You will be installing the Java Development Kit (JDK) and Eclipse Integrated Development Environment (IDE) on your computer, which must meet the following minimum requirements:

Computer Hardware

Your computer must meet the following minimum specifications:

	Minimum
CPU	1.6GHz or faster processor
RAM	1024 MB
Display	1024 x 768 or higher resolution
Hard Disk Size	3GB available space
DVD Drive	DVD-ROM drive

Operating Systems

Your computer operating system must match one of the following:

Windows XP (x86) with Service Pack 3 or above (except Starter Edition)
Windows Vista (x86 and x64) with Service Pack 2 or above (except Starter Edition)
Windows 7 (x86 and x64)
Windows 8 or Windows 8 Pro (excluding Windows 8 RT)
Apple Mac OS X (10.6 or above)

Conventions Used in This Text

This course will use certain styles (fonts, borders, etc.) to highlight text of special interest.

```
Source code will be in 11-point Consolas font, in a single box like this.
```

Variable names will be in **12-point Consolas bold** text, similar to the way they will look in your development environment. For example: **myVariable**.

Function names, properties and keywords will be in **bold face** type, so that they are easily readable.

This picture highlights important concepts within a lesson.

Sidebars may contain additional information, tips, or background material.

This icon indicates a hands-on activity that you will complete on your computer.

What You Will Learn and Do In This Course

TeenCoder™: Java Programming will teach you the fundamentals of writing your own computer programs. You will be writing both console-based and graphical programs using the Java programming language. This course is geared for high-school students who have expressed an interest in computer programming or who are looking for college-preparatory material.

Starting with the second chapter, you will complete a hands-on programming project at the end of each chapter. These projects will increase in complexity as you learn more about the Java language.

What You Need to Know Before Starting

You are expected to already know the basics of computer use before beginning this course. You need to know how to use the keyboard and mouse to select and run programs, use application menu systems, and work with your Windows operating system or Apple Mac OS. You should understand how to store and load files on your hard disk and how to navigate your file system and directory structures with Windows Explorer or Mac OS Finder. You should also have some experience with text editors and using web browsers to find helpful information on the Internet.

Software Versions

You will be using the free *Java Development Kit (JDK)* and the free *Eclipse IDE for Java Developers* software to complete this course. You will download and install these free programs from the Internet. Your course contains links to download and install instructions in PDF format on our website, http://www.HomeschoolProgramming.com. 3rd party websites may from time to time change their download process or release newer versions of their software. Our website will contain updated versions of the instructions as needed.

Getting Help

All courses come with a Solution Guide PDF and fully coded solutions for all activities. Simply install the "Solution Files" from your course setup program and you will be able to refer to the solutions as needed from the "Solution Menu". If you are confused about any activity you can see how we solved the problem! You may also contact us through the "Support" area of our website for further assistance.

Course Errata

We welcome your feedback regarding any course details that are unclear or that may need correction. Please contact us using our online "Getting Help" form. You can find a list of course errata for this edition on our website, http://www.HomeschoolProgramming.com.

Support for Multiple Operating Systems

This course was developed for use both on Microsoft Windows and Apple Mac OS X operating systems. The Java platform is compatible with both environments (and others). We will point out in text or by screen shots any differences between the operating systems. Where necessary, we will provide dedicated sets of instructions for handling each operating system. Be sure to follow the instructions that are right for the operating system you are using!

Directory Naming Conventions

On Wthe directory pathsg systems, directory paths are traditionally represented with backslashes ("\") between folder names like this: "**TeenCoder\Java Programming**", but forward slashes ("/") work also. Mac OS directories use forward slashes as in "**TeenCoder/Java Programming**". In order to avoid cluttering the textbook with both representations, each time we specify a path, we will simply use one style. Be sure to change that style to match your operating system requirements if needed.

Advanced Placement Students

Your course Student Menu contains a variety of "bonus" material, including additional lessons and information for students studying for the Advanced Placement[1] (AP) "Computer Science A" exam. The College Board has changed the requirements for this exam starting in the 2014-2015 school year! For updated supplemental lessons needed for the 2014-2015 AP CS A exam, please visit our website. You will find a link to the current AP resources on the *TeenCoder: Java Programming* product description page.

---

1 AP and Advanced Placement Program are registered trademarks of the College Entrance Examination Board, which was not involved in the production of and does not endorse this product.

Chapter One: Introduction to Java Programming

In this chapter we will describe the major characteristics of high-level computer programming languages. You will learn about the history of Java, the programming language used in this course. We will also introduce you to the tools you will use to write Java programs.

Lesson One: Overview of Computer Programming and Java

What language does your computer speak? It doesn't speak English, or Spanish or French. Your computer only speaks one native language: Machine Language. This language is a binary language, as it only uses two symbols: the numbers 0 and 1.

So, will you ever have to program your computer in machine language? If you plan on studying Computer Science in college, you can count on it. Every Computer Science department has at least one professor who loves to torture freshmen with machine language exercises. However, would you want to write machine code for all your programs? To answer this question, let's take a look at an example.

Let's say you needed to write a program to compute the cost of a shirt, plus tax. The computation on paper would look like this:

```
shirt cost = shirt price + tax
```

That's pretty simple and straightforward. Now let's take a look at that same computation in an imaginary machine language:

```
0010 0000 0000 0100
0100 0000 0000 1100
1001 0000 0001 0110
```

That's clear as mud! How do you come up with those numbers? Well, first you need to know the binary code for the addition instruction. Then you would need to figure out exactly where in your computer's memory the cost and tax for a shirt are stored. After that, you need to find an empty slot in memory to save the result of your addition. Once you have all this data, you simply arrange the binary digits in the precise order that your computer understands. Then, voila! This simple computer computer only takes about 5 days to write.

That's not much fun, but fortunately we have *high-level* programming languages. These languages allow us to write a program in a human - readable form called *source code*. When the source code is completed a *compiler* program takes care of translating the human-readable source code into machine language.

Most programming languages that we use today are high-level languages. These languages hide all the internal details about the Central Processing Unit (CPU) and much of the Operating System (OS). Each language defines powerful objects and operations that may take many CPU instructions to complete.

 High-level languages evolved in the late 1970s and 1980s. These languages allow a programmer to write programs in a human-readable language. A compiler then transforms this English-like program code into machine language.

Even though high-level languages are easier to read than machine language, the programs written in these languages still must follow strict rules in order to make the computer do exactly what you want. Computers do not have the ability to reason independently. They do *exactly* what they are told to do! For this reason, programming languages cannot have any unclear or fuzzy statements that may be interpreted in different ways. For instance, you cannot tell your computer that you want it to "add some numbers, or something". A computer does not know how to identify "some numbers", nor does it know how to do "something". Computers require direct and specific commands.

Let's revisit our shirt example and look at the same statement written in a typical programming language:

```
shirtPrice = shirtCost + tax;
```

This is much easier to understand than machine code! Instead of referring to data with binary digits, we can use descriptive names such as **shirtPrice**, **shirtCost** and **tax**. We are also using easily-recognizable math operators, like the plus sign, to describe the operation that is being performed.

A Brief History of Java

There are many high-level computer programming languages available today. This diversity of languages is due to both the variety of computer hardware and the needs of computer users. Different programming languages exist to solve different types of problems. Some languages are used to create quick and easy graphical applications. Other languages may be specialized to perform extremely precise computations, or support business needs, or run small handheld electronic devices. Some languages are used primarily to write Internet applications. You may have heard of older languages such as Pascal, COBOL, or FORTRAN. More modern languages such as Visual Basic, C, C++ and C# are widely used today.

In the early 1990s, a company called Sun Microsystems created a new programming language called "Java". Java was created from the ground up to use the most modern programming concepts such as object-oriented development. Java was easier to use than some previous languages such as C++, which made it instantly popular with new programmers.

Java also allowed programmers to write a program one time and then run it on many different operating systems. Earlier languages such as C++ would need to be re-built or re-compiled from source code each time you wanted to deploy it on a different operating system or hardware platform. In the early 1990s, the Internet connected many different computers together, and Java was able to fill the programming needs of this environment. For many years, Java was the king of Internet programming languages.

The name "Java" came from a design meeting at Sun Microsystems in the early 1990s. Scores of designers and programmers were brainstorming about possible names when someone yelled out "Java". The name was unique and non-technical – and it stuck!

Java Versions

The Java language has undergone many changes since it was first created in the early 1990s. The first version of Java (version 1.0) was publicly released in January of 1996. For the next two years, Sun Microsystems released a new version of Java each year with versions 1.1 in 1997 and 1.2 in 1998. During the next 8 years, they would release a new version every two years, with versions 1.3 (2000), 1.4 (2002), 1.5 (2004) and 1.6 (2006). When Java version 1.5 was released, Sun also decided to refer to the JDK releases by the minor release number. This means that version 1.5 was commonly called Java 5 and the subsequent release, version 1.6, was called Java 6.

In 2009, a company called the Oracle Corporation purchased Sun Microsystems and became the new owners of the Java language. The process of changing companies caused a delay in the next version of Java. Java 1.7 (or Java 7), was released in the summer of 2011, and Java 8 is planned for late 2013.

In this course you can use any Java version from 1.5 or higher. In our examples, we will be using Java version 1.7, or Java 7. However by the time you are taking this course a later version of Java may be available. If you are using a Mac computer with OS X version 10.6 or above, you will likely have Java 1.6. Nearly all parts of the Java language that we cover in this course are identical between Java 1.5, 1.6, and 1.7, or other versions of Java you may encounter.

Later versions of Java may change the recommended approach in some areas. Our course uses code that will work across all versions, though you may see some build-time warnings in our solution code if using Java 1.7 or later. These warnings may be safely ignored.

Why are we using Java?

Java is the programming language we will use in this course! Why?

- Java is widely used in academics and businesses today, with a large active community of programmers.
- Java is modern and powerful, yet easy to use.
- Java is free to install on your computer!
- High-quality development software is freely available.
- Java is cross-platform, meaning it will work on Windows, Apple Mac OS, and other platforms.
- Java can be used for many interesting tasks, such as writing applications for Android™ mobile phones as you will see in our second-semester *TeenCoder: Android Programming* course!

Legal and Ethical Computing

We cannot go too far into computer programming without first discussing the important topic of *ethics* in computers. Computers are powerful instruments, especially in today's advanced information age. The use of such an instrument should always be guided by good legal, ethical standards.

The Association for Computing Machinery (ACM) has compind a general list of good ethical practices for the field of Computer Science (CS).

The Association for Computing Machinery was formed in 1947 to allow professionals in the (then) new field of computers to meet and share ideas. This group continues this focus today, with members who are either CS or equivalent college graduates or experienced professionals in the field. Computer Science students are also welcome to join as Student Members!

In this list they make the following important points for programmers.

1. Contribute Positively

First and foremost, contribute positively to society and humanity. This principle deals with the quality of life of all people. As people, we have an obligation to protect fundamental human rights and to respect the diversity of all cultures. As programmers, we should always attempt to minimize negative consequences of computing systems, including threats to health and safety. For instance, when you are designing or implementing a software program, you should make every attempt to ensure that your product will be used in a socially responsible way. This means that you should be aware of what users will do with your software and make sure that you agree with the principles of this use. You should never create a software program that has the potential to harm the health or welfare of another person.

2. Do No Harm

The second principle is to always avoid harm to others. "Harm" is any negative consequence, such as an undesirable loss of information, loss of property, or property damage. This principle prohibits use of computing technology in ways that result in harm to users, the general public, employees, or employers. This speaks directly to the creation of viruses and malicious software. These programs have the potential to cause great harm to any user by creating havoc on their personal computer. Creating a program that harms in this way is no different than walking into someone's home and destroying personal property.

All programmers should be aware that even well-intended actions, including those that accomplish assigned duties, may lead to unexpected or un-intentional harm. If this happens, you should make every effort to help fix the resulting damage.

The best way to avoid harming others with your programs is to follow generally accepted standards for system design and testing. As a programmer, you should also make an effort to ensure the program works as advertised. If system features are misrepresented to users, coworkers, or supervisors, you could be personally responsible for any resulting injury.

3. Ensure Software Reliability

A piece of software is only useful if it is reliable. As a programmer, you must ensure that your software is able to perform its required functions under stated conditions for a specified period of time. The reliability of a software system is often measured as the probability that it will experience a failure during normal operating conditions. Software released with errors or "bugs" may not work properly.

4. Honesty

The fourth principle is to be honest and trustworthy. This is true in most things in life and programming is no different. If you are an honest and trustworthy programmer, then it stands to reason that you will not violate the ethics of computing.

Hopefully this is self-explanatory to most people. Computers can be extremely helpful, entertaining devices, but in the wrong hands can be easily used to cause harm. Hackers are programmers who use their talents to invade and disturb the computers of others.

5. Respect Property Rights

The next principle is to always honor property rights, including copyrights and patents. This principle speaks mainly about *software piracy*. This is the theft of software by copying software illegally. Software is created by programmers that get paid for their work. If you obtain their software without paying, you are effectively stealing the software. You should always make sure that the software you are using is a legal, licensed copy. This supports the interests of programmers everywhere.

Programmers should also be sure to give proper credit for *intellectual property*. Intellectual properties are the properties of the mind: artistic works, symbols, music, etc. They are often abstract and difficult to protect, but are property nonetheless and subject to protection under the law. The Internet is a great place to find code samples that solve various programming problems. If you use these samples, be sure to credit the original author in your code. If you do not, then you are effectively plagiarizing or stealing their product.

6. Respect Privacy

The next principle is to always respect the privacy of others. This point is most important when dealing with the distressing topic of identity or personal information theft. Any use of a computer to steal and/or publish the private information of others is wrong and unethical. Any information that you have not been given explicit permission (from the owner) to use should be considered private information. If you have access to private information, always treat this information with the respect that it deserves.

7. Respect Confidentiality

The last principle is to always honor confidentiality. If you have made an explicit promise to honor someone's confidentiality or if you stumble across confidential information in the course of your programming, you have a responsibility to honor that confidentiality. The ethical rule is to respect all obligations of confidentiality to employers, clients, and users unless relieved from such obligations by requirements of the law.

Lesson Two: Parts of a Programming Language

A programming language is fully defined by its *specification*. A language specification typically contains a number of key elements: *syntax*, *semantics*, *data types*, *core library*, and *implementation*.

Syntax

The *syntax* of a programming language describes the possible combinations of letters or symbols that are used to form statements and expressions in a program. The syntax of most programming languages uses letters, numbers, and symbols arranged in a meaningful manner to a human reader. This means that the programming language uses text similar to a natural spoken language. The Java language syntax uses a lexical structure where individual keywords are combined to form larger expressions. With well-written code, these larger expressions should be easily readable and understood by humans.

Semantics

The *semantics* of a programming language is the meaning given to a combination of keywords or expressions. This is an important addition to the syntax of a language, since the semantics make sure that the language is understandable. Without good semantics, it is entirely possible to string together a syntactically correct expression that has no meaning. Let's look at an example of this in everyday English. The following sentence is complete, syntactically correct English.

"Needless feet color simply."

This sentence has a subject and a predicate, a noun and a verb. But there is no meaning; it is complete gibberish. This is why we need semantics. Semantics force the language to be both correct and meaningful.

Data Types

Data types are the next key element in a high-level programming language. A data type describes a piece of information that a program can use. For instance, a language may call a number an **integer** type, or it may refer to some text as a **string** type. This distinction allows a programmer to perform different kinds of operations on information based on its type. For instance, if you wanted to mathematically add two pieces of data together, both pieces of data should be some sort of numerical type. You would not want to add a number to a letter; this would not make any real sense. A language with strong data type rules will not allow you to even attempt to add a letter type to a number type, since the language understands that this is not a valid operation.

There are two ways that a programming language checks a program's code for type-related problems: *static* and *dynamic*. Static checking is done by the compiler portion of the programming software. This is done while the source code is being converted into machine code. If any of the operations on data types are illegal according to the language definition, the compilation will fail and you will not be able to run the program. By contrast, dynamic checking is done while the program is running. Dynamic checking may catch errors that are not visible when the program is being compiled, but become evident when the program is running.

Core Library

Another key element to most languages is the existence of a *core library*. A core or standard library is a set of common code that can be used by all programmers for a given language. This common code is typically broken up into *functions* or *objects* which perform useful jobs.

To understand this concept better, let's first define a simple *function*. A function is the name given to a section of code that performs a specific task. For example, consider the function below in Java syntax:

```
double calculate_circle_area(double radius)
{
    return 3.14159265 * (radius * radius);
}
```

This function simply calculates the area of a circle using the formula "area = PI x (radius x radius)". So, if you needed to calculate the areas of circles from different parts of your program, you could just call this function instead of typing out the full formula every time. You can think of functions as programming shortcuts. Common, often-used code is written once and then referenced whenever it is needed. We will talk more about functions in future chapters.

The core library contains many common functions for you to use. Some commonly used functions are those which collect user input and display output, perform mathematical calculations, manage organized groups of data, convert between different data types, and so on. Core libraries are a great addition to any language, as they cut down the amount of time that a programmer has to spend writing functions for common tasks.

Implementation

The final element to any programming language is its *implementation*. The implementation of a language provides a way to execute or run a program. Programs can be either *compiled* or *interpreted*. Programs that are compiled convert the original source code to an executable file filled with machine language. The executable file can be run only on one specific operating system or CPU. Older programming languages like C and C++ are compiled languages.

Programs that are interpreted are not compiled into machine code for a specific operating system. Instead the source code or an intermediate *bytecode* is run within some interpreting software on the target computer. The Java language is an interpreted language. Interpreted programs may run slower than compiled programs because the interpreter must perform the compilation from source to machine code "on-the-fly". However modern Java platforms will perform this conversion to machine code quickly one time and generally avoid re-converting the same piece of source code over and over again.

Implementation is an important concept when you are dealing with multiple platforms for your programs. A platform is a specific configuration of both hardware and software. A Windows operating system running on an AMD processor is one type of platform. An Apple Mac OS computer running on an Intel processor is another possible platform. Each environment may have its own unique machine language and operating system APIs. Part of the job of the compiler is to translate a program's source code into the "native tongue" of the target platform. If your compiled program will be run on multiple platforms, you must re-compile it once for each target platform. Or, you could use an interpreted language where the interpreter itself is native to the target platform, and you just provide the source code or intermediate bytecode to the interpreter.

Lesson Three: The Java Platform

The *Java Platform* contains a number of different components. Some components are used by all Java programs that run on any computer. Other components are used by developers (such as yourself) who are writing the Java programs in the first place. In this lesson we are going to take a look at each of the major components and explain how they all tie together to form the Java Platform.

The Java Runtime Environment (JRE)

One of the central features to the Java programming language is the ability for a programmer to write one program that will run exactly the same way, without any extra effort, on many different operating systems. Each operating system has its own unique mixture of "native" Application Programming Interfaces (APIs) that let programmers interact with the operating system and underlying hardware.

When you write a "native" program for one operating system, that program has been compiled down to machine code that talks directly to the APIs for that operating system.

As you can see in the diagram below, a native application for one platform will interact with the API exposed by that operating system. The operating system will then manage the hardware for that specific platform.

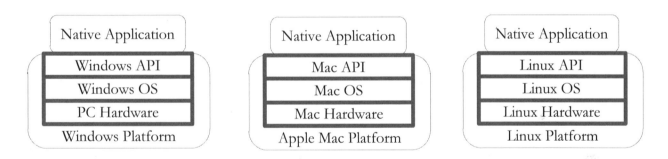

A native program compiled for one platform cannot run on any other platform because it is so tightly tied to the native APIs.

Java programs, on the other hand, are not tightly tied to any one operating system's APIs! Instead Java programs are written to a generic standard called the *Java Virtual Machine* (JVM). Each operating system will have its own JVM that translates Java bytecode down to the native operating system APIs. This is how the Java platform allows programmers to write and build a program once, and have confidence that it will work the same way on any operating system that has a JVM.

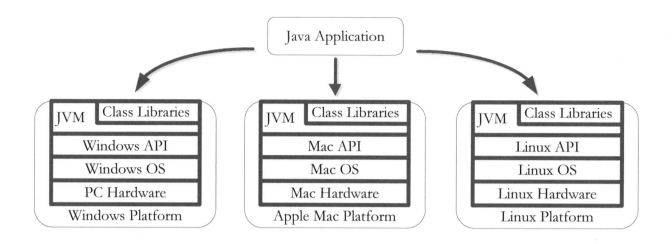

In addition to the JVM itself, Java programs can rely on the *Java Class Library*. The Class Library is a large collection of useful, pre-built objects that make your programming job easier. You won't have to re-invent the wheel each time you need to perform some common task, because the odds are that someone has already written that code for you!

The combination of the JVM and Java Class Libraries is called the Java Runtime Environment or JRE. Your job as a Java programmer is to write code using the standard Java language and class libraries, and let the JRE take care of translating your code to a native application that will run on any operating system.

 = Java Runtime Environment (JRE)

Before any Java program will run on a computer, the JRE must first be installed on that computer! Most likely your own computer already has some version of the JRE installed. If not, you can download and install the JRE in order to let Java programs run on your computer. End users typically don't perform this process themselves – a professionally written Java program will come with an installer that will add the JRE to the target computer if it does not already exist.

The Java Development Kit (JDK)

The second significant part of the Java Platform is the *Java Development Kit* (JDK). As you might expect from the name, this component is used by developers or programmers who are writing Java applications. When you install the JDK, you also get all parts of the JRE as well, so you can run your programs as soon as you build them!

The JDK contains a number of programs useful for developers. We'll describe just a few of them below.

javac	This is the "compiler", a program which takes your source code (*.java) and coverts it to the generic bytecode (*.class) that can be run by any JVM.
javadoc	This utility can scan your Java source code looking for specially formatted comments, and turn those comments into HTML documentation for other programmers to read.
jar	This utility allows you to package together a number of different Java objects (*.class files) into a single *.jar file. It is often more convenient to distribute an application by packaging together all of the pieces into a single JAR file.

As a Java programmer you are responsible for writing *source code*: one or more text files ending in a *.java extension. This source code is the human-readable program that follows the Java language syntax. By reading the .java source code you should be able to tell exactly what a program will do!

Once you have finished writing your source code, the "javac" compiler will be used to turn that source into the generic bytecode that will run in a JVM. This bytecode is stored in a *.class file that has the same name as your *.java source code.

Taken together, the JRE and JDK are called the *Java Platform*. Over time, updated versions of the Java Platform have been released. Recent versions are Java 5, 6, and 7 (also called 1.5,

1.6, and 1.7 by developers), and newer versions may be released by the time you are taking this course. You may already have some version of the JRE on your computer from the installation of other Java applications.

Using a Command Prompt or Console

Some of your intial Java tasks will be completed from a *command prompt* or *terminal console*. Unlike a familiar graphical application, command prompts use text commands to interact with the operating system. Your first job will be to figure out if your computer has Java installed, and you'll do that from a command prompt.

You might not have used a command prompt before! If not, the process of finding and launching the command prompt or using commands from the prompt may be confusing. Please see our "Getting Started with Command Prompts" document from your Student Menu for extra help on using command prompts in Windows and Mac OS.

Identifying Your Java Platform on Windows

On a Windows computer, to figure out what JRE you might already have, open a "Command Prompt" from your Windows Start Menu. Select "Start → Programs → Accessories" and click on the "Command Prompt".

Then from the command prompt line, type "**java -version**" and hit "Enter". If you already have Java installed on your computer, the java version will be displayed as shown.

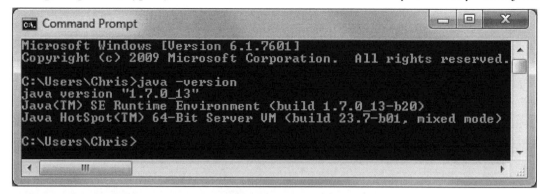

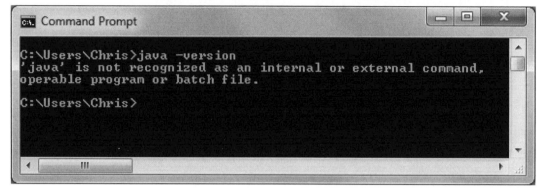

If Java is not installed then you will get an error message indicating that "java" is not recognized.

You can also open the Windows Control Panel to look for a Java Control Panel icon. If you find this icon then Java is installed, and you can double-click on the Java icon to bring up a configuration dialog allowing control of Java behavior on your computer.

Finally, on a Windows computer you can also open the "Programs and Features" or "Add/Remove Programs" icon in the Control Panel and look for a Java entry from Oracle or Sun Microsystems like this:

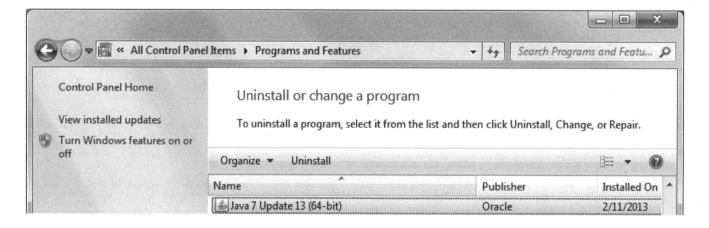

Any of these steps should tell you what version of Java (if any) is installed on your Windows computer. Notice that the "Java" icons only represent the JRE portion of the Java Platform! You most likely do not have the JDK installed on your computer prior to starting this course. When we finish installing the JDK you will see additional lines in the panel above showing the "Java SE Development Kit…".

Identifying Your Java Platform on Mac OS

On a Mac computer, you can figure out the Java version by opening the Terminal program by choosing "Go → Utilities → Terminal". Then you can type "java -version" and hit "Enter".

If Java is not installed you may see the following dialog, especially if you are running Mac OS X version 10.7:

To install Java on your Mac, just choose the "Install" button and follow the directions on the screen.

Multiple Java Versions

It is actually possible to have more than one version of the JRE and JDK installed on your computer. Some early Java programs may be written that require an early version, while a later Java program might require a more up-to-date version. Usually later versions of the JRE are backwards-compatible, meaning the later JRE will run bytecode compiled by earlier JDKs. However over time some of the earliest parts of the Java language or class library have changed enough that the latest JREs cannot support the earliest Java programs.

If you have multiple versions of the JRE or JDK installed on your computer, when running the Java program or using the JDK components you need to be sure which version you are using. This is typically done using environment variables within your operating system or carefully specifying fully-qualified paths when launching programs.

Lesson Four: The Java Integrated Development Environments

Writing a Java application involves a number of distinct steps. First you have to create the text file (*.java) containing the source code. Then you have to compile that source file into Java bytecode (*.class). Finally you have to run the application and see if it works!

Building Programs Manually

You can write your source code entirely in a basic text editor that comes with your operating system. This is, in fact, exactly what you will be doing in the next chapter. A text editor is any software where you can create and edit text files, like Notepad on Windows or TextEdit on Mac OS. When you want to compile and run the program, you can then go to a command line and run the **javac** command to compile the program, and then use the **java** JVM to run the compiled bytecode. Let's look at an example on Windows:

```
> "\Program Files\Java\jdk1.7.0_13\bin\javac" MyProgram.java
> java MyProgram
```

The example above shows the commands you would type into a Windows command prompt window. The first line will use the "javac" compiler from the JDK to change the "MyProgram.java" source code into "MyProgram.class" byte code. The second line will then run the "MyProgram.class" bytecode in the JVM installed on the computer.

To do the same things on a Mac computer, you would open a Terminal window, navigate to the folder with your code files and type in the same commands (but you don't need the full path to your javac compiler):

```
> javac MyProgram.java
> java MyProgram
```

For simple programs with a few source files, this command-line procedure is not hard to do. However, programmers have come up with automatic systems to make writing, building, and running code much easier!

Integrated Development Environments

Today, most programmers use *Integrated Development Environments* or IDEs to build computer programs. IDEs are graphical software packages that combine a fancy text editor to write your code, integrated help systems, and project settings that keep track of all your source files. IDEs also support an automatic *build process* to run all of the source files through the compiler to produce output files that are ready to run. Most IDEs will have a *debugger* tool you can use to examine and find errors in your program while it is running. Everything you need as a programmer can be found in your IDE. There are many different IDEs for the Java language. In this lesson, we will just cover a few of the more popular programs.

Open Source IDEs

Open-source software is source code published and made available to the public. This makes it easy for anyone to copy, enhance and improve the code without paying royalties or fees. Open source code is improved over time through community contributions and cooperation. These communities are composed of individual programmers as well as larger companies.

The concept of open-source products is not new. In fact, the idea was pioneered back in the early 20th century as car manufacturers worked to create newer and more efficient engines and parts for the new automobiles. By freely sharing ideas, these manufacturers were able to innovate faster and more efficiently. Open-source software follows a similar theory: by sharing ideas and source code, we can work together to create better and more powerful software systems.

Java is an open standard that can be implemented on any operating system. So, naturally, a number of open-source IDEs have been developed over time. The Java programming community is very passionate about the language and has released high-quality open-source IDEs that are free for anyone to download and use! These IDEs can usually be modified or extended by specialized plug-ins written by other programmers to do some creative things.

NetBeans and Eclipse

Two of the most popular Java IDEs are NetBeans and Eclipse. These IDEs are both open-source software  written in Java. They are easy to use, have powerful built-in features, and include endless plug-ins to handle the latest programming trends like mobile applications. In addition to the Java language, a programmer can actually use these IDEs to write code in other languages like C, C++, Perl, HTML, XML and PHP.

NetBeans and Eclipse both include standard IDE features like smart code completion, a fully-customizable editor and access to help files for a specific language. The Eclipse IDE is slightly more popular for the Java language, and is the IDE that we will be using in this course.

Other Java IDEs

There are, of course, many other Java IDE software packages available on the market today. Some of these packages are open-source and some are not. The most notable IDEs are JCreator, which is similar in look-and-feel to the Microsoft Visual Studio products, JBuilder, originally created by Borland Software, and IntelliJ IDEA from JetBrains, which is available in both a commercial and open-source edition.

Activity: Install Course Software and JDK

In this activity you will be installing the course files and the JDK on your computer.

Course files	The files that come with this course include material for the student (chapter sample programs, activity starters, instructional documents) and for the teacher (activity solutions, tests, answer keys, etc.).
JDK	The Java Development Kit is a free download from Oracle's website.

Installing the Course Files

The first step to this activity is ensuring the course software is installed on your computer. You may have already run the course setup program to install the Student Files and/or Solution Files before reaching this point. If so you can skip this step and move on to installing the JDK.

The course files are installed by a single setup executable that came with your course. The setup program is called "TeenCoder_JavaProgramming.exe" (for Windows) or "TeenCoder_JavaProgramming.pkg" (for Mac OS). If you received a printed textbook then the course CD in the back of the book contains this setup program, and the setup program should launch automatically when you place the CD in your Windows or Mac OS computer disc drive. Ensure that you are logged in using an administrator account when you launch the setup program. If the setup does not launch automatically, or if you received your course setup program through some alternate process, simply use Windows Explorer or Mac OS Finder to find your setup program and double-click on it to start the process.

The setup executable will offer you the choice of installing the Student Files and/or Solution Files. You may install these components on the same computer (if the student should have free access to the solutions) or on different computers (so the teacher can maintain control over the solutions). For a better understanding of the setup process and the files present in the course material, please refer to the "Getting Started Guide" on our website at http://www.HomeschoolProgramming.com.

Go ahead and perform this setup process now. We recommend installing to the default "C:\TeenCoder\Java Programming" directory for Windows or "/TeenCoder/Java Programming" under your Mac OS user's Home directory. We will refer to this default directory structure in the textbook. The setup program will automatically create a "My Projects" directory under the target directory – this is where all of the student projects will go!

Windows Course Menu Shortcuts

On a Windows computer, once installation is complete you will have a new "TeenCoder" group on your Windows Start Menu. Underneath "TeenCoder" is a "Java Programming" folder. Within that folder are one or two menus for the Student and Solution files (depending on your choices during setup). The look and feel of the Windows Start Menu may change between versions of Windows, but your final menu system should look something like the image to the right (assuming both Student and Solution files were installed).

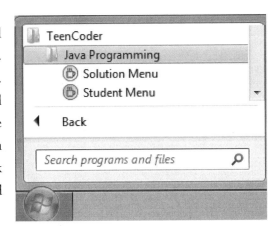

You can find your student "TeenCoder\Java Programming\My Projects" directory from Windows Explorer. Windows 8 users may see the Solution and Student Menu links appear directly on the desktop.

Mac OS Course Menu Shortcuts

Once the installation is completed on your Mac OS computer you will see a new "TeenCoder" image in your user's Home folder.

When you double-click on this image, you will see the "Java Programming" folder and the links to the "Java Student Menu" and the "Java Solution Menu" (depending on your choices during setup). Your "My Projects" working directory is located underneath the "Java Programming" folder.

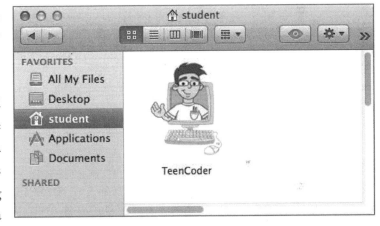

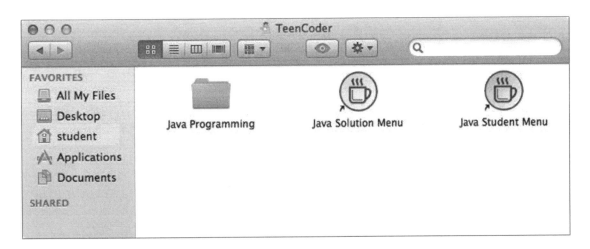

Course File Structure

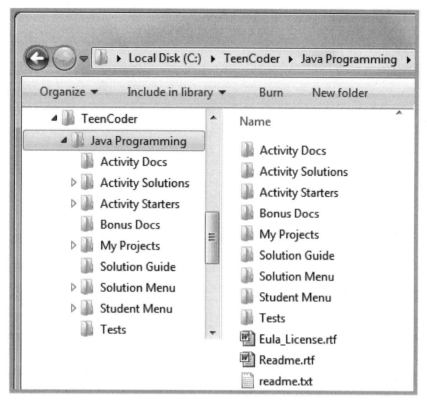

You can run the Student and Solution Menus for easy, HTML-based access to all of the instructional documents (PDFs), activity solutions, and other material distributed with the course.

You may also simply run Windows Explorer or Mac OS Finder and navigate to your target install directory and launch these files on your own! Use of the Menu systems is optional. The example screen shot on the left from Windows Explorer shows the directory structure and files in your target directory.

Most supplemental documents are in PDF format. A ".PDF" file is a common document format that requires the free Adobe Acrobat program to read. Your computer should already have the Acrobat reader installed. If you cannot view the PDF documents, you will need to install Acrobat reader first from http://get.adobe.com/reader/.

Installing the JDK

Your Student Menu contains a tab called "Software Install Instructions". Click on that tab and you will see a button called "Get Online Documents". Click that button and you will be directed to a page on our website that contains PDF documents with the current download and installation instructions. Find the document titled "Java JDK Install Instructions" (for your operating system) containing complete, step-by-step instructions on downloading and installing the JDK. Please follow the instructions to install the JDK on your computer now. You can also directly access all install documentation from our website, http://www.HomeschoolProgramming.com. *Your computer will need to be connected to the Internet during this activity.*

The Working Directory for Projects

Each project you create should be placed in a new sub-folder within your "My Projects" working directory. You may select a different working directory or even create additional working directories on your own; just remember your directory location when you want to save and load your projects.

Multiple students may use the same computer for this course by creating different working directories (using Windows Explorer) or installing the course under different user Home folders (Mac OS).

Chapter Two: Getting Started with Java

In this chapter we will introduce the Java programming language. You will learn the steps involved in transforming source code to an executable program. You will also write your first Java program!

Lesson One: Writing Your First Program

Programming languages are like spoken languages; they need to be standardized to be universally understood. What does that mean? To answer that, let's look at the standards for spoken language. In order for languages such as English to be effective, everyone needs to agree on a common set of rules for spelling, grammar, and vocabulary. Otherwise English-speakers in different parts of the world could not understand each other. Programming languages such as Java are no different. A common set of rules defines how to write Java source code and compile that source code into programs.

Source Files

Source code is human-readable text that follows the rules of a programming language. Source code can be written in a simple text editor and saved in text files on disk. To identify the contents of these files, each language uses a special file extension to show what programming language is in the file. All Java source files end with the ".java" extension. The Java compiler knows that all files saved with a ".java" extension contain Java source code.

Nearly all files on your hard drive have some sort of file extension. Executable programs end in ".exe" or ".app", images might be ".jpg" or ".gif", and audio files may come as ".wav" or ".mp3". Sometimes operating systems such as Windows or Mac OS will hide these file extensions from the end user. This may be fine for normal users, but you are a programmer! Programmers care a great deal about the file extensions because each one means something important.

If you cannot see file extensions in your Windows Explorer or Mac Finder, please refer to our "Un-hiding File Extensions" bonus document from your Student Menu. Those instructions will guide you through the configuration changes necessary to see your file extensions.

In this chapter we will be creating our source files in a simple text editor, like NotePad on Windows or TextEdit on Mac OS. Go ahead and open up a text editor from your operating system now and we will start writing our first program!

Comments

Let's begin by exploring the use of *comments*. Place your cursor in the text editor window and type the following line:

```
// This is my first program.
```

Any text from a double forward slash ("**//**") through the end of the line is a comment. The compiler knows to ignore comments when it is building your program. These comments are only added to describe different parts of your program. If you have multiple comment lines, make sure that each comment start with "**//**".

There is one other way to create a large comment across multiple lines. Instead of using the "**//**" sequence on each line, you can surround the entire multi-line comment with "**/***" to start the comment block and "***/**" to end the comment block. Let's try this in our program. Type in the following code in your text file:

```
/* This is a multi-line comment.
   The comment will continue until I end
   with another asterisk and slash.
*/
```

The compiler knows that anything that comes after a "**/***" is a comment, including a return or newline. The comment only ends with the "***/**" combination. This is extremely helpful when you have many lines of comments and you don't want to keep typing "**//**" at the beginning of every line. You can start a large comment block with "**/***" and end it with "***/**".

Now that you understand comments, we can go over some good commenting techniques. It is always a smart idea to start out every source file with a small block of comments that describes the name of the programmer (you) and what the program is supposed to do. This is helpful for anyone else that reads the file later or for yourself if you don't remember earlier programs.

For your programs, we recommend using the following comment block at the top of each source file:

```
/* TeenCoder Java Programming
   Chapter 02
   HelloWorld Application

   <your name>
   <the date, e.g. March 30th 2013>
*/
```

Now anyone reading your file will know who wrote it, when, and what the file contains.

Do you want to learn about JavaDoc, which can turn your comments into HTML help files? Check out our bonus lesson "JavaDoc" from your Student Menu! There we describe how to format your comments with JavaDoc tags and run the JavaDoc utility to produce HTML output. Bonus material is not required to complete this course, but you may find it useful!

Statements and White-space

Now let's take a look at code statements. A *statement* is a piece of code that performs some specific action and ends with a semicolon. For example, this is a single statement:

```
radius = 1;
```

You could type multiple statements (or even your entire program) together on the same line of text. The compiler doesn't need the code to look pretty; it just insists that you obey the rules for correctly forming statements.

```
radius = 1; diameter = 2 * radius;
```

However, as a human being you would like the code to be formatted in such a way that it's easy to read! We use *white-space* to make the code easier to read. White-space refers to characters like spaces, tabs, carriage returns, or line-feeds (what you get in the text file when you press Enter to go to the next line). These characters do not add any meaning to the program; the compiler ignores them completely. For instance, if you have two statements in your program, you can separate them on different lines by adding white-space (pressing Enter) between the statements:

```
radius   = 1;
diameter = 2 * radius;
```

All the space between the end of the first statement and the beginning of the second statement (including the return) would be considered white-space and ignored. You could have one carriage return between the two statements or a hundred, the compiler doesn't care. White-space is just there to make things easier to read.

If the compiler ignores white-space, including returns, how does it know we have reached the end of our statement? The end of a statement is marked with semicolons ";". Semicolons are to code statements what periods are to sentences. They tell the compiler that the statement has ended. So if the compiler understands that the semicolon is the end of the statement, could you just start your next statement right after the semicolon? Yes, but don't! No one wants to read a single paragraph that spans 10 pages and no one wants to read code that is all jumbled together. That's what white-space is for.

Classes

Every Java source file contains a *class*. A class is a group of statements and data that work together to perform a task. You will learn a great deal about classes by the time you complete this course. But for now, our programs will be very simple. You just need to start your source code with a **class** statement like this:

```
class HelloWorld
{

}
```

This statement declares that our class will be named "HelloWorld". The class name in this statement must match the source code file name. So in this example, our source file must be named "HelloWorld.java". If you do not name the file the same as our class, the program will not compile.

The opening and curly braces { and } define the beginning and ending of the **HelloWorld** class. All code and data belonging to this class must go in between the curly braces.

The "main" Function

Now we are going to write a section of our code that will run as soon as the program starts! Inside the **HelloWorld** curly braces, add the following lines:

```
class HelloWorld
{
    public static void main(String[] args)      // main entry point to the program
    {
        System.out.println("Hello, World");   // a program statement!
    }
}
```

Let's examine this simple program line-by-line, starting with the first new line:

```
    public static void main(String[] args)      // main entry point to the program
```

This is the declaration of the **main()** function, which is the block of code that will run when the program starts. The JVM will start executing your program with the first statement in the **main()** function.

The first word, "**public**", means that this function can be called by anyone outside of the **HelloWorld** class itself. This is important to allow the JVM to call your **main()** successfully.

The second word, "**static**", means that you don't have to create a new instance of your class in order for someone to call the function. Anyone can call it by simply referring to the class name. Again this is important to let the JVM easily call your **main()** function. The next word "**void**" means that this function will not return any data when it is finished running. The words **public, static,** and **void** are *keywords* in the Java language, which means they have special meaning to the Java compiler.

The word "**main**" is the name of your function. "**main**" is a special, well-known function that will be called by the JVM to start your program. The function name must be followed by a pair of parentheses "**(**" and "**)**". Inside those parentheses are any parameters (pieces of data) passed into your function. The **main** function parameters are "**String[] args**". You will learn later on how to use these parameters, but you can just ignore them for now.

In the next line, you see a left curly brace "**{**":

```
{
```

This indicates the beginning of the code for the **main()** function. All statements belonging to the **main()** function go in between the opening and closing curly braces. Your program will execute each statement *sequentially*, step-by-step from the top to the bottom unless something happens to change the program flow.

The next line is the first statement in the **main** function:

```
System.out.println("Hello, World");          // a program statement!
```

This statement calls the **System.out.println()** function to display some text to the screen. **System.out.println()** is part of the standard Java library. "println" is short for "print line", so notice that the next-to-last character is a lower-case "L" and not a number 1 or capital "I". This function will be described in greater detail later. It's important to note that the double-quotes used to enclose a literal string such as "Hello, World" must be "straight" quotes as shown above! Modern text editors may try to use fancier "curved" quotes, but curved quotes are not allowed in Java source code.

At the very end of our **main()** function will be a right curly brace "**}**" to signal the end of the function.

```
}
```

Great! That's the end of your first program! Your completed code should now look like this:

```
/* TeenCoder Java Programming
   Chapter 02
   HelloWorld Application


   <your name>
   <the date, e.g. March 30th 2012>
*/


class HelloWorld
{
    public static void main(String[] args) // main entry point to the program
    {
        System.out.println("Hello, World");    // a program statement!
    }
}
```

Once you have finished your source code, you need to save it as "HelloWorld.java" on your hard drive. But where? We recommend you place all of your projects in a dedicated sub-directory underneath your "TeenCoder\Java Programming\My Projects" directory. So first use your Windows Explorer or Mac Finder programs to create a new directory called "HelloWorld" under "My Projects".

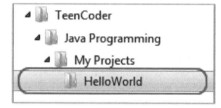

Once you have created a new "HelloWorld" subdirectory, from your text editor save your file as "HelloWorld.java" in your "TeenCoder\Java Programming\My Projects\HelloWorld" directory. If you are

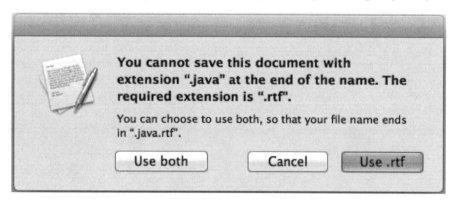

using a Mac, you may see a warning message when you try to save your file as ".java".

If you see this message, click on "Cancel" and then exit the "Save" screen. Now click on "Format" on the top menu, and then choose "Make Plain Text". Now you can save your file as "HelloWorld.java" from Mac TextEdit.

Common mistakes at this early stage include forgetting to create your project's sub-folder within "My Projects" or not paying close attention to exact names of your folder or files. You will need to create your folder and files exactly as shown in order to build the program successfully with our instructions!

Lesson Two: Building and Running from the Command Line

Now that you have written your first ".java" source file, we'll learn to turn it into a ".class" file containing Java bytecode. After that we can run the program in the JVM and see the output! Everything you need to build and run a Java program was included in the free download of the Java Development Kit (JDK) you installed in the last chapter. You do not need to install any other software to build your Java applications. You can just use the simple compiling tools that came with the JDK.

You will need to use two different command line programs to create and run a Java program. The first program is called **javac**. This program will compile your Java source code into Java bytecode that can then be run within a JVM.

Using the "javac" Compiler

The compiler included in the JDK is a command-line compiler. This means that you will need to open a Command Prompt window in either Windows or a Terminal window in Mac OS to build your program. We will introduce a fancier graphical environment in our next chapter, but for now we'll concentrate on the command-line tool.

 **Please see our bonus document "Getting Started with Command Prompts" from your Student Menu for extra help on command prompts in Windows and Mac OS. Command line interactions may be unfamiliar to you, so use this supplemental documentation if needed.**

Let's use the **javac** program to compile the "HelloWorld.java" program that we created in our last lesson. To do this, open a Command Prompt (Windows) or Terminal window (Mac OS) and change to the directory where you saved your "HelloWorld.java" file. We will use the "cd" command to change directories from wherever the command line was initially focused to our new "HelloWorld" folder.

These examples assume you have installed your course material to the default directory and have created the "HelloWorld" directory underneath your "My Projects" folder. First, from a Windows Command Prompt:

Pay close attention to all spaces, double quotes, and slashes. Each is important!

Similarly, from a Mac OS Terminal, the "cd" command works almost the same way, except the slashes are forward-leaning (/).

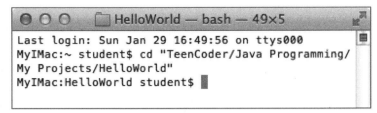

In each case, when finished your command prompt or terminal will be focused on your "HelloWorld" directory, and should reflect that in your command line prompt. Now we can compile our program!

On the Mac, you can just type the following line and the Mac OS will automatically find the **javac** compiler:

```
javac HelloWorld.java
```

On Windows, you will have to give the location of the **javac** program to the operating system. The system PATH does not automatically include the directory where you installed the JDK on your computer. So if you just typed "**javac** HelloWorld.java" you will likely see an error like this, which means Windows cannot find the **javac.exe** program:

```
C:\TeenCoder\Java Programming\My Projects\HelloWorld>javac HelloWorld.java
'javac' is not recognized as an internal or external command,
operable program or batch file.
```

The **javac** program is installed in the "bin" directory wherever you installed your JDK. By default the JDK is located in the "C:\Program Files\Java\JDK<version>\bin" directory, where <version> may be something like "1.7.0_13" depending on the exact version you downloaded. If you don't remember your JDK installation directory from the last chapter activity, pull up Windows Explorer and go confirm the exact directory name now.

Once you are sure of your JDK path, type the following line (replacing "1.7.0_13" with your actual version):

```
"C:\Program Files\Java\jdk1.7.0_13\bin\javac" HelloWorld.java
```

Make sure you use double-quotes to enclose a path containing spaces as shown above!

The compile process should be fairly quick. When it is complete, you should see your file prompt again, with no messages or reports. When you are compiling programs through the command line, no news is really good news! This means the program compiled without errors and you will now have a new file named "HelloWorld.class" in your directory. This is your compiled Java program.

Until you get the hang of it, you may encounter a variety of errors. One common error is "file not found":

```
javac: file not found: HelloWorld.java
```

This means you attempted to compile the "HelloWorld.java" file, but it could not be found. Your command line is most likely not currently focused within the correct "HelloWorld" subdirectory, or your "HelloWorld" subdirectory does not contain the "HelloWorld.java" source file.

If you see others errors, open the "HelloWorld.java" file in your text editor and make sure the code was entered exactly as it appears in the last lesson. Pay specific attention to misspelled words, missing curly braces, missing semi-colons, and accidental curly quotes instead of straight quotes.

Once your program compiles without any errors, you are ready to run!

Using the "java" JVM

To run a Java program from the command-line, you will use the **java** command followed by the name of your java class, in our case: "HelloWorld". The **java** command will load your "HelloWorld.class" bytecode into the JVM. When your program is loaded, the JVM will automatically call the **main()** method in your class to begin the program.

While the "**javac**" compiler was part of the developer tools installed by your JDK, the "**java**" program is simply part of the JRE that all users will have installed on their computer.

In most cases for both Mac OS and Windows, the JRE installation will update your system information so the JRE's "bin" directory is well-known, so you do not need to use the full path to the program. Just type the following line from your command prompt:

```
java HelloWorld
```

If you get the familiar "java is not recognized as an internal or external command…" error on Windows then you will need to include the full path like this (use your actual JRE version if it is not "7"):

```
"C:\Program Files\Java\jre7\bin\java" HelloWorld.java
```

When your Java program runs, you will see the following output:

```
Hello, World!
```

Here is a complete command-line example for Windows that shows how to change to your source code directory, run the **javac** compiler to create your "HelloWorld.class" bytecode, and then run that bytecode with the **java** command to produce the output:

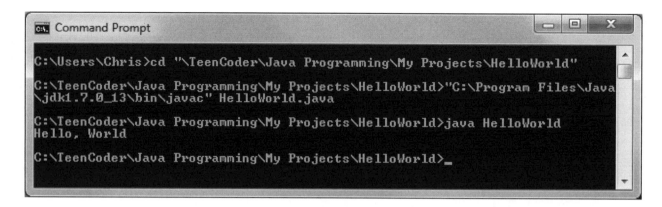

The same the Mac OS example is shown to the right.

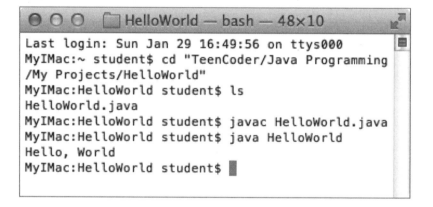

Congratulations, you have compiled and run your first Java program! If you receive errors along the way, remember to double-check your directory and filenames using Windows Explorer or Mac Finder. If you have not already un-hidden your file extensions so you can see the difference between "HelloWorld.java" and "HelloWorld.class", be sure to do so according to the instructions within your bonus documentation.

Lesson Three: Java Classes and Packages

All Java programs contain one or more *classes* or *objects*. Each programmer writes their own classes in addition to possibly using classes written by others or provided in the built-in Java class libraries. Your first program contained a single class called "HelloWorld":

```
class HelloWorld
{
}
```

In the Java language, each class must be located in a **separate** source file where the filename matches the class name. For instance, if you created the **Widget1** and **Widget2** classes, you should have two source files:

```
Widget1.java
Widget2.java
```

As you can imagine, it's quite possible that programmers end up creating classes with the same name. You might even duplicate a class name that is present in the built-in Java class libraries. So how do you tell the difference between identically-named objects? That's where Java **packages** come in handy!

Java Packages

In Java you can group together related classes into something called a "package". You might also hear the concept referred to as a "namespace". You can picture a package as a fully-qualified name that distinguishes your classes from all other classes in the world. A package name is simply a string that you choose such as "**teencoder**". It may contain multiple words separated by a period such as "**teencoder.joe**" to define a package hierarchy. When making a package hierarchy, the most general category is all the way to the left and the most specific name is all the way to the right.

For instance, you might create a package called "**teencoder.joe.utility**". The "**teencoder**" portion states that the classes are part of your effort in this TeenCoder course. The "**joe**" part might be your name to separate your package from your brother or sister who is also taking the class. Finally, the "**utility**" name indicates that the package holds a collection of useful things you might want to re-use from project to project.

By convention, many companies that write Java objects will create packages based on their Internet domain name such as "**com.homeschoolprogramming**", since that is guaranteed to be unique. Why does this look backwards? Remember that the most general category ("com" in this case) is to the left, and you get more specific as you go towards the right. So if we wanted to get really fancy we might create packages like:

> com.homeschoolprogramming.teencoder
> com.homeschoolprogramming.teencoder.android

Built-in Java Packages

The Java platform contains many built-in Java classes. These classes are well-organized into package hierarchies that make them easy to find and use. Most of the built-in classes you will use are in one of these two top-level packages: **java** or **javax**

Each top-level namespace has a number of sub-packages which may contain actual classes or further package sub-divisions. Here are some of the first-level highlights:

java.awt	Classes in the original Java "AWT" graphics library
java.io	Classes dedicated to input and input from the console, files, etc.
java.lang	Fundamental language classes such as data types and system access
java.math	Classes for handling very large or precise numbers
java.net	Classes for handling all sorts of network (socket) operations
java.sql	Classes for dealing with relational databases
java.text	Classes for performing fancier management and operations on strings and text
java.util	Many useful classes commonly used throughout most Java programs
javax.swing	Classes in the more recent Java "Swing" graphics library
javax.xml	Classes to handle XML text files

You will learn about classes from some of these packages in this course. There are a great many built-in Java classes and packages that we will not cover, but you can explore the Java API documentation on your own.

Declaring Packages in Your Source Code

If you decide that your Java classes belong in a package, it's very easy to declare that package within your source file. At the top of each *.java file, simply put the following single line at the *very top*, before anything else except possibly comments:

```
package <your package name>;
```

For example:

```
package com.homeschoolprogramming.teencoder;
```

That package declaration will make your Java class part of the specified package. Your java class now has a fully qualified name of "**<your package name>.<your class name>**". For example, if you created the **MyWidget** class in the package shown above, the full name of the class would be **com.homeschoolprogramming.teencoder.MyWidget**.

Notice we did not declare a package for "HelloWorld". What happens if you do not declare a package? In that case your class automatically belongs to the **default** package. This is simply an anonymous package where all classes have simple names. The **default** package is fine for very small programs such as those we will be writing in this course. We will usually have only a small handful of classes in our overall program, and we don't expect anyone else to be using the classes we write. However since you will be using classes from other packages in the built-in Java class library, it's very important to understand package concepts!

Importing Packages

In order to use any class from in the same package in your code, you can use the "simple" class name without the full package on the front. So if you created **Widget1** and **Widget2** in the same package, you could simply use the class names **Widget1** and **Widget2** within the source code to refer to those classes.

However, if you would like to use a class such as **LinkedList** in another package like **java.util**, then you would use the fully qualified name **java.util.LinkedList** in your source code. This makes it crystal clear to the Java compiler exactly which class you want to use, just in case there are any other **LinkedList** classes running around that might be accidentally chosen instead.

It can be quite cumbersome to type in a bunch of fully-qualified class names all the time, especially when you are frequently using classes from the built-in Java class library or other packages. Fortunately, Java provides a shortcut you can use! Near the top of your source file, between any optional **package** declaration and the beginning of your **class**, you can add one or more **import** statements. Each import statement gives the fully qualified name of a particular class or entire package that you want to access through the simple names of those classes.

For example, let's say we knew we wanted to use a bunch of classes from the **java.util** package as well as a particular class from **java.text**. Here's how you would import those items:

```
import java.util.*;    // * means we are importing all classes within the package
import java.text.SimpleDateFormat;// direct access to just SimpleDateFormat
```

Now in your source code you can refer to any class in the **java.util** package such as **LinkedList** by its simple name. Notice the "*" does not extend to sub-packages, so if you also wanted to use simple class names from a sub-package like **java.util.zip**, simply importing **java.util.*** is not enough. You would need a separate import statement for each specific package like this:

```
import java.util.*;
import java.util.zip.*;
```

There is one package you never need to import – **java.lang**. This package is always automatically imported and all Java programs have simple-name access to classes in the **java.lang** package. In fact you have already used this feature without even knowing it! Recall in your "HelloWorld" program, you used the line:

```
System.out.println("Hello, World");    // a program statement!
```

The **System** class is actually a part of the **java.lang** package, so the fully qualified name is **java.lang.System**. However you can simply use **System** because **java.lang** is automatically imported.

Package Directory Structures

If you create classes with a package name, you must also store those class files in a very specific directory structure on your disk! This allows programmers to carefully categorize and separate the actual source files to avoid naming collisions. If you created two classes with the same name such as **Circle** in different packages, then the "Circle.java" source files must be stored in different directories.

Always identify a root directory in which all of your source files for a project will live. In your case we recommend starting with the "My Projects" directory under your "\TeenCoder\Java Programming" directory. For each new project, create a new subdirectory just like we did for "HelloWorld". So a full directory path for a new project such as "ShowTime" would be:

"\TeenCoder\Java Programming\My Projects\ShowTime"

Now that we have identified a root directory for our project's source code, where to the *.java files go? If you are using the **default** package, then your source files go right into the root directory like this:

"ShowTime\DefaultClass1.java"
"ShowTime\DefaultClass2.java"

However any classes that are part of a package must go into a directory structure that exactly mirrors the package name! Consider the **com.homescholprogramming.teencoder** package name. A new subdirectory must be created for each part of the package name like this:

"ShowTime\com\homeschoolprogramming\teencoder\MyTeenCoderClass.java"

This directory structure might seem like overkill for small projects. But once you start working with very large projects and a team of programmers, it becomes more useful and natural to ensure your classes are carefully separated by package name.

For this course we recommend you always use the **default** package for your classes, so you can store your "*.java" files in the root of your project's source directory.

Activity: Show Time!

In this activity you will create a new program called "ShowTime.java". This program will print the current time to the screen using the **System.out.println**() method. If you have completed the bonus "JavaDoc" lesson, you can also add JavaDoc comments to the code to produce HTML help for your class.

Your activity requirements and instructions are found in the "Chapter_02_Activity.pdf" document located in your "TeenCoder\Java Programming\Activity Docs" folder. You can access this document through your Student Menu or by directly clicking on it from Windows Explorer (Windows) or Finder (Mac OS).

Complete this activity now and ensure your program meets the requirements before continuing!

Chapter Three: The Eclipse IDE

In this chapter we are going to move beyond command-line tools and start learning how to use the Eclipse *Integrated Development Environment* (IDE). You will install Eclipse on your computer, take a tour of the software, create your first project, and configure your help system. This is a big chapter with plenty of new information, so buckle up!

Lesson One: The Eclipse Online Community

In the early days, a programmer would write their program code in one application, compile and run it in another application, and test it in yet another application. Today, programmers have *Integrated Development Environments*. The IDE is a single place where you can type in your code, build, run, and debug your program. Everything you need as a programmer can be found in your IDE.

In this course we will be using an IDE called **Eclipse™**. This lesson will discuss the history and use of the Eclipse software. Eclipse is a free, open-source package hosted at http://www.eclipse.org/.

Eclipse was started in the late 1990s by the IBM Corporation. IDE software was becoming a very popular and indispensable tool in programming. IBM had a vision at this time to create a new kind of IDE – an *open-source* IDE. Open source software is developed by the individual programmers from all over the world instead of within one company's lab. This means that all programmers are allowed to view, change, and compile the source code at any time. IBM thought that relying on many public contributions would create a flexible, powerful, and innovative IDE that could also change quickly to keep up with the current programming trends. Programmers would be able to add new functionality at any time to the IDE.

Initially, IBM attempted to take a parental role in the development of this new IDE. The code was created and maintained by the open-source community, but other companies were invited to partner with IBM to create improvements and innovations to the software. The intent of IBM was simply to provide oversight and some control over the process, but their involvement made other programmers and software companies nervous. Many questioned whether the software was open-source at all!

Since so many companies and individuals were reluctant to accept Eclipse as open source, IBM created the Eclipse Foundation in 2004 and released control of the Eclipse project to this new foundation. Soon after, the first major release of Eclipse (Eclipse 3.0) was born.

With the advent of the Eclipse Foundation, more and more independent vendors were willing to invest the time and money required to create new improvements to the Eclipse system. Finally, Eclipse was becoming a flexible, powerful, open-source IDE.

Currently, the Eclipse Foundation releases new versions of Eclipse every June. Here is a brief look at the historical releases and forthcoming versions:

Release	Year	Version
Eclipse 3.0	2004	3.0
Eclipse 3.1	2005	3.1
Callisto	2006	3.2
Europa	2007	3.3
Ganymede	2008	3.4
Galileo	2009	3.5
Helios	2010	3.6
Indigo	2011	3.7
Juno	2012	4.2
Kepler	2013	4.3

We will be using the **Kepler** release of the Eclipse IDE for this course. Even when newer versions become available, we advise using the Kepler version so your experience will match the lesson instructions.

Innovations in the Eclipse system tend to be implemented as "plug-ins". Plug-ins are small pieces of software that can be plugged-into the IDE to provide additional functionality. For instance, the current version of Eclipse has plug-ins for developing in other programming languages like C and Python, managing databases, and even supporting Android™ application development!

Activity: Install Eclipse

We want you to have the Eclipse IDE installed on your computer so you can follow along as we introduce the software in this chapter. So let's take a quick break and complete this activity!

Installation of Eclipse involves downloading the software from the Eclipse Foundation website (Internet connection required), unzipping it onto your computer, and creating a shortcut to the IDE so you can find it easily. You can find step-by-step instructions linked from your Student Menu. Click on the "Software Install Instructions" and then the "Get Online Documents" button to access the documentation on our website. Locate the "Eclipse Install Instructions" PDF to match your Windows or Mac operating system.

Follow the instructions to install Eclipse on your computer! If at any point in the process you experience something that does not match the documentation, contact us for an updated version of the installation docs.

When you are done you should have Eclipse installed on your computer and a shortcut icon on your desktop to launch the IDE easily. In the next lesson we'll walk you through the Eclipse software step-by-step.

Lesson Two: Eclipse Java IDE

To launch the Eclipse software, simply run the Eclipse executable that you installed during the last activity. You should have created a convenient shortcut on your desktop so you can find it easily.

Eclipse Workspaces

The first time you run Eclipse, you will see a pop-up dialog asking you to select a *workspace*:

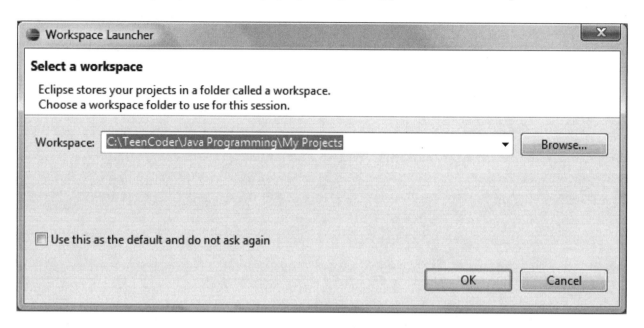

The first time you run Eclipse, the default workspace path will be different, so you should type in the path to your working directory. Your Windows path should be "C:\TeenCoder\Java Programming\My Projects" while Mac OS users should type in "/Users/<your name>/TeenCoder/Java Programming/My Projects".

What is a workspace? Conceptually, an Eclipse workspace is a collection of individual projects. A workspace may contain zero, one, or more projects. All of the projects in your workspace should be physically stored on your hard drive under a particular root folder. The workspace location Eclipse is asking for above will be that root folder containing all of the projects in the workspace. If you want to pick the workspace once and then not be bothered each time you start Eclipse, check the "Use this as the default and do not ask again" box.

So what workspace strategy do we want to use for this course? We could choose to make a separate workspace that holds each activity or programming project, and you could then switch between workspaces in Eclipse to see individual projects. Or, we could make one workspace that will hold all of our projects. Since we recommend putting all of your class projects underneath the "My Projects" directory, we are going to create just one workspace located at "My Projects". That way you can see all of the projects you make for this class and easily switch between them without changing workspaces. Go ahead and type in the path to your "My Projects" directory for your operating system click the "OK" button now.

Notice that your actual path may not be exactly the same as the example above if you are have chosen a different install location when running your course setup program.

When you select a folder as a workspace location, Eclipse will create a sub-folder called ".metadata" to hold information about the workspace settings and the projects in the workspace. So whenever you see a ".metadata" folder you will know that the parent folder has been chosen as an Eclipse workspace.

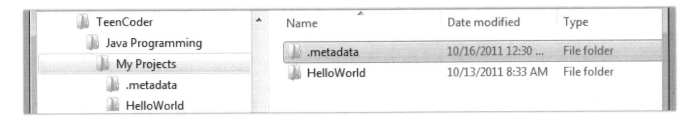

Eclipse Workbench

Once you click the "OK" button to select your workspace, your main Eclipse window will appear. The first time you run Eclipse you will see a "Welcome" screen that contains a number of links to helpful information such as tutorials, samples, and the Eclipse website. You can ignore all of those (unless you are curious) and simply click on the arrow button on the right that says "Open Workbench".

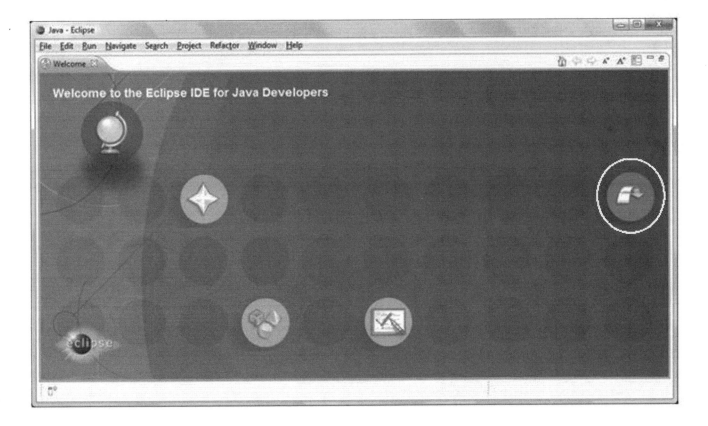

Your first look at the main Eclipse IDE screen is probably overwhelming! There are many different areas (or window panes) within the screen. It's important to understand that you can easily make windows appear, disappear, or move to a different location. So if you begin customizing your Eclipse software to suit your personal preferences, your screens may not match our exact screen shots in this textbook. We are also showing Windows-based images, and Eclipse under Mac OS will use Mac-style window frames and menus. But Eclipse running on both Windows and Mac OS will behave the same way with the same features.

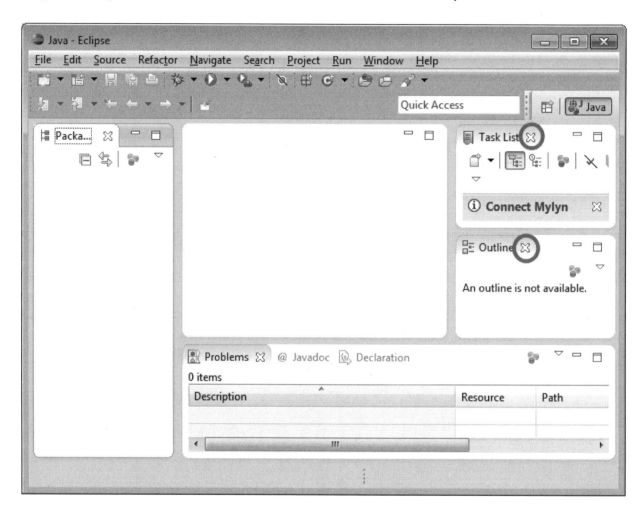

The first thing we want to do is de-clutter your work area by getting rid of some windows we won't use. So click on the two "X" locations circled above to close out the "Task List" and "Outline" tabs.

Now your main view is somewhat cleaner. We have added the circled numbers in the image below so we can talk about the different areas.

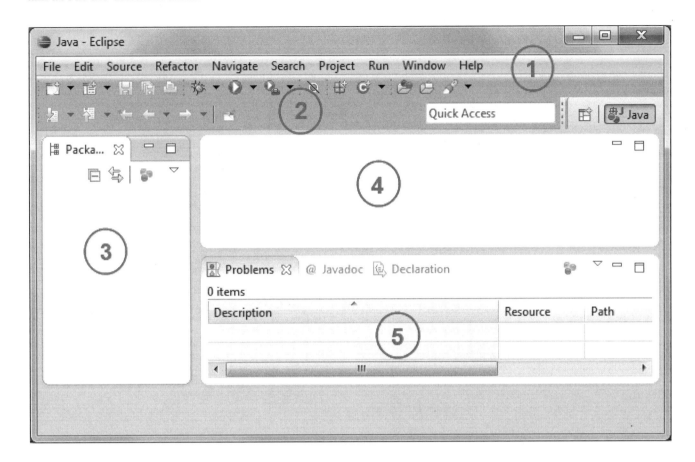

The first area (1) is simply a menu bar where you can access every feature of Eclipse. We will introduce some of the features over time as we explore the IDE, and there are many other interesting areas you can examine on your own. The second area (2) is a toolbar that gives you one-click access to some of the more commonly used features of the software. All of the buttons look pretty mysterious right now, but we'll show you how to use the important ones as we go along. To one side you may see the third area (3) which is called the "Package Explorer". This panel will eventually show you the contents of each project in your workspace, but it will be empty for now and possibly missing altogether because we haven't created any projects yet.

The fourth area (4) is your main working area. When you have a project loaded this area will be subdivided into additional windows containing your source code. The fifth area (5) is where Eclipse gives you feedback about your project. In the "Problems" tab you will find a list of errors that the Java compiler has found in our source code. We don't have a project loaded yet, so thankfully this is an empty list.

Notice that the top-right part of each windowed area contains some common buttons that let you minimize or maximize the window (plus possibly other tasks). Simply move your mouse over each of the buttons to get a tool-tip pop-up that describes what the button does.

Lesson Three: Creating an Eclipse Project

In this lesson, we will recreate our simple "Hello, World!" program from the last chapter. This time, we will create and run the program entirely in the Eclipse software – no more command lines!

Your First Eclipse Project

To begin, launch the Eclipse IDE and make sure you have selected the same "My Projects" workspace as described earlier. Then, create a new Java project by selecting "File → New → Java Project" from the menu.

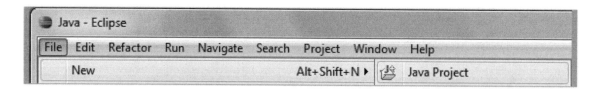

You will then see a pop-up dialog asking for the project name. Enter "HelloWorld2" for the **Project name** since "HelloWorld" was already used in the last chapter. Use only letters, numbers, spaces, and underscores for your project name and avoid all other special characters that may not work well as part of a folder name.

You can leave all of the other settings at the default values. Notice the **Location** is automatically set to the "HelloWorld2" folder under your "My Projects" directory. This is where your new project will live.

Click the "Finish" button at the bottom when done to create your project! If you

see pop-up messages about "EGit" (which is a source control system) or your HOME environment variable, just check "Do not warn again…" and click "OK".

What happened? The IDE screen may not have changed that much after your project was created. This is because Eclipse doesn't yet know what windows you want to show on your screen. The *Package Explorer* is a very useful window, so if it's not already visible let's enable it now. From your menu, select "Window → Show View → Package Explorer".

Now you can see a window called "Package Explorer" on the left side of your IDE:

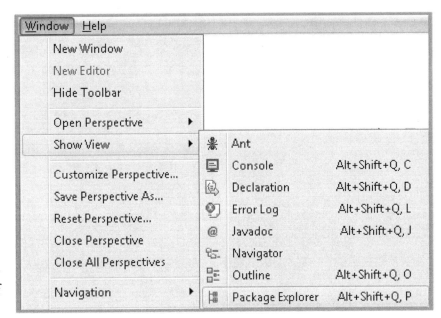

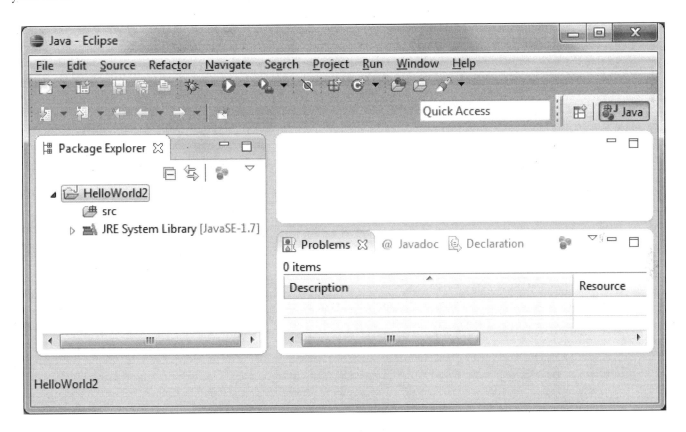

The Package Explorer will allow you to look through all of the projects in your workspace. Right now we have just one – the "HelloWorld2" project. Underneath that project you can see a "src" directory, which is a standard sub-folder from the root that will store all of your source files (*.java). You can also see a listing of the JRE that will be used. In this example we have JRE version 1.7 installed, though your own version may be different.

The Package Explorer within the IDE will not show you all of the files that are related to your project, however, so let's take a quick look at what is actually on your hard drive. Using Windows Explorer or Mac Finder, look within your "HelloWorld2" directory to see the following files and subdirectories:

Directory or File	Description
.settings	This folder contains your personal configuration choices for the IDE settings related to your project. You do not need to view, edit or manage anything in this directory, and it is not important to share as part of your source code.
bin	This folder will contain the compiled output (*.class) of all the objects in your program. If you are trying to send your program to someone without a JDK, you need to send this output (*.class files), but you do not need to share anything in this directory when just sending your source code to another programmer.
src	This folder can also be seen in your IDE Project Explorer. It holds all of the *.java source files for your project. When sending your project to another programmer, it's important to include all of the files in your "src" directory.
.classpath	This file is automatically created by Eclipse to track your project build settings such as the input libraries and output directory. It should be sent along with your source files when sharing your code with another Eclipse-based programmer.
.project	This file is automatically created by Eclipse to contain basic information such as the name of your project. It should be sent along with your source files when sharing your code with another Eclipse-based programmer.

To summarize, when sharing your project source code with others or asking for help, you should send (in a ZIP, or as email attachment) the following files and directories:

- The "src" directory and everything in it
- The .classpath file
- The .project file

If you want to run your program on another computer that just has a JRE installed (but not the JDK), then you should copy all of the *.class files from the "bin" directory to the target computer. Then you can run the program with the **java** command from the command line.

Your First Eclipse Class

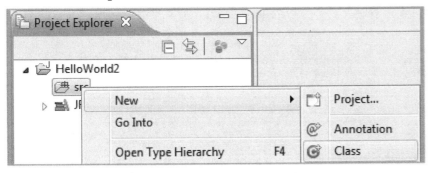

Remember that all Java programs are simply one or more classes that do useful work, so our next step is to create a new class. Right-click on the "src" folder in Project Explorer and select "New → Class":

The "New Java Class" dialog will give you many options for creating a class. For all classes created during

this course, you can leave the **Source folder** at the default value and the **Package** name empty. You can ignore the warning at the top about using default packages. We already learned about package names and decided for our course to use the default.

The first thing you have to pick is your **Name** for the class, so enter "HelloWorld2" in that field. Class names cannot contain any spaces, and you should usually avoid special characters too.

You can ignore all other options with one important exception!

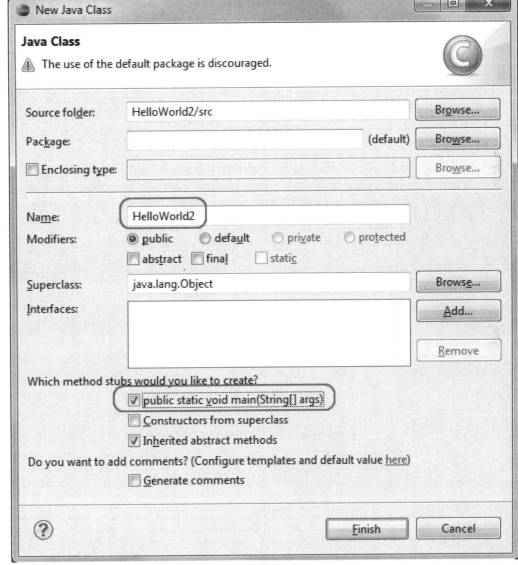

For the main class in your program, check the "**public static void main(String[] args)**" box under "Which method stubs would you like to create?" This will ensure your class has a **main**() function that will get called when the program starts. Then click the "Finish" button to create your **HelloWorld2** class.

Now we're getting somewhere! You can see a new "HelloWorld2.java" source file has been created for you using the default package underneath the "src" directory in the Project Explorer.

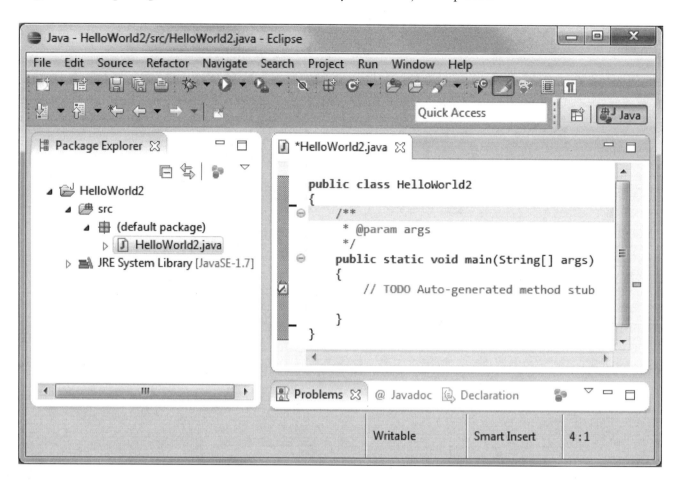

The main right side window should now show your source file contents. This editing pane is a full-featured text editor, so you can modify your source code right here in the IDE instead of using some external program. This right-side window has a tabbed interface across the top, so you can have more than one source file open at the same time. You can close out a source file by just clicking the "X" within the tab next to the file name. If you ever accidentally close a source file and want to re-open it for editing, just double-click on the file name (such as "HelloWorld2.java") in the Package Explorer.

Now that your main program class is created, go ahead and fill in the **main()** function with the code that will be executed when your program is run. You may remove the auto-generated "TODO" comment. Use the same "Hello, World" output as in the last chapter, or be creative!

```java
public static void main(String[] args)
{
    System.out.println("This is my first Eclipse program!");
}
```

If your curly braces are not vertically aligned as shown above, from your Student Menu's "Software Install Instructions" page, go to our online documents area. Complete the steps in the "Eclipse Configuration Instructions" (Configuring_Eclipse.pdf) document to change the default alignment of your curly braces.

When you finish typing your **main()** function logic, notice that the "HelloWorld2.java" tab now contains an asterisk. This means the source file 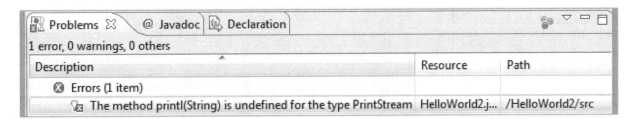 has changed but has not yet been saved to disk. To save your source file, simply click on one of the "save" icons up on your toolbar . The single-disk icon will save just the current file, while the multiple-disk icon will save all modified files in your project. You can also use the menu "File → Save" command.

Building an Eclipse Program and Understanding Errors

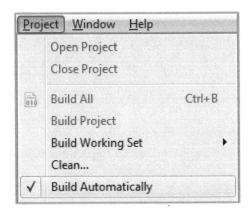

Now that you have completed and saved your code, how do you get the *.java source file compiled into a Java *.class file? Actually, using the default Eclipse settings, this is done for you automatically every time you save your file. Look under your "Project" menu and you will see the "Build Automatically" option checked.

If you uncheck this option, then you need to select "Build Project" from this menu each time you want to build. We recommend leaving "Build Automatically" enabled because that's one less thing to do!

At any point if the automatic build process detects an error in your program, you will see an error message or warning in the "Problems" tab at the bottom of your IDE. For example, let's say we didn't spell the "println" function name correctly (dropping the final letter):

```
System.out.printl("This is my first Eclipse project!");
```

Now you are trying to call a function that does not exist, and the error description will tell you exactly that.

Problems ⊠ @ Javadoc Declaration		
1 error, 0 warnings, 0 others		
Description	Resource	Path
⊗ Errors (1 item)		
The method printl(String) is undefined for the type PrintStream	HelloWorld2.j...	/HelloWorld2/src

You will also see the red "X" symbol in your text editor to the left of the line of code containing the error and next to your source filename in the Project Explorer. This is Eclipse's way of letting you know there is a problem that needs to be fixed. If you double-click on the error in the "Problems" tab your cursor should automatically go to the error line in your source window. Correct the problem, save the file, and you will see the error go away.

Running an Eclipse Program

All right, now that your source code is finished and error-free and has been built automatically for you, it's time to run the program. You could, if you wanted to, open a command line and manually run **java** against your .class files. But part of the fun and convenience of using an IDE is that Eclipse can do all of that for you with just one button click!

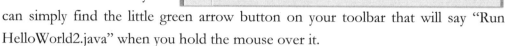

You can run the program by selecting "Run → Run" from the menu. Or you

can simply find the little green arrow button on your toolbar that will say "Run HelloWorld2.java" when you hold the mouse over it.

Click the "Run" button now and let's see what happens! If your source file is not saved, Eclipse will prompt you to save it. You can check the "Always save…" box to automatically save your files before running. You may also see a "Run As" pop-up dialog asking what kind of Java program you have. If so just select "Java Application" and click "OK".

The output looks a bit different than the command-line doesn't it? Eclipse did not start an external command line window. Instead it simply created a "Console" tab at the bottom of the IDE to hold the output.

You can also see more information at the top such as the phrase "<terminated>" (which means the program has ended), the name of the project ("HelloWorld2"), and so on. There are also quite a few buttons on this tab to manage your console, but you shouldn't have to use any of them right now.

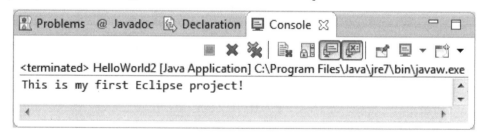

What is Debug Mode?

Notice right next to the "Run" command is "Debug". We will learn all about Debug mode later in the course. This mode allows you to run your program step-by-step and watch each line execute. It's a great way to find run-time errors and understand how your program flows. For right now we don't need it, but you may accidentally select the Debug option instead of the normal "Run". If you are using the Windows OS you may get a Windows Firewall warning; just click "Allow Access" to allow the program to continue

In many cases you won't notice a difference between "Debug" mode and a normal "Run". However if there is an error in your program, or it stops at a breakpoint, or simply because the IDE remembers your preferences, there is a good chance that your IDE may change itself completely in Debug mode! This new look is called the Debug *perspective*, and is the IDE's way of showing you useful windows and commands that are specifically related to debugging your program.

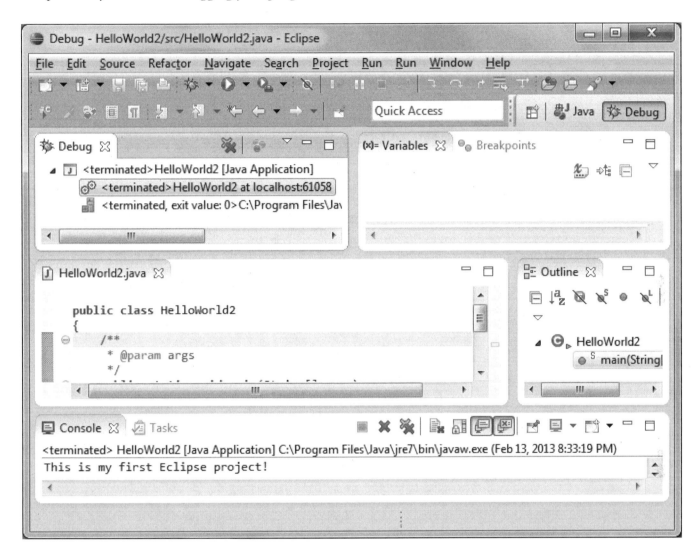

Wow, that is completely different! What happened to your Project Explorer and what do those other windows mean? Don't worry, you haven't lost anything, the IDE has just decided to hide some windows and show you different things instead. If your program is stuck in Debug mode and is still running, you can find the red square under the "Console" tab or the "Debug" tab and click it to terminate the program.

Now you probably want to get out of the Debug perspective and back into your normal Java perspective. To switch perspectives, just click the "Java" button at the top-right corner next to your new "Debug" perspective. You can also switch perspectives at any time from the menu by selecting "Window → Open Perspective → Java".

Whew, that's better; you have now returned to your familiar IDE with Project Explorer and source code!

Lesson Four: Help and Reference Documentation

Programmers love to have useful documentation right at their fingertips. While this course will teach you many things, there is always more to learn and understand. You may also want an alternate explanation for a certain concept or more detail about how to use a particular built-in class from the Java library. The Eclipse IDE works hard to provide this information for you in several easy ways.

Getting Help on Eclipse

Eclipse itself is a powerful software program with many options. If you have any questions about how Eclipse works, you can find help from the "Help" menu.

Selecting "Help Contents" will lead you to a full-featured help system containing information about the Eclipse workbench and developing Java in Eclipse. You can also select the "Search" option from the "Help" menu and type in keywords to find within the Eclipse help system.

Getting Help on Java

Once you are comfortable with Eclipse itself, you may need to look for help on the Java programming language and the classes in the Java class library. The Java Eclipse IDE has built-in context-sensitive help for all of the included Java classes.

When you are typing your Java code you should notice tool-tip pop-ups giving you more information about the package, class, or function. For example, just typing "System" and then a dot "." will display a list of all the objects in the **System** package.

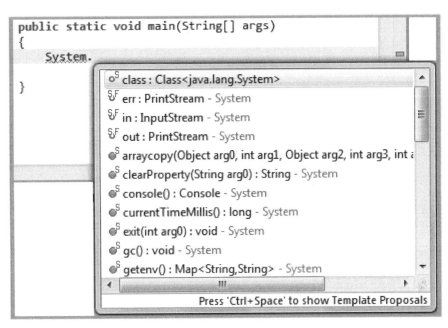

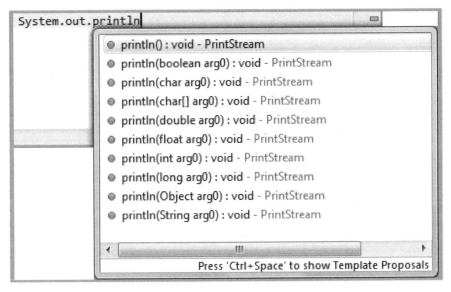

Continue typing "System.out. println" and you will see the help popup change automatically after each dot. You will next see all of the functions on the **out** class and then finally all of the different types of **println()** functions.

Detailed JRE Documentation

While the pop-ups described above give useful hints as you type in code, you don't really have great descriptions of each class or function. Once your code is typed in, you can hover your mouse cursor over a particular package, class, or function to get a pop-up with a more detailed description.

In this example we held the mouse cursor over the **println**() function and received an automatic popup that described the function and the parameters to the function. If the description is longer than will fit in the pop-up you can hit the "F2" key to focus on the pop-up and scroll up and down.

```
public static void main(String[] args)
{
    System.out.println("This is my first Eclipse project!");

}
```

● void java.io.PrintStream.println(String x)

println

```
public void println(String x)
```

Prints a String and then terminate the line. This method behaves as though it invokes print(String) and then println().

Parameters:
    x - The String to be printed.

Press 'F2' for focus

So far we have figured out how to get help on code that we have just written. But where do you go if you don't know what classes or functions to use and just want to explore your available options? Let's find out!

Online Java References

You may wish to explore the Java class library, Java tutorials, or the Java language specification online. Complete reference documentation for the Java class library exists at the following locations (choose the correct one for the version of the JDK you installed):

http://download.oracle.com/javase/6/docs/api/

http://download.oracle.com/javase/7/docs/api/

These web pages are hosted by Oracle, a company who purchased Sun Microsystems, the creators of the Java language. While the links are well-known and stable, it is possible they may change in the future. In that case you can easily find the new online locations with any Internet search using keywords like "Java API documentation".

Here is an example of the main Java API help web page for version 7:

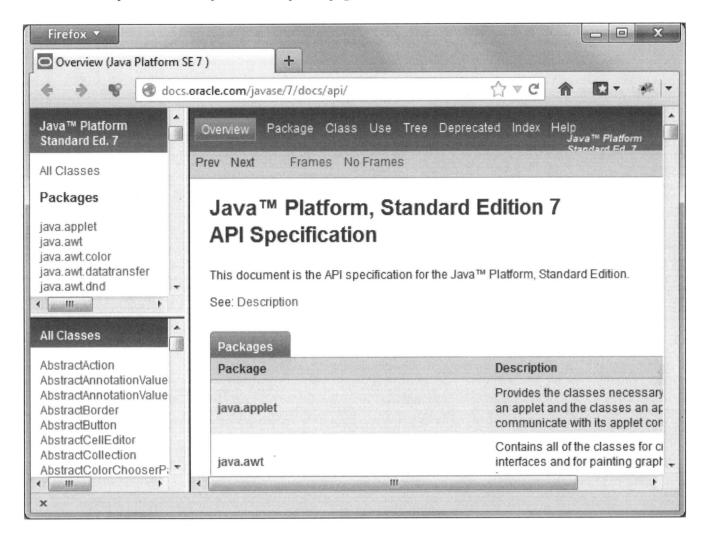

The top-left pane contains a list of all the Java packages such as **java.awt, java.lang, java.net, java.io**, etc. Click on one of the package names and the bottom-left pane will narrow to show just the individual classes in the selected package. In the main right window is a large description of the package or class you have clicked on in one of the left panes.

In addition to pure reference documentation, you can find a wealth of Java tutorial topics and other how-to information online. This site, also hosted by Oracle, contains many tutorials or "trails" on different subjects.

http://download.oracle.com/javase/tutorial/

The tutorials are kept up-to-date with the latest Java release, but for most practical purposes you can apply the tutorial information to earlier Java versions also.

Activity: Eclipse "ShowTime" Project

In this activity, you will incorporate the "ShowTime.java" program from the last chapter in an Eclipse project. You will then build and run the program from within the Eclipse software.

Your activity requirements and instructions are found in the "Chapter_03_Activity.pdf" document located in your "TeenCoder\Java Programming\Activity Docs" folder. You can access this document through your Student Menu or by directly clicking on it from Windows Explorer (Windows) or Finder (Mac OS).

Complete this activity now and ensure your program meets the requirements before continuing!

Chapter Four: Data Types and Variables

This chapter will introduce the different types of numeric and character data you can use in your program. You will also learn how to print these data types out to the screen.

Lesson One: Primitive Data Types

Computer programs use many kinds of data! An email application needs to send and receive lines of text, a spreadsheet application knows how to store and manage numbers, and a video game needs to use graphical images, sound effects, and music. Computer programs must carefully understand the exact format of each piece of data. In this lesson we will cover some of the basic Java *data types*. All of the data types described in this lesson are *primitive* data types. Each time you declare an instance of a primitive data type in your code, the computer will reserve enough memory to hold the entire data type. Every copy of a primitive data type can hold a different, unique value.

Numeric Data Types

One very commonly used category of data types is the numeric data types. These types of data contain just what you expect – numbers! Why does Java have more than one type of numeric data? Because there are many different kinds of numbers: whole numbers, fractional numbers, large numbers and small numbers. You should choose the numeric data type that best matches your expected program data. There are two general categories of numeric data: *integer* and *floating point*.

Integers are positive or negative whole numbers. There are no fractions or decimal places in an integer value. Some example integer values include: a student's age (17), the number of MP3 music files in a collection (412), or the scores in a football game (24 to 17). You can perform basic mathematic functions like addition, subtraction, multiplication and division on integer values and get integer results. Any fractional division results are discarded.

Floating point data are real numbers that contain an integer plus a fractional part, separated by a decimal point. Some examples of floating point values are: PI (3.14159), the number of seconds shown on an accurate stopwatch (12.32), or the cost of a pizza ($7.95). Floating point values might not have a fractional part...in that case the digits to the right of the decimal point are all zeros (4.00).

Java defines specific data types to deal with integer and floating point numbers, both large and small. Each data type takes up a certain amount of computer memory (measured in *bytes*). That memory size will set limits on the number's *range* (maximum and minimum possible values) and *precision* (number of digits). The following tables define the main numeric data types for the Java language. Here are the integer data types:

Data Type	Bytes in Memory	Range
byte	1	-128 to 127
short	2	-32,768 to 32,767
int	4	-2,147,483,648 to 2,147,483,647
long	8	-9,223,372,036,854,775,808 to 9,223,372,036,854,775,807

This table shows the floating point (or real) numeric data types:

Data Type	Bytes in Memory	Range
float	4	$1.40239846 \times 10^{-45}$ to $3.402823467 \times 10^{38}$
double	8	$4.94065645841246544 \times 10^{-324}$ to $1.79769313486231570 \times 10^{308}$

Now you may be wondering why there are so many numeric data types defined. Why not always use the biggest one? The answer is in the speed and efficiency of the program. Operations on larger data types take slightly longer than smaller data types. It also takes more bytes of memory to store the larger data types, as shown in the tables above. It's a good practice to choose the smallest data type that will *for sure* hold the data your program will be using. Also, floating point operations are more complicated than integer operations, so only use floating point if you truly need decimal data.

Non-Numeric Primitive Types

There are two additional primitive data types that are not numeric: **char** and **boolean**. A **char** represents one letter, numeric digit, or keyboard symbol such as 'a', '3', or '*'. Notice that individual characters are surrounded by single quotes. A **boolean** variable can hold either a **true** or **false** value.

Data Type	Bytes in Memory	Range
char	2	One text character
boolean	1	**true** or **false**

Each **char** data type is two bytes because it stores characters in a "Unicode" format. This format supports not just English characters, but a huge range of characters and symbols from other languages. Later on we will describe how to build **strings** (lines of text) from characters.

Lesson Two: Variables

In addition to telling the compiler what kind of data type to use, we need to tell the compiler the *name* we will use to refer to the data in our program. When you create an instance of a data type and give it name, that instance is called a *variable*. Variables are places where you store data in your program. You can change a variable's contents while running the program (that's why they are called "variables").

Declaring a Variable

In order to create a variable and give it a name, you "declare" the variable in your source code. A variable declaration consists of a data type, then some white-space, and then the variable name, ending with a semicolon. In this example we declare an **int** variable and a **float** variable:

```
int myInteger;
float myFloat;
```

Another example variable declaration is this character representation of a student's grade. We are using the **char** data type to store a single letter like 'A' or 'B'.

```
char student_grade;
```

If you know for certain that a value will never change while the program is running, you may make a special variable declaration that will tell the compiler never to let that variable change. You do this by adding the **final** keyword in front of your data type. You cannot change the value of any final variable while the program is running. For example:

```
final int NUM_GAMEBOARD_ROWS = 8;    // this variable will always contain 8
NUM_GAMEBOARD_ROWS = 7;        // ERROR: you cannot change a final variable!
```

You should make **final** variables out of values that you use throughout your program that you may want to change in between compiles. In the above example we have decided that a game board will have 8 rows, and we can write lots of code that uses that constant value to build the game board screen. But perhaps later you decide that 10 rows would be better. All you have to do is change your **final** declaration from 8 to 10 and then recompile! This is a much better approach than hard-coding the value "8" everywhere in your code, and then having to find and change all of those places if you want to alter the value.

Rules for Naming a Variable

The Java language has specific rules about how you can and cannot name your variables. Your variable names may contain any mixture of upper and lowercase letters (including non-English characters). By convention a **final** variable is declared with all capital letters, but this is not a requirement.

```
int CAPITAL;        // capital letters are fine
int lowercase;      // lowercase letters are fine
int MixedCase;      // mixed case names are fine
```

It's important to understand that the names of variables are case-sensitive. This means that names with the same letters in different upper or lower-case mixtures are treated as different variables.

```
int ShirtCost;      // Even though the words are the same
int shirtCost;      // The case of the letters is different!
int shirtcost;      // This variable is different too!
```

By convention you should use capitalization to help visually identify different words in a variable name. In the example above, the two words are "shirt" and "cost", and the first two examples show different conventions for capitalization. You could capitalize the first letter of each word, as shown by **ShirtCost**. The normal Java style, however, is to leave the first letter lower case and then capitalize the first letter of any remaining words as in **shirtCost**.

You can also use the underscore character (_) in your variable name. Often this is used to visually separate words but can also be used as leading or trailing characters.

```
int shirt_cost;     // embedded underscores are ok
int _pants;         // leading or trailing underscores are ok
```

Numbers are also acceptable in variable names as long as they are not at the beginning. They can be either embedded in the middle or at the end of the name.

```
int area51;         // embedded or trailing numbers are fine
int 42aliens;       // ERROR: can't begin with a number!
```

The dollar sign character can be also be used in anywhere in the name, although the Java specification recommends avoiding the dollar sign completely. You might see dollar signs in some automatically generated code, but don't use it yourself.

```
int $help;          // dollar signs are permitted, but not recommended!
```

All declarations must have names that are one continuous string of letters and symbols. Declarations cannot contain spaces.

```
int no spaces;      // ERROR: can't contain spaces or other whitespace
```

All declarations must have unique names. You cannot use the same name for two different variables that exist in the same place at the same time.

```
int same;         // once is ok, but...
int same;         // ERROR: can't declare the same variable twice
```

The Java compiler has a list of key words that have specific meaning to the compiler; these are called "reserved" words. You cannot use any reserved words as a variable name.

```
int return;       // ERROR: can't use a reserved keyword as a name
```

Assigning Values to Variable

Once you declare a variable, you can assign a value to the variable later in your program. Assigning values to variables is very easy. Just type the variable name, an equals sign ("="), and a value followed by a semicolon. You may also have white-space before and after the equals sign, and before the semicolon. For example:

```
// declare some variables
char    myChar;
int     myInt;
long    myLong;
float   myFloat;
double  myDouble;
boolean myBoolean;

// assign some values to the variables
myChar      = 'A';
myInt       = -42;
myLong      = 1234567890123L;
myFloat     = 3.14F;
myDouble    = 6.02E23;
myBoolean   = true;
```

Notice that you can enter **float** (or **double**) decimal numbers in more than one format. You can use the simple decimal notation or you can use the scientific (exponential) notation with the E character representing "10 raised to the Nth power". So **myDouble** above contains 6.02×10^{23}.

Whenever you enter a decimal number the compiler will assume it is a **double** type unless you add an "F" to the end of the number to indicate a **float** as shown above in "3.14F". If you tried to just assign "3.14" to a **float** variable you would get a "type mismatch" compiler error, because you cannot assign what is assumed to be a **double** value to a smaller **float** variable without possibly losing data.

Similarly, any integer value you type in is assumed to be an **int** data type. If you want to treat it as a **long** you need to append an "L" after it, as shown in the example "1234567890123L" above. If you tried to type in just "1234567890123" the compiler would give you an "out of range" error because that value is too large to store as an **int**.

Also notice that characters must be assigned to the **char** data type by surrounding the character with single quotes ('A'). If you tried to use double quotes, the compiler would give you an error.

```
myChar = "A";    // ERROR: Can't use double quotes for a char data type
```

Using double-quotes indicates a **string**, which is a series of multiple characters strung together. We'll talk more about strings shortly. If you want to assign a character value that you can't type from your keyboard (such as a Chinese character), you can use Unicode notation '\uXXXX' where XXXX is the hexadecimal numeric Unicode value representing the character. You can find tables of Unicode characters online.

Default Variable Values

All of our variables so far have been declared without initializing to any particular value, like this:

```
int     myInt;
char    myChar;
```

Primitive Type	Default Value
byte	0
short	0
int	0
long	0L
float	0.0F
double	0.0
char	'\u0000'
boolean	false

What value do these variables hold? Java will assign a default value to each un-initialized variable as shown in the table to the left.

Many earlier programming languages such as C++ do not assign any default value to un-initialized variables, meaning their contents are completely random. However Java assigns the above default in an attempt to help you avoid errors due to random data. It is still considered bad practice to rely on these default values, so always make sure your variables are initialized to some known data before you try to use them.

Initializing Values during Declaration

You can set initial values at the same time you declare the variable. This is a great way to do two tasks with a single statement! On the declaration line, just add an equal sign and the data before the semicolon like this:

```
char    myChar    = 'A';
int     myInt     = 42;
long    myLong    = 1234567890123L;
float   myFloat   = 3.14F;
double  myDouble  = 6.02E23;
boolean myBoolean = true;
```

Now you know for sure exactly what each variable contains as soon as you declare them.

Simple Mathematical Operations

Many computer programs will need to perform simple math such as addition, subtraction, multiplication, division, or modulus (remainder). In Java, and most programming languages, this is very easy to do! You can use the following symbols to perform these math operations:

Symbol	Description	Example	
+ (plus sign)	Addition	`int myInt = 1 + 2;`	`// myInt = 3`
- (minus sign)	Subtraction	`int myInt = 2 - 1;`	`// myInt = 1`
* (asterisk)	Multiplication	`int myInt = 2 * 3;`	`// myInt = 6`
/ (forward slash)	Division	`double myDouble = 7.0 / 4.0;`	`// myDouble = 1.75`
% (percent)	Modulus (remainder)	`int myInt = 7 % 4;`	`// myInt = 3`

The modulus operator will divide the first number by the second and then return the *remainder* of the operation. You can of course use variables instead of hard-coded numbers for your math; usually you'll be looking at equations involving some mixture of variables and numbers:

```
double rectangleArea = myWidth * myHeight;
double triangleArea  = myBase * myHeight / 2.0;
```

Shortcut Operators

Everybody likes a good shortcut, and programmers are no different. Over the years programmers have found themselves doing certain things so often that shortcuts were invented to save a few keystrokes. The assignment shortcuts allow you to combine any of the mathematical operators with the equals sign. This means that the value in the variable you are *assigning to* is used as the *left side* of the math operation!

Symbol	Description	Example (assuming variable contains **5** to start in all cases)	
+=	Plus-equals	`myInt += 1;`	`// myInt = 6`
-=	Minus-equals	`myInt -= 2;`	`// myInt = 3`
*=	Multiplication-equals	`myInt *= 3;`	`// myInt = 15`
/=	Division-equals	`myDouble /= 4.0;`	`// myDouble = 1.25`
%=	Modulus-equals	`myInt %= 4;`	`// myInt = 1`

Two operations are so frequent that there is an even shorter way to write them! You can add or subtract 1 from a variable and store the result back into that variable with the increment and decrement operators:

Symbol	Description	Example (assuming variable contains **5** to start in both cases)	
++	Increment	`myInt++;`	`// myInt = 6`
--	Decrement	`myInt--;`	`// myInt = 4`

We will use these shortcuts in our example code, and you will find them useful when writing your own too.

Type Casting and Truncation

You may sometimes need to convert data from one type to another. This process is called *casting*. You can cast data from one type to another by putting the target data type in parentheses before the original value:

```
double value1 = 7.2;          // start with a double
int    value2 = (int)value1;  // manually cast the double to an integer
```

What happens to the fractional part of the **double** if you cast it to an **int**? The fractional part is simply *truncated* or dropped, leaving you with an integer value. Because you lose data doing this, the manual cast with parentheses is required to let the compiler know that is exactly what you want to do.

If the cast cannot possibly result in data loss, the compiler will auto-cast for you without needing any data type in parentheses. If you convert from an **int** to a **double**, for example, that is always safe:

```
int    value1 = 7;          // start with an integer
double value2 = value1;     // auto-cast the integer to a double
```

You may need to cast integers to doubles in order to perform more accurate math. Consider this example:

```
int value1 = 5;
int value2 = 2;
double result1 = value1 / value2;                      // result1 = 2.0
double result2 = (double)value1 / (double)value2;      // result2 = 2.5
```

Why is **result1** equal to 2.0 and not 2.5? The expression "**value1 / value2**" will be evaluated first. Dividing two integers will give an integer result, with the fractional part dropped. Then Java will assign the integer result to the **double**, auto-casting it from 2 to 2.0.

In order to get a more accurate result, you can cast **value1** and **value2** to double within the equation. That way Java will perform a division with two doubles, resulting in 2.5 that simply gets stored in **result2**.

Want to learn more about numbers and math in Java? Check out our bonus chapter "Numbers and Math" from your Student Menu! There we describe how numbers are stored in a computer, how to convert between different numeric bases, and how to use the java.lang.Math object to perform rounding and other mathematical operations. The bonus material is not required to complete this course, but you may find it useful.

Java Wrapper Classes

Since the Java language is completely object-oriented, each primitive data type is also represented by its own Java class. These classes are often called "wrapper" classes because they wrap a basic data value into a class that provides some extra functionality. You can always use either the class name or the primitive data type name – they are completely interchangeable!

Here is a list of the primitive data types and their corresponding **java.lang** wrapper class:

Primitive Type	Wrapper Class
byte	Byte
short	Short
int	Integer
long	Long
float	Float
double	Double
char	Character
boolean	Boolean

Let's take a look at some example code using both a primitive and its corresponding wrapper class:

```
int myInt1 = 4;        // declare int variable and initialize to 4
myInt1 = myInt1 + 1;   // add one to that variable
```

```
Integer myInt2 = 4;      // declare Integer variable and initialize to 4
myInt2 = myInt2 + 1;     // add one to that variable
System.out.println(myInt2);   // print value to the console
```

The primitive **int** data type can hold a number and accept the results of mathematical operations on that number. The **Integer** wrapper class can do those same things and also has extra functions you can call to do things like converting the number to a string for display on the screen.

Since the primitive data type and the wrapper class can be mixed together interchangeably, you can set the values directly between one and the other like this:

```
int myInt1 = 42;
Integer myInt2 = myInt1;
```

At this point, both variables contain the same value: 42.

Each wrapper class has some special functions (also called methods) and properties. You can access these functions and properties with the class name and the dot operator (.). Two commonly-used properties are:

- **MAX_VALUE** – This property holds a constant value with the biggest number the type can hold.
- **MIN_VALUE** – This property holds a constant value with the smallest number the type can hold.

These properties are very helpful in determining if you will be able to store a certain value into your variable. The following code demonstrates the use of the **MAX_VALUE** property:

```
// set myInt1 to the maximum possible value for the data type
int maxIntegerValue = Integer.MAX_VALUE;
```

Each wrapper class also has a "value" method that will return the underlying data as the correct primitive type. The following example shows the **Integer.intValue()** and **Double.doubleValue()** methods:

```
Integer myInt1 = 4;
int myInt2 = myInt1.intValue();   // myInt2 now contains 4

Double myDouble1 = 4.0;
double myDouble2 = myDouble1.doubleValue();  // myDouble2 now contains 4.0
```

Lesson Three: Reference Data Types

In the last lessons you learned about "primitive" or "value" data types and variables. When you declare a primitive data variable, you automatically get a spot in computer memory reserved for that value. Each time you declare a new primitive variable, you get a new "instance" or copy that can be set to a different value.

In this lesson, you will learn about *reference* data types. These data types are called "reference" types because declaring them as variables does not create space for the data in memory. Instead the variable name is merely a "reference" to wherever the data actually resides. When you first declare a variable for a reference data type, the variable's value is **null**, which means "nothing". The variable literally refers to nothing and has no data at all associated with it. All reference data types are objects or classes instead of primitive data types.

Think of a reference variable as an entry in your cell phone's contact list. When you meet someone, you can put their phone number in your contact list. Now you have a "reference" to this person, though you didn't make a clone of that entire person just for your own use!

You declare a reference variable just like primitive data; write the data type first and then the variable name. Let's imagine that we have defined a **Contact** object to contain some data. All objects are reference types.

```
Contact myContact;     // myContact is null
```

If you try to use a reference variable that contains **null**, you will cause an error in your program. So how do you set a reference variable so that it refers to actual data? In order to create a new instance of your reference data type, you must use the **new** keyword like this:

```
Contact myContact = new Contact();
```

This creates a new place in memory that will hold an instance of the data type (object). The reference variable **myContact** is merely a link to that place in memory, but the variable itself does not "own" the memory. Notice we added a set of parentheses after the data type when using the **new** keyword. When you create a new instance of a data type, you can sometimes add parameters just like a function to help initialize the data type. The empty parentheses mean there are no parameters needed to create a new instance of that data type.

Another way to set a reference variable is to assign the variable equal to some other reference that has already been initialized with a valid data object.

```
Contact myContact1 = new Contact();
Contact myContact2 = myContact1;  // myContact2 now refers to valid data
```

This does not mean that we are copying the existing object into a new instance! We are merely pointing our reference variable at that existing object. You can imagine sharing the information about "Joe" with your best friend and the guy next door. You have not copied your friend, but he appears in more than one contact list. You now have two references to the same person!

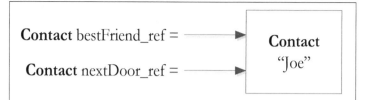

In this same way, two or more reference variables can point to the same object in memory:

```
Contact myContact1 = new Contact();
Contact myContact2 = myContact1;
```

Now, both **myContact1** and **myContact2** refer to the same object in memory! It's like having two names or an alias for the same person.

Since a reference variable can possibly contain **null** instead of a valid reference, you should ensure in your program that your reference variables are not **null** before you use them. You may, on occasion, want to remove the variable reference to some object. In this case simply assign the variable to **null** and it will no longer refer to anything!

```
myContact = null;          // myContact reference variable is now null
```

String Reference Data Type

One of the most common reference data types in the Java language is the **String** data type. A *string* is a series of characters that form a line of text. It can be a short string like someone's name, or a very long string like an entire book. The **String** data type is a reference data type.

To create a **String** variable, you would declare it just like any built-in data type:

```
String myString;
```

In this example, we declare a **String**, but do not initialize it to any value. This means that our **myString** reference variable will start out with a **null** value. In order to use this variable in a program, we will have to initialize it by assigning a text value to it. All text values must be surrounded by double-quotes!

```
myString = "You're a better man than I am, Gunga Din!";
```

Now we can use the string variable in our program.

Notice that we did not have to use the **new** keyword to create a new **String**. The **String** is a special case because it is so heavily used. To initialize a **String**, you only need to assign a value within double-quotes.

Of course, you can declare and initialize a string at the same time:

```
String myString = "Greetings";
```

Now our **myString** variable is created, initialized and is ready-to-use in a program. The **String** is frequently used in Java programs and we will spend more time exploring this useful class later!

Primitive Wrapper Classes

The primitive data type wrapper classes such as **Integer** and **Double** are also reference data types. Just like **String**, they are very commonly used, so Java supports declaration and initialization of them either as a primitive or reference data type. Both sets of code below actually do exactly the same thing:

```
Integer myInt1 = 4;                  // declare & initialize Integer with 4
Integer myInt2 = new Integer(4);     // declare & initialize Integer with 4

Double myDouble1 = 4.0;              // declare & initialize Double with 4.0
Double myDouble2 = new Double(4.0); // declare & initialize Double with 4.0
```

Lesson Four: Printing Data

Now that we have discussed the different Java data types and variables to hold data, let's explore a function to print these variables to the screen. This function will be used in many of our programs during this course.

Introducing System.out

For programs run from a command line (console), the easiest way to print data to the console is through a built-in Java class called **java.lang.System**. The **System** object contains a property called **out**, which itself is an object representing output to the console. To print a line of text to the console, you can call a function on the **System.out** object called **println()**. The function is defined as follows:

```
public void println(String text)
```

The **println()** method will print a string to the console, followed by a newline character to advance the cursor to the next line. If you pass in a primitive data type such as an integer, that value will be automatically converted to text string. This method should look familiar to you, since we used it to write our first program.

```
System.out.println("Hello, World!");
```

In the "Hello World" program, this statement caused the text "Hello, World!" to be printed on the console.

```
Hello, World!
```

If you want to print some text but stay on the same line, you can use the **print()** function instead:

```
System.out.print("abc");
System.out.print("def");
System.out.print("ghi");
```

Now all of those input strings would appear on the same line:

```
abcdefghi
```

Escape Characters

There are some special cases when building text that require the use of *escape sequences*. Escape sequences allow you to put something in a string that would be hard to represent otherwise. For example, tab characters, carriage returns, and linefeeds are difficult to represent in a text string. Also, characters like the double-quote are difficult to represent in strings because the Java language uses these for special features. How would you display a double quote? You could not print a string like this:

```
System.out.println(" " ");     // ERROR:  compiler error
```

The compiler would not understand where the string stops (second quote or third?). To represent these special characters you need to use an escape sequence. Escape characters start with a backslash (\) and finish with one character. These two characters combined are translated by the compiler into a single character and are then stored in the output string. For example, the string: "\n" is a string of length 1 that holds the "new line" character. This causes your output to skip down to the next line.

Here is a list of Java escape characters:

Escape Character	Description
\b	Backspace
\f	Form Feed
\n	New Line
\r	Carriage Return
\t	Horizontal Tab
\'	Single Quote (')
\"	Double Quote (")
\\	Backslash (\)

Now let's use these escape characters in some example code. Notice we are using the "\n" escape character at the end to advance to the next line instead of using **println()**:

```
System.out.print("New line:\n#\n");
System.out.print("Carriage return:\r#\n");
System.out.print("Tab:\t#\n");
System.out.print("Single quote:\'\n");
System.out.print("Double quote:\"\n");
System.out.print("Backslash:\\\n");
```

The examples would output the following lines:

```
New line:
#
Carriage return:
#
Tab:      #
Single quote:'
Double quote:"
Backslash:\
```

Activity: Your First Variables

In this activity you will create a project that declares, initializes and prints values for common data types.

Your activity requirements and instructions are found in the "Chapter_04_Activity.pdf" document located in your "TeenCoder\Java Programming\Activity Docs" folder. You can access this document through your Student Menu or by directly clicking on it from Windows Explorer (Windows) or Finder (Mac OS).

Complete this activity now and ensure your program meets the requirements before continuing!

Chapter Five: Working With Strings

We previously introduced **Strings** as a data type that can hold a line of text. **Strings** are very common variable types that most programs will need to use. In this chapter we take a closer look at **Strings** and the methods you can use to transform, format, and convert them.

Lesson One: Comparing Strings

In this lesson, you will learn how to compare two strings to see if they are equal. String comparisons are useful when you are accepting any type of user input in your program. Validating user IDs, passwords, and answers to questions are all examples where you will need to compare a user's input to some other string.

String Equality

In the Java language, two **char** variables have the same data if they each contain the same character with the same case. The characters must truly be identical in every way: the letter and its case must match. For instance, the characters 'y' and 'Y' are not equal. **String** variables contain many characters in a row. Strings are equal if every character matches the corresponding character in the other string, including case.

The Java **String** class provides the **equals()** function to see if all the characters in one string match the characters in another string.

```
boolean equals(Object inputString)
```

You would call this method on one string and pass in another input string for comparison. The function will return **true** if the strings are identical or **false** if the strings are not equal. If the object you pass in is not already a **String**, Java will do its best to convert it to a string representation.

Let's look at some example string comparisons:

```java
String myString1 = "abc";
String myString2 = "abc";
String myString3 = "ABC";
String myString4 = "abcd";

boolean isEqual1 = myString1.equals(myString2);    // true
boolean isEqual2 = myString1.equals(myString3);    // false
boolean isEqual3 = myString1.equals(myString4);    // false
```

First, we create and initialize four string variables. The first two variables contain identical strings, while the third and fourth variables contain different strings due to case or extra letters.

Next we compare the first string, **myString1**, to the other three strings and store the result in a **boolean** variable. As you can see, the first call to **equals()** will return **true** because the second string is equal to the first. The other two comparisons will return **false** because the strings are not equal.

Case-Insensitive String Comparison

The **String.equalsIgnoreCase()** function gives us another way to compare strings. This function works exactly like the **equals()** function, except that it doesn't care about case-sensitivity. This is a great function to use if you are trying to match string data regardless of the characters' cases.

For example, if our program asked a user a simple yes or no question, we could prompt them like this:

```
Do you want to continue? (YES/NO):
```

The user should then enter either a "YES" or "NO". But what if the user enters "yes" or "Yes" instead of "YES"? You could make multiple calls to the **equals()** function to check possible inputs, or you could just make one simple call to the **equalsIgnoreCase()** function like this:

```java
boolean isEqual = userInput.equalsIgnoreCase("yes");
```

This will return **true** if the user types in "YES", "Yes", "yes", "yEs", or any other value that differs from "yes" only by case.

Lesson Two: Common String Operations

In this lesson you will learn about some common **String** class functions to manage your string data. You will also learn how to access individual characters within the string by using a numeric index.

Characters in a String

A **String** object contains a series of **char** data in a line. You can visualize each character in its own little box, and each box is represented by a number or *index*.

The very first character in the string always has an index of zero! Each character after that increases the index by one. **String** methods that deal with index values for characters use this numbering system.

You can access the individual characters in a **String** by using the **charAt()** method. This method will allow you to grab a specific character by using the index of the character. In the examples below we try to get the characters at index 3 and index 9 from **myString**, which contains "Look out!":

```
String myString = "Look out!";
char result1 = myString1.charAt(3);  // result1 contains 'k'
char result2 = myString1.charAt(9);  // EXCEPTION - index out of range!
```

The first line will run successfully and return the character at index 3, which is the lowercase 'k'. But what happens on the second line? The string "Look out!" only contains 9 characters, so the valid index range is 0 through 8. Attempting to access a character with an invalid index will result in a runtime exception!

 Remember that the first character in the string is index 0, not index 1! The last valid character index is equal to the string length minus one.

String Methods

Programmers have been working with strings for a long time, and the Java **String** class contains many very useful methods that let you manage your string data. We'll describe the more common methods now and you can refer to the Java API documentation if any more unusual methods are needed. Often one method will have several variations that each take input parameters of different data types.

While discussing the **String** methods below, we'll assume these **String** variables have been initialized:

```
String myString1 = "goofy";
String myString2 = "moon";
String myString3 = "MOON";
```

The first useful **String** function we'll examine is **contains()**. This method will accept an input string and search the target string for any match. If a match is found it will return **true**, otherwise it will return **false**. In these examples we search for the strings "n", "oo", and "ooo" in "moon". The first two results are **true** because those strings are found in "moon", but the last result is **false** because "ooo" is not found.

```java
boolean result3 = myString2.contains("n");   // result3 = true
boolean result4 = myString2.contains("oo");  // result4 = true
boolean result5 = myString2.contains("ooo"); // result5 = false
```

The next **String** function, **indexOf()**, is used to determine where a character or substring is within a larger string. For example, the following lines will look at **myString3**, which contains "MOON", and find the first character 'O' at index 1 and the string "MO" starting at index 0. Remember that individual characters are surrounded by single quotes and strings are surrounded by double quotes.

```java
int result6 = myString3.indexOf('O');     // result6 = 1
int result7 = myString3.indexOf("MO");    // result7 = 0
```

Similarly, the **lastIndexOf()** function is used to find the last instance of a character in a string. This is useful when you believe there might be more than once instance of a character in a string, and you are looking for the last instance. In this example we find the last 'O' in **myString3** at index 2:

```java
int result8 = myString3.lastIndexOf('O');     // result8 = 2
```

You can find the number of characters in a **String** by calling the **length()** method. This example looks at **myString1**, which contains "goofy" and returns the number of characters, 5:

```java
int result9 = myString1.length();     // result9 = 5
```

The **replace()** function creates a new string, starting with a source string and replacing all the instances of one character with another character, or one substring with another substring. The following line will create a new string replacing all of the 'o' characters in **myString2** with the letter 'a'. The original contents of **myString2** are unchanged!

```java
String result10 = myString2.replace('o', 'a'); // result10 = "maan"
```

The **substring()** function is used to pull out a piece of a string. This function is given either a starting index or a starting and ending index. Characters will be copied out starting at the first index and continuing to the end of the string or, if provided, to the ending index minus one. In the following code, the **substring()** function will pull characters from **myString2**, which contains "moon", starting at index 1 and continuing either through the end of the line or up through and including index 2. Make sure your input index values represent a valid range in the string!

```
String result11 = myString2.substring(1);        // result11 = "oon"
String result12 = myString2.substring(1, 3);      // result12 = "oo"
```

The **toUpperCase()** and **toLowerCase()** functions will create new strings from a source string, turning all of the characters to upper or lower case. The original contents of the source string are unchanged.

```
String result13 = myString2.toUpperCase();        // result13 = "MOON"
String result14 = myString3.toLowerCase();        // result14 = "moon"
```

String Method Summary

The table below summarizes the **String** methods we have discussed so far:

String Method	Description
equals(X) equalsIgnoreCase(X)	equals() returns **true** if **String** X is equal to the current **String** object. This is a case-sensitive comparison. You may perform a case-insensitive comparison using equalsIgnoreCase() instead.
charAt(X)	Returns the **char** value at the string location specified by the numeric index X. The first **char** in a string is index 0.
contains(X)	Returns **true** if the current string contains the substring X, or **false** if not found.
indexOf(X)	Returns the numeric index of the first occurrence of the character or string X in the string, or -1 if the character or string X is not found.
lastIndexOf(X)	Returns the numeric index of the last occurrence of the character or string X in the string, or -1 if the character or string X is not found.
length()	Returns the number of characters in the string. An empty string returns 0.
replace(X,Y)	Returns a new **String** formed by replacing all occurrences of the character or string X with the character or string Y.
substring(X)	Returns a new **String** copied from the current **String** starting at index X and running through the string end
substring(X,Y)	Returns a new **String** copied from the current **String** starting at index X and ending at index Y-1
toLowerCase()	Returns a new **String** where the contents of the current **String** have been converted to all lower case. The original **String** is unchanged.
toUpperCase()	Returns a new **String** where the contents of the current **String** have been converted to all upper case. The original **String** is unchanged.

Lesson Three: Formatting and Building Strings

There are times you will want to create a **String** based on variable parameters. You may also want to carefully guide how numbers in the string look by setting the number of digits, decimal precision, monetary symbols, and so forth. The Java **String** class has a **format( )** method that allows you to build a new string with variable parameters in several different ways. The **format()** method is static, which means you do not need to create a **String** variable to use it. Simply use the class name followed by a dot and the method name like this: **String.format().**

The **String.format()** method returns a **String** object. As parameters it requires a **format** string and then 0, 1, or more optional parameters:

```
String format(String format, Object param1, Object param2,...)
```

The input **format** parameter can contain a mixture of fixed text and *format specifiers*. Each format specifier will let you control exactly how the individual parameters are displayed within the output string. An trivial input **format** string without any format specifiers such as "Three blind mice" will be returned exactly as-is from the **format()** function, and any optional parameters will be ignored.

```
String result = String.format("Three blind mice", "ignored");
```

The **result** variable will contain "Three blind mice" and the extra parameter is discarded. But that's not very useful… we want to learn how to insert our parameters into the format string!

Simple Format Specifiers

A simple format specifier looks like this: "**%1$s**". What do all these characters and symbols mean?

All format specifiers start with a percent sign (**%**). You then can follow with a numeric index and dollar sign that identifies which parameter value (**1$, 2$**, etc.) you want to display in that location. "**1$**" corresponds to the first parameter, "**2$**" references the second optional parameter, etc. After the dollar sign comes a character that controls how the input data will be formatted to the output string. In this example we used "**s**" which means the inputs will be converted to strings if they are not already strings.

Here are a few examples that use one or two parameters and the "s" conversion:

```
String result1 = String.format("Three %1$s mice", "blind");
String result2 = String.format("%1$s blind mice", 3);
String result3 = String.format("%2$s %1$s mice", "blind", "Three");
```

Can you guess what values will be in the three result strings? Here they are:

```
Three blind mice
3 blind mice
Three blind mice
```

In the first example the format specifier "%1s" is replaced with the string "blind" at that location within the format string. In the second example the same format specifier converts the number 3 to a string "3" and places it at the beginning. Finally, we demonstrated a trickier example using two parameters. Notice that we used the "**2$**" first to substitute the second parameter near the beginning, then used the "**1$**" to pull in the first parameter later. Of course in your code the parameters most likely will be variables instead of hard-coded values, but the substitution pattern works the same way.

Advanced Format Specifiers

You can make your format specifiers more powerful by adding some optional pieces. Here is the complete set of options that can be used for a specifier:

% [parameter_index$] [flags] [width] [.precision] conversion

Everything that is written within the square brackets is optional. This means that the only required parts of the format specifier are the percent sign (%) and a conversion character. If you do not use a numeric index, then the first format specifier will use the first parameter, the second format specifier will use the second parameter, and so on. Here is an example:

```
String result = String.format("Three %s %s", "blind", "mice");
```

The returned string will contain "Three blind mice", as the "%s" format specifiers pull the first and second parameter into their respective locations in the format string.

The **[width]** option is a number that sets the minimum output width the parameter value will occupy, using blanks to pad the output as needed. It does not imply any maximum width however.

```
String result1 = String.format "The %1$3s musketeers", 3);
String result2 = String.format "The %1$3s musketeers", "three");
```

These examples produce the following strings, where you can see the parameter substitution takes at least 3 characters but may use more if needed:

```
The   3 musketeers
The three musketeers
```

The **[width]** option can be used to easily align columns of numbers on the screen. If the specified width is positive then the text is right-aligned. If the width is negative, the text is left-aligned. If the width is smaller than the string, the alignment indicator is ignored. The text will not be truncated to fit the specified width. Here are some additional examples using the width to left and right-justify columns of numbers.

```
String result1 = String.format("#%5s#", "123");
String result2 = String.format("#%-5s#", "123");
String result3 = String.format("#%5s#", "1234567");
```

The resulting strings will contain:

```
#  123#
#123  #
#1234567#
```

Conversion Characters and Conversion Flags

The "conversion" character is required at the end of your format specifier. So far we have used "s" which produces simple strings, but there are many more conversions to choose from! The following table lists some of the more common conversion characters:

Conversion Character	Description	Example	Results
s	Displays a simple string	**String.format**("%s", "hello");	"hello"
S	Converts string to upper case	**String.format**("%S", "hello");	"HELLO"
d	Displays value as base-10 integer	**String.format**("%d", 12);	"12"
E or e	Formats the number in scientific (exponential) notation.	**String.format**("%E", 12.4); **String.format**("%e", 12.4);	"1.240000E+001" "1.240000e+001"
f	Formats the number as a decimal	**String.format**("%f", 12.4);	"12.400000"
tD	Displays the date in month/day /year or other local format.	**String.format**("%tD", **Calendar.getInstance**( ));	"11/31/2011"
tF	Displays the date in year-month-day format.	**String.format**("%tF", **Calendar.getInstance**( ));	"2011-11-31"
tT	Displays the 24-hour time from the input **Calendar**.	**String.format**("%tT", **Calendar.getInstance**( ));	"13:34:18"
tr	Displays the 12-hour time with AM/PM.	**String.format**("%tr", **Calendar.getInstance**( ));	"1:34:18 PM"
%	Displays a percent character	**String.format**("%%");	"%"
n	Adds a newline character to the string	**String.format**("hop%nscotch");	"hop scotch"

The "t" character represents a time and date value held in a **Calendar** object. In order to use the **Calendar**, you will first need to **import** it at the top of your source file:

```
import java.util.Calendar;
```

Notice that the "t" has an additional character after it to describe what part of the date/time value to display and in what format it should appear. The format of the time and date display will be automatically adjusted to match the preferred style in the local country, which may order the month/day/year values differently or use different symbols. There are many, many more options available for conversion characters, especially around the date/time display, so please refer to the Java API documentation for more details if you are curious.

The **[.precision]** option is not valid for characters, integers, or date/time values. It only works for conversions like "f" that produce decimal numbers or general-purpose strings. In the case of decimal numbers, the precision controls the number of digits after the decimal point. For general strings, the precision controls the overall maximum width of the field.

```
String result1 = String.format("%.4f", 12.4567);
String result2 = String.format("%.4s", 12.4567);
String result3 = String.format("%.4s", "longer");
```

In the first example we have formatted the input value as "f" which is a fractional number, so the precision ".4" will ensure there are four decimal places after the dot. In the second case we treated the input as a string with "s", so the same precision just sets the overall string length to 4 characters. Similarly in the last example the longer input string is truncated to just 4 characters on output!

```
12.4567
12.4
long
```

You can, of course, combine the width and precision options:

```
String result = String.format("%10.3f", 12.4567);
```

Here we have specified that the overall width is 10 characters and the floating-point precision is 3 characters. The resulting output has 10 total characters and 3 digits to the right of the decimal point:

```
"    12.457"
```

Before the **[width]** value you can add some optional **[flags]** to further guide the output format. The table below describes the common **[flags]** you can add to a format specifier.

Flag	Description	Example	Results
'-'	The dash flag will cause the result to be left-justified within the specified width.	String.format("%-10.3f", 12.4567));	`"12.457      "`
'+'	The plus flag will cause the numeric result to always include the + or – sign.	String.format("%+10.3f", 12.4567));	`"   +12.457"`
'0'	The zero flag will cause the numeric result to be zero-padded to the left.	String.format("%010.3f", 12.4567));	`"000012.457"`
','	The comma flag will cause the numeric value to have a thousand's separator.	String.format("%,12d", 12345678);	`"  12,345,678"`
'('	The open parenthesis will put negative numbers within in parentheses.	String.format("%(10.3f", 12.4567)); String.format("%(10.3f", -12.4567));	`"    12.457"` `"  (12.457)"`

We have shown you many powerful formatting options that are available with the **String.format()** command. However there are more detailed options available and we can't possibly cover them all! So if you need to format output in a certain way that was not mentioned above, please refer to the Java API documents for the **String.format()** command for a detailed description of all options.

String Concatenation

Concatenation is the process of putting together two pieces. You can put together two smaller strings to make a larger string. This is a common task, so Java allows you to "add" two strings together using the plus sign (+).

```
String myString = "hello" + "goodbye";
```

The above example places the value "hellogoodbye" into the **myString** variable. Notice that there is no natural space between words because we didn't specify one inside the quotes. This is important to remember when you are combining text: Java will not add natural spaces around words; you must do it yourself.

If you have a variable with some string contents already, and you want to add more to the end, you can use the plus-equals operator (+=). Notice that we placed our own space before the word " there".

```
String myString = "hello";
myString += " there";              // myString contains "hello there"
myString = myString + " there";    // myString contains "hello there there"
```

The result after the second line is the string "hello there". The += operator does the same thing as a full assignment statement where the left value is added to the right value and stored back in the left variable. The third line shows the equivalent assignment, adding " there" again to the end of the current **myString** value.

Lesson Four: Converting Between Strings and Numbers

You will often need to convert a **String** variable to a number or a numeric variable to a **String**. The Java language makes both of these operations very easy.

Converting Numbers to Strings

Every data type in the Java language has a method called **toString()**. The **toString()** method is used to do just what it says – change any data value into a string value. Remember that each primitive data type such as **int** or **boolean** has a corresponding **java.lang** class like **Integer** and **Boolean**. You call the **toString()** method on these classes and pass in the primitive data to be converted. For example:

```java
int myInt = 42;
String myString1 = Integer.toString(myInt);    // myString1 = "42"


double myDouble = 3.14159;
String myString2 = Double.toString(myDouble); // myString2 = "3.14159"


boolean myBool = false;
String myString3 = Boolean.toString(myBool);  // myString3 = "false"
```

If you attempt to concatenate a primitive number onto a **String** using the (+) operator, then the **toString()** method will be automatically called on the corresponding wrapper object! Take a look at this cool feature:

```java
int intAge = 18;
String stringAge1 = intAge;      // ERROR - cannot assign a number to a string
String stringAge2 = "" + intAge; // OK - string concatenation calls toString
System.out.println("My age is: " + intAge);   // OK - string concatenation
```

You can see the second line is an obvious compiler-time error because you cannot simply assign one data type like an **int** to another incompatible data type like a **String**. However, the last two lines work fine because the string concatenation operator (+) will automatically wrap the primitive **int** with an **Integer** class and call **toString()** to obtain the string "18" from the wrapper object.

Converting Strings to Numbers

To convert a **String** into a numeric data type is slightly more complicated than converting a number to a string. When looking at a string that may (or may not) contain a number, we need to *parse* the string to see what number might be inside. Again we will use the data type **java.lang** wrapper classes to do the job. Each numeric wrapper class has its own parsing method that will scan the input string and pull out a number of the correct data type, if possible.

Let's take a look at an example. To convert an integer into a string, we would use the **Integer** class method called **parseInt()**.

```
String myString1 = "42";
int myInt1 = Integer.parseInt(myString1);    // myInt1 = 42
```

If you wanted to translate a string into a **boolean** value, you would use the **Boolean** class method called **parseBoolean()**.

```
String myString2 = "true";
boolean myBoolean = Boolean.parseBoolean(myString2);  // myBoolean = true
```

Here is the full list of Java numeric primitive classes, their parse methods, and an example.

Class Name	Parse Method	Example
Integer	parseInt(String)	int myInt = Integer.parseInt("56");
Short	parseShort(String)	short myShort = Short.parseShort("56");
Long	parseLong(String)	long myLong = Long.parseLong("56");
Byte	parseByte(String)	byte myByte = Byte.parseByte("56");
Float	parseFloat(String)	float myFloat = Float.parseFloat("56.78");
Double	parseDouble(String)	double myDouble = Double.parseDouble("56.78");
Boolean	parseBoolean(String)	boolean myBoolean = Boolean.parseBoolean("true");

It's important to keep in mind that the parse methods will only work properly if you are trying to convert a string with the right numeric data for the target data type. For example, you cannot take a string value of "904" and parse it into a **Byte** data type! The **Byte** data type will only hold values up to 127.

The following code will compile without any errors:

```
byte myByte = Byte.parseByte("904");
```

But when you try to run your program, this statement will cause an error or exception! You will likely see the error printed to your console like this:

```
Exception in thread "main" java.lang.NumberFormatException: Value out of range.
Value:"904" Radix:10
```

In addition, the parsing methods are not smart enough to translate words into numbers. So we could not translate a string to a number with code like this:

```
int myInt = Integer.parseInt("fifty-six");
```

This line of code will also generate a run-time error in your program, since Java cannot interpret the string "fifty-six" as a number:

```
Exception in thread "main" java.lang.NumberFormatException: For input string:
"fifty-six"
```

So what happens if you don't know what data is in a string before you try to convert it? If you try to parse incorrect data, the program will raise exceptions like we have shown above. We will discuss how to handle and avoid exceptions later on in this course.

 **Activity: String Theory**

In this activity, you will create, compare and change **String** values.

Your activity requirements and instructions are found in the "Chapter_05_Activity.pdf" document located in your "TeenCoder\Java Programming\Activity Docs" folder. You can access this document through your Student Menu or by directly clicking on it from Windows Explorer (Windows) or Finder (Mac OS).

Complete this activity now and ensure your program meets the requirements before continuing!

Chapter Six: User Input

In this chapter, we will take a more in-depth look at some different ways to read and validate user input from a command-line program.

Lesson One: Using Command Line Parameters

Command-line parameters are values supplied when a program is run from the command line or console. In the early days of computing, most programs were run from the console, so command-line parameters were very common. For example, if you entered a program name followed by the word "-help" on the command line, most programs would have printed out a list of the accepted command line parameters. In fact, "-help" was a parameter itself!

Today you can still pass command-line parameters to a Java program running in the console. After you type "java" and the class name, add any number of values you like separated by spaces. For example, typing "java HelloWorld Chris" on the command line would pass the parameter "Chris" to the HelloWorld program. By changing the code inside HelloWorld slightly we can echo that parameter back out to the user:

```
C:\TeenCoder\Java Programming\My Projects\HelloWorld>java HelloWorld Chris
Hello, Chris

C:\TeenCoder\Java Programming\My Projects\HelloWorld>_
```

Command-Line Parameters in the main() Function

In Java, the command line parameters are given to the program as parameters to the **main()** function. Let's take another look at the **main()** function you have seen at the beginning of each of your classes so far:

```
public static void main(String[] args)
{

}
```

There is only one parameter to the **main()** function: a variable called **args**. Due to the square brackets "[ ]", this parameter is a special data type called an *array*. We will talk more about arrays in a future lesson, but for now you should understand that an array is a group of values that all have the same type. These values can be accessed by an index number or the position in the group, starting with zero. So the first value in the **args** array is value **args**[0], the next value is **args**[1], and so on. All of these individual values are **String** objects.

Let's say we create a class named **ParamTest** with a **main()** function. We then add some code to the **main()** function that makes use of two command-line parameters:

```java
class ParamTest
{
    public static void main(String[] args)
    {
        System.out.println("Parameter 1: " + args[0]);
        System.out.println("Parameter 2: " + args[1]);
    }
}
```

This simple program just prints out the value of the first two parameters passed from the command line. What would happen if you were to run the program with parameters "howdy" and "partner!"?

```
java ParamTest howdy partner!
```

You would get in the following output:

```
Parameter 1: howdy!
Parameter 2: partner!
```

Verifying Command-Line Input

You cannot be certain ahead of time how many parameters a program will receive. Users may not know what your program expects, or they may not follow even the clearest directions! If you attempt to run our **ParamTest** program without any parameters, you will receive a runtime exception. Why? The input **args** array will not contain any data, but the code attempts to access the first element **args**[0] on this line:

```java
System.out.println("Parameter 1: " + args[0]);  // possible exception!
```

The program will generate an error, since the **args** array does not contain an element at index 0. The same error would occur on the next line if we only passed one parameter and tried to print the second parameter.

```
System.out.println("Parameter 2: " + args[1]);  // possible exception!
```

So if you want to use command-line parameters, you should always check to make sure you have the number of parameters expected! You can get the number of values in an array by reading the **length** property:

```
int numArgs = args.length;  // numArgs will contain the number of values
```

The **length** property may return 0, 1, or more depending on how many values are in the array.

Now we can re-write our simple **main()** function so that we only print out an argument value if we know for sure it exists. We are going to use a little bit of "decision-making" logic using something called an **if()** statement. You will learn all about decision making and flow control in the next chapter, but for now just understand that the **if()** statement asks a question that evaluates to **true** or **false**, and if the result is **true** then the code within the curly braces after the **if()** statement will be executed.

```java
public static void main(String[] args)
{
    if (args.length > 0)  // is args.length greater than zero?
    {
        System.out.println("Parameter 1: " + args[0]);
    }
    if (args.length > 1)  // is args.length greater than one?
    {
        System.out.println("Parameter 2: " + args[1]);
    }
}
```

Now we are only printing parameters 1 and 2 if we are sure there is enough data in the **args** array. If there is only one parameter, then only that first parameter will be printed and the second will be skipped. If there are two parameters then both will be printed. If there are no parameters then nothing will be printed!

Lesson Two: Interactive User Input

Now we know how to get command-line arguments when the user starts a program, but how do we get input while the program is already running? We would like our program to be able to interactively ask the user questions, receive their answers, and process the data according to the needs of our program.

In order to get user input from a console program, we can use a handy Java class called the **Scanner**. The **Scanner** class will allow you to read inputs of different data types into your program. There are many different methods available for this class – many more than we can discuss in one lesson. We will focus on the methods that allow us to get information that a user types on the keyboard.

Using the Scanner Class

Before using the **Scanner** class you'll want to add the class package to your import list at the top of the source file. The **Scanner** class is in the **java.util** package, so import that package as follows:

```java
import java.util.*;
```

The next thing you will need to do is create a new **Scanner** variable. Since a **Scanner** is a class that means it is a reference data type, so we will use the **new** keyword to create this variable.

```java
Scanner input = new Scanner(System.in);
```

The **Scanner()** class needs one parameter when it is created: a source from which the input data will be read. In our case we want to read the input from the console where the user is typing, so we use the value **System.in**. **System.in** is something called an **InputStream** and it represents everything the user is typing into the console through the keyboard. You have already used **System.in**'s cousin, **System.out**, in order to print text back to the console!

Now our **Scanner** is ready and waiting for input. We need to tell our user what data we are expecting them to enter, so let's print some instructions to the screen:

```java
System.out.print("Type your name and press Enter: ");
```

Notice that we used the **print()** method and not the **println()** method. This is because the **println()** method will put the cursor on the next line on the screen. In our case, we want the cursor to remain after the colon (:) until the user enters their data, so we use the **print()** method.

Next we need to retrieve our user's name. We can do that with the **Scanner.nextLine()** method.

```
String username = input.nextLine();
```

nextLine() will wait for the user to type in some characters to the console and press the "Enter" key. All of those characters are then stored in the returned **String**. When the user presses the "Enter" key a "newline" character ('\n') is added to the input stream. This is the signal that the end of the line has been reached. When calling **nextLine()**, the newline character is discarded and will not be returned in the resulting string.

Finally, when you are done with the **Scanner** object, it's good practice to call the **close()** function on it to release any resources held by the **Scanner**.

```
input.close();
```

Here is a complete example that shows how to create a **new Scanner** object, read in a couple of lines of text, and print the results back out to the screen:

```java
public static void main(String[] args)
{
    Scanner input = new Scanner(System.in);

    System.out.print("Type your name and press Enter: ");
    String username = input.nextLine();
    System.out.println("Hello " + username);

    System.out.print("Type your city and press Enter: ");
    String cityName = input.nextLine();
    System.out.println("You live in " + cityName);

    input.close();
}
```

When running console programs in Eclipse, a "Console" tab will appear at the bottom of the IDE.

```
Problems  @ Javadoc  Declaration  Console ☒
                                          ■ ✖ ✖  ▣ ▤ ▣▣  ▣ ▣ ▾ ▫ ▾
<terminated> HelloWorld2 [Java Application] C:\Program Files\Java\jre7\bin\javaw.exe (Feb 16, 2013 5:12:59 PM)
Type your name and press Enter: Wrascally Wrabbit
Hello Wrascally Wrabbit
Type your city and press Enter: Atlanta, GA
You live in Atlanta, GA
```

When you are trying to type in user input, make sure to click on the "Console" tab first so the console has the focus, otherwise your keyboard typing will not go to the console.

Scanning Multiple Data Fields

You might want the user to enter more than one piece of information on the same line. Each piece of information must be separated by a *delimiter*. A delimiter is a character (or characters) that separate different data fields from a single line of text or an input stream. If you used a space as a delimiter, then each word in the input would be considered a different data value. The **Scanner** object by default recognizes any whitespace characters (such as spaces, tabs, or newlines) as delimiters. It is possible to change the delimiter to a more complicated pattern, but that is beyond the scope if this course, so let's stick with the defaults.

Since **Scanner.nextLine()** reads all of the values on a line as a single string, we'll clearly need a different way to get individual data fields from the same line. The **Scanner.next()** method will do exactly this.

```
Scanner input = new Scanner(System.in);
String username = input.next();
```

The **next()** method will wait until the user has typed in some data followed by any delimiter, and will then return that value. You can call the **next()** method more than one time to retrieve as many values as you like from the input stream. By the way, our remaining examples in this chapter will all assume **input** has been initialized as a **Scanner** object, and you will call **close()** when you are done with it.

```
System.out.print("Type your name and city, then press Enter: ");
String name = input.next();
String city = input.next();
System.out.println(name + " in " + city);
```

If the user types in "Wrabbit Atlanta" in this example, the "Wrabbit" will be returned by the first call to **next()** and "Atlanta" will be returned by the second call.

Scanning Numeric Data

The **nextLine()** and **next()** **Scanner** methods will return **Strings**. But what if you wanted the user to enter numbers instead, or a mixture of numbers and strings? Instead of using **next()**, you can use one of several methods that will scan the input and automatically convert it to a different primitive data type. The following table lists the most common primitive methods and examples using them from the **Scanner**.

Data Type	Method Name	Example
boolean	nextBoolean()	**boolean** result = input.**nextBoolean**();
byte	nextByte()	**byte** result = input.**nextByte**();
double	nextDouble()	**double** result = input.**nextDouble**();
float	nextFloat()	**float** result = input.**nextFloat**();
int	nextInt()	**int** result = input.**nextInt**();
long	nextLong()	**long** result = input.**nextLong**();
short	nextShort()	**short** result = input.**nextShort**();

Let's look at a simple example:

```
System.out.print("Type your age and favorite color, then press Enter: ");
int age = input.nextInt();
String color = input.next();
System.out.println("Your age is '" + age + "'");
System.out.println("Your favorite color is '" + color + "'");
```

If you entered "18 green", the output would be:

```
Problems  @ Javadoc  Declaration  Console

<terminated> HelloWorld2 [Java Application] C:\Program Files\Java\jre7\bin\javaw.exe (Feb 16, 2013 5:35:03 PM)
Type your age and favorite color, then press Enter: 18 green
Your age is '18'
Your favorite color is 'green'
```

Using next() Across Multiple Lines

You may want to use mixture of **next**() and **nextLine**() in your code. Sometimes you want to get an entire line and other times you need to parse out a numeric data value. Or perhaps you want to call one of the methods like **nextInt**() to parse data on several different lines. Consider this reasonable-looking example:

```
System.out.print("Type your full name and press Enter: ");
String name = input.nextLine();
System.out.print("Type your age and press Enter: ");
int age = input.nextInt();
System.out.print("Type your nickname and press Enter: ");
String nickname = input.nextLine();
System.out.println(name + "(" + nickname + ") is " + age + " years old");
```

What happens after the user enters their age and presses "Enter"? Surprise! They don't get a chance to enter their nickname, the last **nextLine()** call returns immediately with an empty string.

```
Problems  @ Javadoc  Declaration  Console
<terminated> HelloWorld2 [Java Application] C:\Program Files\Java\jre7\bin\javaw.exe (Feb 16, 2013 5:36:45 PM)
Type your full name and press Enter: Wrascally Wrabbit
Type your age and press Enter: 18
Type your nickname and press Enter: Wrascally Wrabbit() is 18 years old
```

What's going on here? The key is that none of the "next" methods except **nextLine()** will remove the newline character itself from the input stream! So when you call **nextInt()** above and the user types in "18" and then hits the Enter key, the 18 is read into the age variable but the newline character is left on the input stream. Then the following call to **nextLine()** sees that newline and returns an empty string immediately.

How do we fix this problem? The secret is to flush the newline character from the input stream after calling one of the "next" methods where the user has hit "Enter" afterwards. To get rid of the newline, just make a call to **nextLine()**! That will read the newline and discard it, leaving your input stream empty and ready for the next input. Here is the example again, corrected with a call to **nextLine()** after calling **nextInt()**:

```java
System.out.print("Type your full name and press Enter: ");
String name = input.nextLine();
System.out.print("Type your age and press Enter: ");
int age = input.nextInt();
input.nextLine();        // CLEAR OUT THE NEWLINE!!

System.out.print("Type your nickname and press Enter: ");
String nickname = input.nextLine();

System.out.println(name + "(" + nickname + ") is " + age + " years old");
```

Now the program will behave as we expect, giving the user a chance to enter their nickname:

```
Problems  @ Javadoc  Declaration  Console
<terminated> HelloWorld2 [Java Application] C:\Program Files\Java\jre7\bin\javaw.exe (Feb 16, 2013 5:28:54 PM)
Type your full name and press Enter: Wrascally Wrabbit
Type your age and press Enter: 18
Type your nickname and press Enter: Blazin' Bunny
Wrascally Wrabbit(Blazin' Bunny) is 18 years old
```

Lesson Three: Validating User Input

You might be wondering what happens if the user enters a string value when you are expecting a number. As you might guess, calling a method like **nextInt()** when there is a non-numeric string waiting will cause an error. You need to learn how to *validate* user input.

It is always important when accepting input from a user to make sure that you are receiving *expected* input. What if the user enters a string when you ask them for a number? Or what if they don't enter any data at all? If this happens, the **Scanner** "next" methods will cause an error in your program. Look at this:

```java
System.out.print("Type in your GPA and press Enter: ");
double gpa = input.nextDouble();
input.nextLine(); // clear the newline when using next methods
System.out.println("Your GPA is " + gpa);
```

Here's what happens if you don't enter a numeric value.

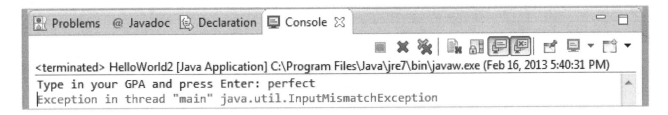

You can see an **InputMismatchException** exception was raised when the unexpected data was read. This type of error will cause your program to exit, so we want to avoid it. Therefore, we need a way to check our user's input before we attempt to read from the input stream.

To do this, we can use a separate set of **Scanner** methods called the **hasNext** methods. There is a "hasNext" method for each of the numeric "next" methods that we discussed in the last lesson. Each "hasNext" method will look at the next data in the input stream and return **true** if that data can be converted to the target numeric type. Only if you are sure that the input stream contains the right kind of data should you call the matching "next" methods to retrieve the data.

Data Type	Method Name	"Has" Method Name
boolean	nextBoolean()	hasNextBoolean()
byte	nextByte()	hasNextByte()
double	nextDouble()	hasNextDouble()
float	nextFloat()	hasNextFloat()
int	nextInt()	hasNextInt()
long	nextLong()	hasNextLong()
short	nextShort()	hasNextShort()

Remember in the last lesson we used an **if()** statement when checking to see if the user entered enough command-line parameters. We will use the same statement here to check the **boolean** result from the **hasNext** methods and only call the matching **next** if the result is **true**. We are also going to extend the **if()** statement with an **else** clause. The **else** clause will specify some section of code to run when the **if()** statement expression is **false** instead of **true**.

In this improved example we are checking for a valid **double** before calling **nextDouble()**:

```
Scanner input = new Scanner(System.in);


System.out.print("Type in your GPA and press Enter: ");
if ( input.hasNextDouble() )  // if hasNextDouble() returns true
{
    double gpa = input.nextDouble();  // pull double from input stream
    System.out.println("Your GPA is " + gpa);
}
else  // hasNextDouble() has returned false
{
    String error = input.next();        // get whatever user did type in
    System.out.println("Invalid entry: " + error);
}
input.nextLine(); // clear the newline when using next methods
```

Now the program will execute your **else** logic if the user types in non-numeric data:

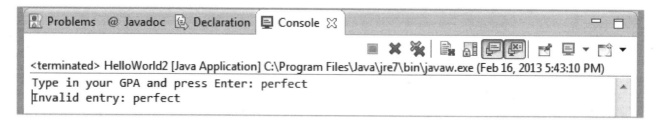

However it will print your GPA if you enter a numeric value:

```
Type in your GPA and press Enter: 4.0
Your GPA is 4.0
```

Remember that even if your user's data does not match your expected type, and the **hasNext** method returns **false**, you will still want to pull that data from the input stream to clear it out! Otherwise it will still be there the next time you try to use the stream. In our **else** clause above we used the **next**() method to pull out whatever bad input the user entered as a **String,** which can handle any data the user can type in.

Don't forget to call **nextLine**() whenever you have used one of the **next**() methods and need to tidy up the input stream. This will clear any remaining characters and the newline entered by the user.

Activity: Conversation Piece

In this activity, you will gather user input to create a short story.

Your activity requirements and instructions are found in the "Chapter_06_Activity.pdf" document located in your "TeenCoder\Java Programming\Activity Docs" folder. You can access this document through your Student Menu or by directly clicking on it from Windows Explorer (Windows) or Finder (Mac OS).

Complete this activity now and ensure your program meets the requirements before continuing!

Chapter Seven: Basic Flow Control

In this chapter you will learn how to test for conditions to see if an expression is **true** or **false**, and change the execution path (program flow) based on the answer. Your programs will frequently use this sort of *flow control* to avoid error conditions, respond to user input, or process data.

Lesson One: Logical Expressions and Relational Operators

In this lesson, we will learn about logical expressions and relational operators.

Logical Expressions

Logical expressions compare values and produce a Boolean value of **true** or **false**. For example:

```
1 < 2
```

This statement is a logical expression that results in **true**, since 1 is in fact less than 2. The '<' symbol stands for "less than" and is one example of a *relational operator*.

Expressions that do not result in either a **true** or **false** are NOT logical expressions. For example:

```
1 + 2
```

This is a *mathematical expression*, not a logical expression, since it results in a number (3) and not **true** or **false**.

Mathematical expressions always result in a number.

Logical expressions always result in either "true" or "false".

You will use logical expressions to compare data in your variables and make decisions in your program based on the variable contents.

Relational Operators

Relational operators are the comparison symbols used in logical expressions. All programming languages including Java generally use the same set of symbols for relational operators. Let's look at some operators that perform comparisons such as "less than", "greater than", "equal to", and so on.

The first relational operator is the *less than* (<) operator. The result of this operator is **true** if the left side of the expression is smaller, or less than the right side. The statement is **false** if the left side of the equation is not less than the right side. For example:

```
1 < 2     is a true statement since 1 is less than 2.
2 < 1     is a false statement since 2 is not less than 1.
1 < 1     is a false statement since 1 is not less than 1.
```

The next relational operator is the *less than or equal to* (<=) operator. The result of this operator in a logical expression is **true** if the left side of an expression is smaller than or equal to the right side. The result is **false** if the left side is not smaller or equal to the right side. For example:

```
1 <= 2    is a true statement since 1 is less than 2.
2 <= 1    is a false statement since 2 is not less than nor equal to 1.
1 <= 1    is a true statement since 1 is equal to 1.
```

The *greater than* (>) operator will return **true** if the left side of an expression is larger than the right side. The result is **false** if the left side is not greater than the right side. For example:

```
1 > 2     is a false statement since 1 is not greater than 2.
2 > 1     is a true statement since 2 is greater than 1.
1 > 1     is a false statement since 1 is not greater than 1.
```

Next, we have the *greater than or equal to* (>=) operator. The result of this operator in a logical expression is **true** if the left side of an expression is larger than or equal to the right side. The result is **false** if the left side is not larger than or equal to the right side. For example:

```
1 >= 2    is a false statement since 1 is not greater than nor equal to 2
2 >= 1    is a true statement since 2 is greater than 1.
1 >= 1    is a true statement since 1 is equal to 1.
```

The next operator is the *equal to* (==) operator. The result of this operator is **true** if both sides of a logical expression are the same. For example:

```
1 == 2     is a false statement since 1 does not equal 2.
2 == 1     is a false statement since 2 does not equal 1.
1 == 1     is a true statement since 1 equals 1.
```

Note the difference between the use of the symbol "=" and the symbols "==". The single equals sign is used to assign a value to a variable, while the double-equals sign is used to compare two values:

```
int a = 1;     // this is an assignment statement
if (a == 1)    // this is a logical expression used in an if() statement
```

If you try to use the wrong symbol, Java will give you the errors shown below.

```
int a == 1;   // Syntax error on token "==", = expected
if (a = 1)    // Type mismatch: cannot convert from int to boolean
```

The first error is straightforward, letting you know you need to use a single equals sign for an assignment statement. The second error means the **if()** statement requires a logical expression that results to **true** or **false** within the parentheses, but the assignment statement results in an integer instead of a Boolean.

The last relational operator is the *not equal to* (!=) operator. This operator returns **true** if the two sides of the expression are not equal to each other. The result is **false** if they are equal to each other. For example:

```
1 != 2     is a true statement since 1 is not equal to 2.
2 != 1     is a true statement since 2 is not equal to 1.
1 != 1     is a false statement since 1 is equal to 1.
```

These relational operators are very important in the use of flow control, since they help the program to make decisions about what statements to execute.

Variables in Logical Expressions

So now that we have discussed logical expressions and relational operators, how are they used in a program? Most of the time, these expressions are used to make decisions about what lines of your program are executed and what lines are not executed. Typically you will not be using hard-coded numbers (e.g. 1 < 2) in your program; you already know that answer in advance! It's much more powerful to use variables in your logical expressions instead.

All of the basic numeric variable types can be used freely in logical expressions. For example, if "age" was a numeric data type, these logical expressions are valid:

```
age > 18
age == 18
age != 18
```

Be aware, however, that it's not so simple for strings! If "name" was a string value containing some text, these expressions are valid and will compile, but they will not do what you expect.

```
name == "Barney"
name != "Wilma"
```

Remember that all **Strings** are objects and therefore are reference data types. If you use the equals-to or not-equal-to operator on object references, that will only tell you if the references point to the exact same object. It will not tell you if the contents of the object are the same! Consider this code:

```
String name1 = "B";        // start with "B"
name1 += "arney";          // now make "Barney"
String name2 = "Barney";
if (name1 == name2)        // compare object references name1 and name2
{
    System.out.println("name1 is equal to name2");
}
```

This code may not produce any output. That is because **name1** and **name2** variables can refer to different **Strings** in memory, even though those strings contain the same text. Remember from an earlier chapter you use the **equals()** and **equalsIgnoreCase()** methods to see if the *contents* of two **Strings** are the same.

Compound Expressions

It is possible to build more complex logical expressions by combining individual **true/false** expressions. You can combine logical expressions with the following logical operators:

Symbol	Name	Description
"&&"	AND	The result of "A && B" is **true** if both A and B are **true** expressions. "A && B" is **false** if either A or B are **false**.
"||"	OR	The result of "A || B" is **true** if either A or B is **true**. "A || B" is **false** if both A and B are **false**.
"!"	NOT	The result of "!A" is **true** if A is **false**. "!A" is **false** if A is **true**.

For example, if you wanted an expression to evaluate as **true** for all the people who are over 18 *and* less than 65, you could use the AND operator "&&":

```
age > 18 && age < 65
```

If you wanted to write an expression to evaluate as **true** for all the people who are either 16, 18, or 20 years old you could use this expression with OR operators "||":

```
age == 16 || age == 18 || age == 20
```

Finally, if you wanted to write an expression to evaluate as **true** for all people that are not 14 years old, you could use the NOT operator "!":

```
!(age == 14)
```

Notice there are often different ways to write an expression to get the same result. These are equivalent:

```
age != 14        // age not-equal-to 14
!(age == 14)     // not (age equal to 14)
```

You can (and should) use parentheses around each logical expression to clarify where the expression starts and stops. You can also use parentheses to ensure the correct grouping of related expressions. For example, if you wanted an expression to evaluate to **true** of a person's age was 16 or 17 and weight was over 100, you could write this:

```
weight > 100 && age == 16 || age == 17
```

However it's not clear at a glance if this will do what you expect. The compiler may evaluate "weight > 100" first, and then AND the result to "age == 16", and then OR that result to "age == 17", which isn't what we wanted at all! We wanted "age == 16" OR "age == 17" to be evaluated as a group, and then the result AND-ed to "weight > 100".

There are rules in each language that specify exactly what the compiler will do in this situation. If you understand all of those rules you can write expressions that will behave correctly. However, it's far better to use parentheses to specify exactly what to do and not leave it to mysterious rules that other programmers might not understand. For example:

```
(weight > 100) && (age == 16 || age == 17)
```

All expressions within parentheses will be evaluated first, and then joined together with the operators between expressions. Now we have made it clear to the compiler and other programmers that we want the two age expressions evaluated and OR-ed together, and then the result AND-ed to the weight expression. Here is how the program will break down this expression, step-by-step, assuming weight = 101 and age = 17.

```
(weight > 100) && (age == 16 || age == 17)
(    true   ) && (   false  ||    true  )
(    true   ) && (            true        )
            true        // final result!
```

Operator Precedence

Operator precedence is the term which describes the order in which operators are carried out by the compiler within a single expression. For example, let's look at a statement with multiple operators:

```
int result = 5 + 2 * 4;
```

So what is the result when this statement executes? Does the program add 5+2 first and then multiply the result with 4 to get 28? Or does the program multiply 2*4 and then add 5 to get 13? The answer to these questions is found in the order of operator precedence. The higher precedence operators are executed first within a statement, followed by the lower precedence operators.

The following table contains a list of operators and precedence (from higher to lower) in the Java language.

Operator Name	Operator Description
( )	Parentheses
!	Logical NOT
* / %	Multiplication, Division and Modulus
+ -	Addition and Subtraction
< <= > >=	Less/Greater Than, Less/Greater Than or Equal To
== !=	Equal To and Not Equal To
&&	Logical AND
||	Logical OR
=	Assignment

Because the parentheses have the highest precedence, we can use them to help group expressions for evaluation as demonstrated earlier. Where there are multiple operators of the same precedence level, the operators are evaluated from left to right in the expression. Let's return to our first example statement.

```
int result = 5 + 2 * 4;
```

We can look at the precedence table and see that the multiplication should execute first. So the program first calculates 2 * 4, which is equal to 8. Then the program will add 5 to 8 and assign the value 13 to the result.

Let's take a look at more complicated statement:

```
int x = 3 * 4 + 6 / 3 - 2;
```

This may look difficult, but we can step through this statement one operator at a time. The highest operators in this expression are the '*' and '/' operators. Since they have the same precedence, the compiler will evaluate them left-to-right. So our first calculation is 3*4, yielding the remaining expression:

```
x = 12 + 6 / 3 - 2;
```

Next the division '/' operator will be executed as we move to the right. So our next calculation is 6 / 3, producing the remaining expression:

```
x = 12 + 2 - 2;
```

The remaining + and - operators have the same lower-level precedence, so they also will be evaluated left-to-right. So our next calculation is 12 + 2, which gives us:

```
x = 14 - 2;
```

Finally, we can perform our final calculation 14 – 2, which gives the answer: **x = 12**.

Using Parentheses

You can make your mathematical expressions easier to read and force the program to perform operations in a certain order. The parenthesis operator is the highest operator on the chart, so we know that any expression in parentheses will be done first! Let's look at our last example and use parentheses to change the meaning:

```
int x = 3 * (4 + 6) / (3 - 2);
```

This may look very similar to the expression above, but the compiler will see it completely differently. Since the parentheses have the highest order, our first calculation is (4 + 6). So now we have the expression:

```
x = 3 * 10 / (3 - 2);
```

Now we will calculate the expression in the second parentheses, which is (3 – 2), resulting in the expression:

```
x = 3 * 10 / 1;
```

The highest remaining operator is the '*', so our next calculation is 3 * 10, resulting in this expression:

```
x = 30 / 1;
```

Finally, we can perform our last calculation, 30 / 1. This gives us the final result: **x = 30**.

As you can see, the use of parentheses has the ability to completely change the outcome of the expression! It's good practice to use parentheses to clarify any complication expression. They make your intended calculation obvious to the compiler and to anyone reading your code. For example, look at these two statements:

```
int result1 = 1 + 2 * 3;
int result2 = 1 + (2 * 3);
```

These statements look different, but they actually do the same calculation. The only difference is that the second statement is easier to read. The precedence in the second expression is made obvious by the use of parentheses; you don't have to go look at an operator precedence table.

Short Circuiting of Logical Expressions

If you have two logical expressions joined by AND (&&) or OR (||), your program may not need to evaluate both expressions! If you are using AND, then both expressions must be **true** in order for the result to be **true**. So if the left-side expression is **false**, then the right-side expression does not matter and will be ignored. This skipping of the right-side expression is called *short-circuiting*. Consider this example:

```
(a != 0) && ((b / a) == 1))
```

You know it's important not to attempt to divide by zero. By checking for "a != 0" on the left side of the AND operation, you prevent the right-side from executing unless the value of "a" is not equal to zero.

Similarly, when using OR, if the left expression is **true** then the overall result is **true**, so the right side does not matter and will be ignored. What happens if the **String** variable **myString** is **null** in this expression?

```
(myString == null) || (myString.length() == 0)
```

If **myString** equals **null** then the overall OR expression is **true** immediately, so the right-side expression is not executed. This avoids an error by trying to call a function like **length**() on a **null** reference variable!

Lesson Two: Using the "if" Statement

In programming, the term *flow control* refers to the order in which your program executes statements. This order can be changed from the natural sequential order by the use of flow control statements. These statements take several different forms. This lesson will focus on *conditional* statements.

The "if" Statement

The **if**() conditional statement allows you to run a certain block of code based on whether a logical expression evaluates to **true** or **false**. We have used the **if**() statement a few times already, but now it's time to explore the concept more formally. An **if**() statement in comes in one of these two forms:

```
if (<logical expression>)
    // the very next statement executes if the logical expression is true


if (<logical expression>)
{
    // all statements in this body execute if the logical expression is true
}
```

The **if** keyword is followed by a logical expression in parentheses. The logical expression can be very simple or very complicated, but it must evaluate to either **true** or **false**. If the logical expression is **true**, and you have no curly braces afterwards, then the very next statement only will execute. If the logical expression is **false**, then the very next statement only is skipped. Remember that the compiler does not care about whitespace, so all of these **if**() expressions do the same thing:

```
if (<logical expression>) System.out.println("result is true");


if (<logical expression>)
    System.out.println("result is true");


if (<logical expression>)
System.out.println("result is true");
```

Use of indentation in the second example makes it easier for humans to understand the intent of the code at a glance, but all statements work the same way. It is good practice to always indent your code to show what is supposed to be covered by an **if**() statement. But don't fall into the trap of thinking that indentation will actually make any difference!

```
if (<logical expression>)
    System.out.println("result is true");
    System.out.println("This gets printed every time!");
```

In this example you may have fooled yourself into thinking the second **println()** was covered by the **if()** statement, but that is not the case! In order to run more than one statement if an expression is **true**, you must use the curly braces to define the body of the **if()** statement.

 For clarity, it's good practice to always use curly braces with your if() statement, just so there is no confusion! But don't be surprised if you see an if() statement without curly braces from time to time.

Using the **if()** statement with a matched set of opening and closing curly braces after the parentheses will define a body or block of code that will run if the logical expression is **true**. If the expression is **false** then the entire body will be skipped, and the program continues on the next line below the ending curly brace.

```
if (<logical expression>)
{
    // all statements in this body execute if the logical expression is true
}
```

The code within your **if()** body may be simple or very complex. You can declare variables that are visible only within that code block. You can call functions, and even run other **if()** statements or loops that we will learn about in the next lesson.

You can use as many **if()** statements in your program as you like:

```
if (<1st logical expression>)
{
    // this code executes if the 1st logical expression is true
}
if (<2nd logical expression>)
{
    // this code executes if the 2nd logical expression is true
}
if (<3rd logical expression>)
{
    // this code executes if the 3rd logical expression is true
}
```

The "if", "else if" Statements

You can also use the **else if** keywords to evaluate other expressions when prior **if()** expressions are **false**. You may add a final **else** keyword as well that takes no logical expression. The **else** statement will run a block of code if none of the prior **if** or **else if** statements are **true**.

```
if (<1st logical expression>)
{
    // this code executes if the 1st logical expression is true
}
else if (<2nd logical expression>)
{
    // this code executes if the 1st logical expression is false
    // AND if the 2nd logical expression is true
}
else
{
    // this code executes if all of the above expressions are false
}
// this is the next line in the program, independent of the ifs above
```

This **if/else if / else** example shows a series of decision making statements. If the first logical expression is **true**, the code in the first set of curly braces will be executed. Once this code is executed, the program will drop all the way down after the end of the "else" statement closing curly brace and will continue the program execution at the next line in the program.

If the first logical expression is **false**, the program will drop down and test the second logical expression. If this second expression is **true**, the code in the second set of curly braces will be executed. Once this code is executed, the program will again drop down to the end of the "else" statement and program execution will continue on the next line in the program.

If the first two logical expressions are **false**, the program will drop down to the last **else** statement. This statement is a catch-all statement that will run if no other expression has evaluated to **true**. Once this set of statements has executed, the program will continue on the next line in the program.

Once you start an **if()** statement, you may follow it with any number (0 or more) **else if** expressions. The final **else** is optional, and you can, of course, only have one **else** clause for a single **if()** statement.

Remember, the expression in the **if()** or **else if( )** parentheses must be a logical expression and not a mathematical or assignment statement! Only expressions that evaluate to **true** or **false** are accepted.

```
    if (a = 5)  // ERROR:  assignment statements are not logical expressions
    {
    }
    if (a + 5)  // ERROR:  mathematical equations are not logical expressions
    {
    }
    if (a == 5) // OK!  This is a logical expression
    {
    }
```

What's the difference? Well, in the first statement, you are not checking to see if **a** equals 5, you are actually assigning the value **5** to the variable **a**. The second statement adds 5 to the value of **a**, which results in another number and not **true** or **false**.

Java will not automatically convert a number to a Boolean **true** or **false**. You need to use a comparison operator if you have an integer containing 0 or 1 that you want to represent **false** or **true**.

```
    int value = 1;
    if (value) { }       // ERROR: 'value' is an integer
    if (value == 1) { } // OK:  comparison operator results in Boolean true
```

The "return" Keyword

You always have the option of immediately returning from whatever function you happen to be in – be it the **main()** method or some other function you have written. You can use the **return** keyword on a line by itself as a separate statement. The program flow will halt at that point and go back to the function that called the one you are in. If you are in the **main()** method then using the **return** keyword will exit your program!

```
    if (myString == null)
    {
        return;  // Oops!  This is an error condition, we can't go any further!
    }
```

In this example we have used the **if()** expression to check for an error condition and then returned if we find a problem. The **return** keyword will halt and return to the calling function even if you are deep inside any of the other program flow control structures we'll talk about later on such as the **for()** loop or the **while()** loop.

If your function has a **void** return type such as **main()**, then you are not expected to return any data, so simply using "**return;**" by itself is enough as we demonstrated above. However, if you are inside some function that has declared a returned data type such as **int** or **String** or some other object, then you must return something that matches that data type!

```
public String fullName(String firstName, String lastName)
{
    if ((firstName == null) || (lastName == null))  // verify inputs
    {
        return "Null input data!";      // return some descriptive error
    }
    return firstName + " " + lastName;  // return the full name
}
```

This example uses the **return** keyword if an error is detected in the input data to hand back *some* **String** because the **fullName()** function must return a **String**! It also uses the **return** keyword to give back the expected data when the inputs are valid.

Lesson Three: For Loops

A program *loop* will let you execute the same block of statements more than one time. Loops can let you avoid cut-and-pasting many duplicate lines of code that all do the same thing. They can also let you continue to do the same things until certain conditions are met.

A **for()** loop is generally used to execute a set of statements repeatedly when you know the number of loop iterations in advance. Let's say you wanted to print all of the numbers from 0 to 99. If you didn't have a loop, you'd be stuck writing 100 individual lines like this:

```
System.out.println("0");
System.out.println("1");
// and so on...
System.out.println("99");
```

Fortunately, the **for()** loop is a perfect replacement for these 100 lines of code.

```
for (int index=0; index<100; index++)
{
    System.out.println(index);
}
```

In this **for()** loop, we initialize an integer variable called **index** to 0 and loop over the **System.out.println()** statement while **index** is less than 100. We increase **index** by one each time through the loop.

for() Syntax

Now let's look at the parts of a **for**() loop a little more carefully. All **for**() loops are based on a numeric index, which can be one of the integer data types (**byte, short, int, long**). The index variable starts at some specified number and is then increased or decreased each time through the loop until the test condition becomes **false**. The loop keyword "for" is followed by three statements inside parentheses, separated by semicolons.

```
for (<initialization statement>; <test expression>; <change statement>)
{
    // statements to be executed within the loop go here
}
```

The *initialization statement* identifies your loop index variable and sets it to some initial value. This statement ends with a semicolon just like any other assignment statement.

You can declare your loop index variable directly within the loop, as we demonstrated above, or you can declare it beforehand and just set the variable to the starting value in the initialization statement like this:

```
int index;
for (index=0;
```

The above technique will keep the **index** variable around after the loop is finished, and it will contain the final value after the end of the loop. Unless you need the final value of the **index** for some reason outside of your loop, it's more common to declare the **index** variable within the initialization statement so it belongs just to the body of the **for** () loop and is not visible outside the loop's curly braces.

```
for (int index = 0;
```

The *test expression* that comes next is a logical expression that compares the value of the loop index variable to some end target. The loop will continue to execute the code within the loop body while the test expression is **true**. In our example we used the expression "**index** < 100" to print up through the number 99.

```
for (int index = 0; index < 100;
```

The test condition will be evaluated at the start of each loop. When the expression is **false** (**index** is greater than or equal to 100 in our example), the program will skip to the next line of code after our loop body. We could have also used the expression "**index** <= 99" to get the same result.

The *change statement* is the third and final statement within the **for**() parentheses. This statement is also an assignment statement and should update the loop index variable. The assignment will happen after the body of the loop has executed each time, but prior to the test condition evaluating the next time through the loop. In our case, we wanted to count from 0 through 99, adding 1 each time. The change statement should not have an ending semicolon, because the closing parenthesis will signal the end of the **for()** line.

```
for ( int index = 0; index < 100; index = index + 1)
```

Here we show the index value is going to be increased by one each time through the loop. Because this is very common, an *increment operator* (++) can be used instead to do exactly the same thing. Writing "**index**++" is the same as writing "**index** = **index** + 1".

```
for ( int index = 0; index < 100; index++)
```

Your change statement can use any valid assignment such as "**index** = **index** + 1" or "**index** = **index** + 5" or "**index** = **index** - 3". In most cases your loop index will go up or down by one each time, but you can design your loop to change your index however you like each time around. You must do *something* to change your index, otherwise your test condition will never go **false** and you will be stuck in an infinite loop!

 It is common to shorten the names of for() loop index variables to just a single character like "i" (for index). While this runs against normal good-programming practice, the shortened names are well-understood by other programmers looking at your code.

The *body* of the loop is between the opening and closing curly braces. The loop body is the group of statements you would like executed each time through the loop.

```
for ( int index = 0; index < 100; index++)
{
    // statements in here will be run 100 times with index = 0 through 99
}
```

The next example **for()** loop prints numbers 4 through 0, counting backwards by 2 each time.

```
// declare a for loop with index "i" starting at 4, decrementing twice each
// time through the loop, and continuing so long as i >= 0
for (int i = 4; i >= 0; i = i - 2)
{
    System.out.println(i);
}
```

The resulting output will show the numbers 4, 2, and 0.

Breaking Free!

Sometimes you may want to end your **for()** loop early, no matter what the index variable or test conditions say! You can use a **break** statement to immediately exit any loop you might be within at the moment. For example, say we wanted to find the first space in a string. We might write a **for()** loop to look over all of the characters in the string. Once we find the first space there is no point in looking at the rest of the string, so we can exit the loop right away.

```java
String target = "Paper or plastic?";
int firstSpace = -1;

// walk over each character in the target string
for (int i = 0; i < target.length(); i++)
{
    // check to see if this character is equal to space
    if (target.charAt(i) == ' ')
    {
        firstSpace = i; // save the index of the first space
        break;          // exit the loop, we're done!
    }
}
```

This **for()** loop will result in the **firstSpace** variable being set equal to the index of the first space character in the target string (5 in this example). If we didn't have the **break** statement our **for()** loop would continue until the end and we'd actually find the last space instead (at index 8). The **break** statement can be used in all loop types, not just the **for()** loop, and it has exactly the same effect.

Lesson Four: While Loops

A second type of program loop is called a **while()** loop. This loop is used to execute a set of statements *while* a condition is **true**. You may not know in advance how many times the loop will execute, but you know the condition under which it should continue executing. For instance, you may want to continue obtaining user input until the user sends some special signal that they are done. So you would loop *while* the user input is *not equal* to that special signal.

"while" Syntax

A **while()** loop is based on a logical expression that evaluates to either **true** or **false**. As long as this expression evaluates to **true**, the loop will continue to execute.

The while loop syntax looks like this:

```
while ( <logical expression> )
{
    // statements to be executed within the loop go here
}
```

The loop begins with the **while** keyword followed by a logical expression in parentheses. Just like the **for()** loop, the body of the **while()** loop is defined by curly braces surrounding the statements to be executed. The logical expression is evaluated at the top to decide whether or not to run the statements within the loop body. If the logical expression is **false** at the very beginning, the loop body will never execute.

Within the loop body you *must* have some statements that will affect the logical expression, usually by modifying one or more variables involved in the expression. Otherwise you will have an *infinite loop* because the logical expression result never changes from **true** to **false**!

Your logical expression may be simple or complex, with multiple logical expressions combined with the AND ("&&"), OR ("||"), or NOT("!") operators. Be sure to use parentheses to make it clear how the individual expressions will combine. For example:

```
while ( ( A < B) || ( (C + D) > 42))
```

This loop will execute while A is less than B, OR the sum of C + D is greater than 42.

Example While Loop

Here is an example using the **while()** loop to echo text entered by the user to the screen in uppercase until the user enters "quit".

```
public static void main(String[] args)
{
    Scanner input = new Scanner(System.in);

    // tell the user what we expect them to do
    System.out.println("Type any text and press enter.
    System.out.println("Type 'quit' to quit.");
```

```
            // declare the variable we'll use in the loop expression
            boolean done = false;

            // Loop until the user enters "quit".  Notice we initialized the
            // variable "done" such that the logical expression is initially true!
            while (! done)     // while not done
            {
                    // read user text and echo to screen in uppercase
                    String userText = input.nextLine();
                    System.out.println(userText.toUpperCase());

                    if (userText.equalsIgnoreCase("quit"))
                    {
                        done = true;  // user wants to quit
                        System.out.println ("\n'quit' entered, leaving program!");
                    }
            }

            input.close();
    }
```

Here is an example run of this program and the resulting output:

```
Type any text and press enter.  Type 'quit' to quit.
hello
HELLO
How's it going?
HOW'S IT GOING?
I'm done
I'M DONE
quit
QUIT

'quit' entered, leaving program!
```

Common Mistakes with While Loops

One common **while**() loop mistake is the dreaded *infinite loop*. This condition is caused by failing to change the inputs to the logical expression in the loop body. You must change the logical expression inputs at some point in order for the loop to exit! If it never changes, your program will be stuck forever in this loop. Always make sure that your loop code contains a way to change the logical expression result to **false**. In our example above we set a Boolean flag **done** to **false** when the user typed in a key phrase.

This example while loop will never end!

```
while (1 < 2)
{
    // this is an infinite loop because 1 is always less than 2
}
```

 You are responsible for changing the result of your logical expression in your while loop body. If you never change the result of this expression, the while loop will never stop running. This is called an infinite loop, since the loop executes infinitely, or forever!

Do-While Loops

The last type of loop that we will discuss is called the **do-while**() loop. This loop is very similar to the **while**() loop, where a logical expression is used to decide if the loop should continue executing. The difference is the logical expression is not tested until the *end* of the loop body. This means that the loop body will *always* execute at least one time.

The **do-while**() syntax looks like this:

```
do
{
    // loop statements here execute while logical expression is true
}
while (<logical expression>);
```

The first statement is the **do** line. This is simple line marks the beginning of the **do-while**() loop body. As in previous loops, the loop body is contained within the curly braces.

The last part of the loop is the **while** statement after the closing curly brace. The **while** keyword is followed by a logical expression within the parentheses. Once again, remember the logical expression must be changed within the loop body. Otherwise, you will end up with an infinite loop! After the closing parenthesis you must add a semicolon to mark the end of the **do-while**() loop.

This example reworks the prior **while**() example where user input will be echoed in upper case until the user types "quit". We know we want to execute the loop body at least once because we need user input in order to test our loop expression.

```
Scanner input = new Scanner(System.in);

// tell the user what we expect them to do
System.out.println("Type any text and press enter.");
System.out.println("Type 'quit' to quit.");

// Loop until the user enters "quit".
boolean done = false;
do
{
    // read user text
    String userText = input.nextLine();
    System.out.println(userText.toUpperCase());

    if (userText.equalsIgnoreCase("quit"))
    {
        done = true;  // user wants to quit
        System.out.println ("\n'quit' entered, leaving program!");
    }
}
while (! done);   // loop until done

input.close();
```

This program will behave just like the earlier **while**() example.

```
Type any text and press enter.
Type 'quit' to quit.
Here we go again!
HERE WE GO AGAIN!
quit
QUIT

'quit' entered, leaving program!
```

Your choice of a **for**() loop, a **while**() loop, or a **do-while**() loop depends on the needs of your program.

Activity: Fun Factorials!

In this activity, you will write a **for**() loop, a **while**() loop and a **do**-**while**() loop to calculate the factorial of a given number. You will also use an **if**() statement to check to see if the user enters valid data.

Your activity requirements and instructions are found in the "Chapter_07_Activity.pdf" document located in your "TeenCoder\Java Programming\Activity Docs" folder. You can access this document through your Student Menu or by directly clicking on it from Windows Explorer (Windows) or Finder (Mac OS).

Complete this activity now and ensure your program meets the requirements before continuing!

Chapter Eight: Writing Methods

All of our code up to this point has been written in the **main()** method or function which is called when your program starts. In this chapter you will learn how to write your own methods!

Lesson One: Writing and Calling Methods

Your program may need to perform a task many times. For instance, you may need to compute the area of a circle several times in your program. Would you want to write many copies of the calculation code? Or would you want to create a single block of code that you can use over and over? Having only one copy of the code makes it much easier to write and maintain. This block of reusable code is called a *function* or *method*. Once a function has been created, it can be called from different places in your code, whenever needed.

You have already written one method, **main()**, as the entry point for each of your programs. This method is called by the JVM when your main class is run. Most of the other methods you have used, such as **System.out.println()**, have been pre-written as part of the standard Java class library. In many languages a method is referred to as a "function" or a "subroutine". In fact, these terms are nearly interchangeable and we will use both in this course. A *method* is really just a function that belongs to an object. Since all Java code belongs to some sort of object, functions in Java are called methods.

Here is a simple example method that will make the computer happy. Can you figure out what it does?

```java
public static void makeSmiley()
{
        System.out.println("        ***        ");
        System.out.println("      **   **      ");
        System.out.println("     *       *     ");
        System.out.println("    *  *   *  *    ");
        System.out.println("    *         *    ");
        System.out.println("    *   *   *  *    ");
        System.out.println("    *  *   *  *    ");
        System.out.println("     *  *****  *     ");
        System.out.println("      **     **      ");
        System.out.println("        ***        ");
}
```

Let's take a look at this code in more depth. The first line is the method *declaration*:

```
public static void makeSmiley()
```

This line tells the compiler that we are creating a method called "**makeSmiley**". The declaration starts with several keywords. The first keyword is **public**. This tells the compiler that our method will be available to all other classes in this program, if any. The keyword **static** tells the compiler that you will be able to use the method without creating an instance of your class first. We will discuss the **static** keyword in more detail in a future chapter. For now, understand that the **main()** method itself is **static**, and therefore any other method belonging to your class that is called by **main()** must also be **static**.

The keyword **void** means that this method will not return any value to the calling code. The parentheses after the method name can include an optional list of parameters. The **makeSmiley()** method does not have any parameters. We'll talk more about other return data types and parameters in the next lesson.

After the method declaration, we have a set of curly braces with our lines of code inside:

```
{
    // All the System.out.println() statements for
    // The makeSmiley () function goes inside these curly braces
}
```

This is the *body* of the method. Any code within the curly braces will be executed every time the program calls this method. You can do anything you like within a method body, including declaring local variables, calling other functions, and so on. Any variables you declare within the method body are only visible to code within the body itself and are discarded when the function exits. We will get into some more complicated methods in the next couple of lessons.

Function Naming Rules

When you are creating your function names, there are some rules that you must follow. First, the function's name must consist only of lowercase or capital letters, numbers and underscores (_). The first symbol in your function name must always be either a letter or an underscore. Do not use any other special characters.

Second, you should always remember that function names are case sensitive. The functions named "**makeSmiley()**" and "**MakeSmiley()**" are different functions! A simple case-mismatch in the function name often causes problems later in the code.

Using meaningful function names makes your code easier to read and understand. If you name a function "**do_it**" then you don't really have any idea what the function will do. But if the function is called "**calculateCircleArea**" then you have a pretty good idea.

Lastly, you should pick one naming style and stick with it throughout your program. If you decide to capitalize the first letter of every word in your function name (**MyFunction**), do this for all your functions. If you decide to capitalize the first letter of every word except the first (**myFunction**), or separate words with underscores (**my_function**), be consistent. Other programmers looking at your code will thank you later!

Here are some examples of valid and invalid function names:

```
myFunction()    // OK
MyFunction()    // OK
my_function()   // OK
_test()         // OK
A1()            // OK
1A()            // ERROR - numbers cannot be first
A 1()           // ERROR - spaces are not allowed
A!()            // ERROR - other special characters not allowed
```

Function Placement within the Class

Just like your **main()** method "belongs" to the class you create for the program, any other methods you write will also belong to that class. Your methods should appear between the class curly braces just like **main()**:

```
public class MyProgram
{
    public static void main(String[] args)
    {
        makeSmiley(); // call this function from main()!
    }

    public static void makeSmiley()
    {
        // statements for function body go here
    }
}
```

Make sure you carefully match the opening and closing curly braces for each function body, and also match opening and closing curly braces for the overall class definition. Otherwise you will get some pretty strange compiler errors! Use consistent indentation so you can find matching braces with an easy glance at your code.

Functional Decomposition

Another good reason to write functions is to break a large task down into smaller pieces. If you have a single function that contains hundreds of lines of code, odds are this function will be very hard to understand! Taking that large body of logic and converting it to a number of smaller, well-defined functions is called *functional decomposition*. It's usually a good idea to "divide and conquer" a complex task by defining a number of smaller tasks that are easy to complete and that together will resolve the larger challenge.

When do you stop breaking a function down into smaller sub-functions? You'll have to use your good judgment! It's safe to say that you probably don't want hundreds or thousands of lines of code in one function, but you also probably don't need a huge number of functions with one or two lines of code each. Stop your functional decomposition at a level where you are comfortable understanding a single function that performs a well-defined task.

Lesson Two: Method Parameters and Return Values

In the previous lesson we demonstrated methods that did not have any parameters or return values. These simple methods may work great for some tasks (or if you want to display a large smiley). However, if you really want to tap into the power of methods, you need to learn how to use parameters and return values!

Function Parameters

It is often very useful to *parameterize*, or provide external data, to your method body. For instance, if you have a method that calculated the area of a rectangle, that method will need to know the width and height of the rectangle. In order to tell the method about this data, you would use method *parameters*. Method parameters are data that you *pass* into your function from the calling code. Parameters are listed inside the parentheses after the name in the method declaration:

```
public static void myMethod(<data type 1> <parameter 1 name>, …)
```

The declaration of a method parameter looks a lot like the declaration of any other variable; you start with a data type (e.g. **int**) and follow with the variable name. If you have more than one parameter then separate them with commas and do not add semicolons. You can use the parameters just like any other variable within the body of your function. Let's look at an example of a method declaration with parameters:

```
public static void calculateRectangleArea(double width, double height)
```

This statement declares a method called **calculateRectangleArea**() that takes two parameters: a **double** variable called **width** and a **double** called **height**. Whenever this method is *called*, or used, from your program, you will need to provide these two parameters in the function call.

Let's look at a possible function body for our **calculateRectangleArea**() method:

```
public static void calculateRectangleArea(double width, double height)
{
    double area = width * height;
    System.out.println("Rectangle area = " + area);
}
```

You can see our function body has only two statements: the area calculation and a **System.out.println**() to output the results. The parameters **width** and **height** are used just like any other variable in our program. Passing data into functions can give them greater power and flexibility.

Function Return Values

Another optional function feature is the *return value*. A return value is data that a function can return to the calling code. For instance, in our **calculateRectangleArea**() function, we could just return the **area** result instead of printing it to the screen. That would allow us to use the result in some other calculation.

To return a value, we create a method declaration that uses a data type instead of **void** for the return type. For instance, instead of a method declaration like this:

```
public static void calculateRectangleArea()
```

We can declare the same method with a **double** return value:

```
public static double calculateRectangleArea()
```

The method return type can be any valid data type such as one of the primitive numeric values, a **String**, or even a more complex object!

As always, after you declare your method, you must implement the body of your function. The difference now that we are using a return type is that the method must use the **return** keyword to send the result back to the calling program. When you are ready to leave your function and return to the calling code, you use the **return** keyword end your method and pass back the specified data. A return statement looks like this:

```
return <expression>;
```

This is an extremely simple statement, but there are some key things to remember: First, the expression that you return must evaluate to the same data type that you declared in your method declaration. You should not declare a method with a return type of **int** if you are going to return a **double**. Your expression may be very easy (e.g. just a variable name) or a more complex expression that will evaluate to the correct data type.

For example, we can calculate the area of a circle and then return the resulting value using this method:

```
public static double calculateCircleArea(double radius)
{
    double answer = radius * radius * 3.14159;
    return answer;
}
```

Notice that the **answer** variable above isn't really used for anything other than returning the result. In this case we could just **return** the expression itself and save ourselves a step. Let's look at an example of this style:

```
public static double calculateCircleArea(double radius)
{
    return radius * radius * 3.14159;
}
```

So far we have shown very simple methods. However the body of the method can be as complex as you like. It may even call other methods!

Method Overloading

You have seen that all methods belong to some object or class. Can you define two methods with the same name on that class? Yes, that is allowed as long as the parameters are different! This is called *method overloading*. Method overloading is often used to support the same general operation against more than one data type. Below we show the same function defined for both **int** and **double** input parameters.

```
public int findMinimum(int i1, int i2)
{  /* implementation not shown */ }

public double findMinimum(double d1, double d2)
{  /* implementation not shown */ }
```

To overload a method, your parameter data types must be different, or you must have a different number of parameters, or the data types must be listed in a different order. Then the compiler can automatically figure out which method to call based on the data from the calling code. Note that simply changing the method *return type* is not enough! The *parameters* themselves must be different.

Lesson Three: Calling Methods

Now that you have learned how to create methods, with or without parameters and return values, let's look at how to use these methods in a program. To run your method from somewhere in your code you *call* it.

Calling Methods with no Parameters or Return Data

Calling a method that does not have either a return value or any parameters is very simple. The statement consists of just the method name, empty parentheses, and a closing semicolon. For instance, if we had a method that was declared as follows:

```
public static void myMethod()
```

We could call the method in our code like this:

```
myMethod();
```

When your method's return type is **void**, that means no data is returned, so you cannot use the method as part of a larger expression! For instance, these statements make no sense and would produce compile errors:

```
System.out.println( myMethod() );   // ERROR
int a = 5 + myMethod();             // ERROR
```

You cannot pass a **void** result into the **println()** function, nor can you add a **void** result into any mathematical or logical expression.

Calling Methods with Parameters

When you call a method with parameters, you must pass a list of values in the parentheses that exactly matches the number, order, and data type of the parameters defined in the method declaration. The values will be separated by commas. If your parameters do not match, the compiler will generate an error on that method call and your program will not build!

Each parameter you pass into a method may be a simple hard-coded value, a variable name, or an expression evaluating to the correct data type. For example, with our area calculation, we could pass the numbers for the width or height, OR we could use two **double** variables with values assigned to them. Both of the following function calls to **calculateRectangleArea()** do the same thing:

```
double width = 2.0;
double height = 3.0;

calculateRectangleArea(2.0,3.0);        // pass in some hard-coded values
calculateRectangleArea(width,height); // pass in some variable data
```

Since our parameters match the required input (two **double** values) these statements will compile just fine!

Ordering of Parameters

In addition to the number of parameters, you must pay attention to the order of the parameters in the method. The compiler doesn't care what variable names you may pass in, it only knows the expected order of parameters and the data types. The compiler takes the first value that you pass into the method and assigns it to the first parameter. The second value that you pass is used as the second parameter, and so on. If you pass in the right number of parameters with the correct data types to match the method declaration, your code will compile. Otherwise you will get a compile error!

 **It does not matter if your input variable names match the parameter names in the method declaration. Only the input order is important. If your method needs a String and an integer, make sure you pass in those data types in that exact order!**

Let's take a look at an example of this key concept. Consider a simple **divide()** method:

```
public static double divide(double dividend, double divisor)
{
    return dividend / divisor;
}
```

The first parameter is the **dividend** and the second parameter is the **divisor**. Both are **doubles**. When we call this function, unless we are careful, we may get the parameters in the wrong order!

```
double top = 4.0;
double bottom = 2.0;


// This is NOT a compile-time error.  The compiler just knows you have
// satisfied the input parameter list with two doubles.
double result = divide(bottom,top);
System.out.println(top + " / " + bottom + " = " + result);
```

Our **divide**() method requires the dividend (top part) to be first and the divisor (bottom part) to be second. However in the method call above we have mistakenly reversed this order! As long as the number, order, and type of the input parameters match the function declaration, it is a valid function call, and the compiler can't warn you about the mistake. In this example the function call will return unexpected results:

```
4.0 / 2.0 = 0.5
```

Of course we know that 4 divided by 2 is not 0.5. We did not get a compile-time error, or a run-time exception, but we observed that the program results were incorrect. These types of errors can be tricky to identify and fix, so be careful when writing your code to provide the method parameters in the right order!

Parameters Passed by Value

One last note on calling methods with parameters: the parameters you use inside the method body are *copies* of the value passed in by the calling program. This is called passing parameters by *value*. You may change the value of the copy inside the method body, but that will not change the original variable contents from the calling program, even if the variable names are the same!

For example, first we will define a method called **threeIsBetter**() that takes one **int** parameter **param**.

```java
public static void threeIsBetter(int param)
{
    param = 3;
    System.out.println("param inside function = " + param);
}
```

Then from our calling code we define a variable **param**, assign it a value, and pass it into **threeIsBetter**().

```java
int param = 2;
threeIsBetter(param);
System.out.println("param outside function = " + param);
```

Now let's look at what happens to the **param** before and after this function is called. First we set its value as 2. We then call the method and pass in our **param** variable. Once the method has completed, we will print the value of **param** again and see if it has changed.

This code would give the following output:

```
param inside function = 3
param outside function = 2
```

139

As you can see, even though the copied **param** variable was changed inside the method, the original variable **param** outside the method was not changed. So for primitive data types, you cannot change the value of the input variable inside the method body.

Reference Parameters

However, consider what happens when your function accepts a reference variable instead. The reference itself is still passed by value, so a copy of the reference is made, but the reference just points to the same object in memory! This example accepts an imaginary class **MyClassType** as the input parameter:

```java
public static void referenceCheck(MyClassType myClass)
{
    myClass.changeMe();  // call an imaginary function on our made-up class
}
```

Now our calling code creates a new instance of **MyClassType** and passes it into **referenceCheck()**.

```java
MyClassType mine = new MyClassType();
referenceCheck(mine);
```

Even though the reference itself has been copied from the **mine** variable on the outside to **myClass** inside the method, both references point to the same instance of **MyClassType**. So the one and only instance of that object will have the **changeMe()** method called on it. The result of that **changeMe()** function (whatever it does) will persist after the **referenceCheck()** method returns. So keep in mind a function body will use a copy of the reference variable that points to the original object, not a copy of that object!

Calling a Method with a Return Value

If a method returns a value instead of **void** you may use that value in a number of ways. Consider this example that returns an **int** value:

```java
public static int myMethod(int p1)
```

You may still call this method on a separate line and ignore the return value completely:

```java
myMethod(42);
```

You may also use the returned data as part of an assignment statement:

```java
int myData = myMethod(42);  // save result of myMethod into myData
```

You can use the result as part of a larger expression, so long as the returned data type is appropriate:

```
int myData = 3 * myMethod(42);   // save 3 times result into myData
if (myMethod(42) > 6)            // use result in a logical expression
```

We can even use the method's return data as input to another function!

```
System.out.println("the answer is " + myMethod(42));
```

Just make sure whatever you do with the returned data value is allowed for that data type.

Activity: Checkerboard

In this activity, you will write your own function! Your function will accept a width and a height parameter and then use these values to print a checkerboard pattern to the screen.

Your activity requirements and instructions are found in the "Chapter_08_Activity.pdf" document located in your "TeenCoder\Java Programming\Activity Docs" folder. You can access this document through your Student Menu or by directly clicking on it from Windows Explorer (Windows) or Finder (Mac OS).

Complete this activity now and ensure your program meets the requirements before continuing!

Chapter Nine: Debugging and Exceptions

In this chapter you will learn how the IDE can help you find problems in your program at runtime. You will also learn some advanced techniques for error handling within your program.

Lesson One: Logic Errors, Runtime Errors and Exceptions

In the past lessons we have talked about compile-time errors. But what happens if your program compiles without a problem and still won't run properly? This means you have found a *logic error* or *exception*. A logic error means you wrote code that doesn't do what you wanted. For instance, you might use the wrong logical expression in an **if()** statement so your program does not flow correctly. An exception means you tried to do something illegal such as call a method on a **null** reference variable, divide by zero, etc. When an exception is *thrown* or *raised*, your program stops immediately unless you have special code in place to handle it.

Example Runtime Exceptions

The following table describes some of the more common runtime exceptions you may encounter:

Exception	Thrown when you have attempted…
NullPointerException	…to call a method on a reference variable that contains **null**.
ArrayIndexOutOfBoundsException	…to access an array element with an invalid index.
ArithmeticException	…an illegal math operation such as divide-by-zero.
ClassCastException	…to cast one class to another unrelated class or data type.
IllegalArgumentException	…to pass invalid input data into a method.

Let's look at some code that will cause runtime errors before talking about how to identify and resolve them. First we are going to generate a "divide by zero" exception. This common runtime error occurs just when you think it does: you try to divide a number by zero! If you recall your math lessons, you'll know this is not a valid operation. Computers can't do it either! The code below demonstrates this problem.

```java
public static void main(String[] args)
{
        // initialize some variables
        int numerator = 14;
        int denominator1 = 3 + 4;    // do some math
        int denominator2 = 7;


        // result is "numerator divided by (denominator1 minus denominator2)"
        int result = numerator / (denominator1 - denominator2);   // Exception
        System.out.println("result is: " + result);
}
```

Of course, you can see that "(**denominator1 – denominator2**)" will equal zero, so we are headed for trouble! When this code is run, you get a runtime error like this in your console output:

```
Exception in thread "main" java.lang.ArithmeticException: / by zero
    at Sandbox.main(Sandbox.java:19)
```

There are three important things to notice here. First, the **System.out.println()** statement after the divide-by-zero attempt did not execute at all. When an exception is raised, program flow is transferred away from the current line and the program will end completely unless you have special handling code in place to "catch" the exceptions. When you get a runtime error that causes a popup message, displays a stack trace, or other abnormal termination, your program is said to have *crashed*. The JVM will quit executing your program at the point where the exception was raised.

Second, see that the exception tells you exactly what went wrong. The exception name is "**ArithmeticException**" and the details it provides states "/ by zero". That's pretty straightforward!

Third, you see what is called a "stack trace" underneath the exception, which will show you exactly where the exception happened. In this case the exception was raised from the function **main()** in the "Sandbox.java" source file at line 19. Now you know where to start looking for the problem.

The "**NullPointerException**" is another example of a runtime error. This error occurs when you attempt to use a reference variable that is empty (contains **null**) instead of a valid object. You must always make sure your object reference contains a valid object before you try to call a function or access a property through that reference. Here is a simple example:

```java
String myString = null;
int length = myString.length();
System.out.println("String length = " + length);
```

When this code is run, we get the following error:

```
Exception in thread "main" java.lang.NullPointerException
    at Sandbox.main(Sandbox.java:12)
```

Again you can see the exact error (**NullPointerException**), the source file ("Sandbox.java"), the function (**main()**), and the line within the source (12) where the exception was raised. Now that you know what a runtime exception looks like, let's learn how to find and fix them in your code!

Lesson Two: Finding Runtime Errors

It happens to the best of us… at some point your program is going to crash or raise a runtime exception. The error cause and fix might be obvious, or it might take a little investigation. We have to find the *bug*, or mistake, in the program that allows the runtime error to happen. There are three common ways to identify the problem: *code review*, *program tracing*, or using a *debugger*

Code Review

The first method to find a runtime error is to use a *code review*. A code review is just what it says: review (read) your code to see if you can spot the error. This can be a tedious process, but is may be your best option for debugging certain scenarios. A good set of human eyes can be great troubleshooters!

To perform a code review, look at your program's source code starting at the beginning of the **main()** function. Look at the first line of code. Do you understand everything that is going on in this line? Is the line formatted correctly and easy to read? What is this line supposed to do? And what are the expected results? Is there any way that user input could cause this statement to do something unexpected (e.g. divide by zero)? If you can answer all of these questions, and feel confident the line performs as intended, go to the next line.

Repeat this inspection process for each line of code in sequence. Code reviews work best for small programs or when you have narrowed the problem down to a small section of code. The examples and assigned programs in this course are small enough to perform a code review, should you have any problems.

Sometimes you can greatly speed up the code review by thinking about the output you saw from your program, and using that to zoom in on a particular area of code. If you have 100 statements in your program you feel confident the first 75 worked fine based on the output you saw before the crash, then start reviewing the last 25 statements first!

Program Tracing

Tracing is another technique for finding runtime errors. This technique uses very verbose output to tell you where your program is executing within the source code. You may use this technique if an exception does not tell you exactly where the error occurs. Or, possibly, some other user is reporting that your program crashed but they can't understand the "techno-speak" exception information.

Remember the **System.out.println()** function is used to display text to the screen. You can also use it to follow a program's execution. In the example below, we add a **System.out.println()** statement after each line of code. When the program runs, we should see these lines display on the screen. When the exception occurs, we will know that the error happens between the last **System.out.println()** output that you see and the next one that you didn't. Let's revisit our divide-by-zero example and add some program tracing:

```java
public static void main(String[] args)
{
    System.out.println("starting program");          // tracing statement

    // initialize some variables
    int numerator = 14;
    int denominator1 = 3 + 4;    // do some math
    int denominator2 = 7;

    System.out.println ("variables initialized");    // tracing statement

    // result is "numerator divided by (denominator1 minus denominator2)"
    int result = numerator / (denominator1 - denominator2);   // ERROR
    System.out.println("result is: " + result);
}
```

As you can see, we have added a couple of **System.out.println()** statements to our code. After every significant line of code, we have used **System.out.println()** to trace our progress through the program. Now, when this code is executed, we will see the following results:

```
starting program
variables initialized
Exception in thread "main" java.lang.ArithmeticException: / by zero
    at Sandbox.main(Sandbox.java:20)
```

So now we know that the runtime error happened after our **System.out.println()** statement "variables initialized" but before the final result was printed. We can go back to our code and look at the line directly following the last **System.out.println()** we saw in the output.

```
int result = numerator / (denominator1 - denominator2);
```

This is where our error occurred! Knowing this, you can take a closer look at the code leading up to this statement to find why it is generating a divide by zero error.

The final handy debugging method we will cover is the use of a *debugger*. This tool will enable you to step through the code line-by-line, watching each statement execute.

Using a Debugger

Normally when you run a program it executes either directly on top of the operating system (for some compiled languages) or on top of the JVM (for Java). You can also run a special program called a *debugger* which sits between your program and the operating system or JVM.

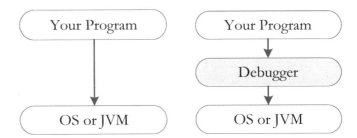

Debuggers will let you walk step-by-step through each line in your program and watch your program as it runs. This is an extremely powerful tool! While you are watching the running program, you can make sure the program is working as you expect. This includes making sure the statements are executing in the correct order and even peeking at the contents of your variables to make sure the data is being stored correctly.

After your program is successfully built with no compile errors, you can run your program in the debugger. Some languages such as C++ have different ways to build your program that make debugging easier, but you don't have to worry about that with Java.

 The debugger is a real time-saver for programmers! Instead of performing a lengthy code review or adding many tracing statements to your program, the debugger lets you watch your program in action, step-by-step, looking at variable contents as you go.

Program States

While running your program in the debugger, the program will be in one of two states: *running* or *in break*. When your program is in the *running* state, it is executing normally. The program starts at the beginning of your **main()** function and follows your normal program flow. This isn't the most useful state for debugging. While running, the program is moving far too fast to watch individual statements or observe the data.

When your program is *in break*, it is paused. The debugger knows the complete state of the program, including which statement is about to be executed and the data contents of all variables. While in break, most debuggers will highlight the line that is *about* to be executed. The previous statement has already been executed. In this example the darker highlighted line has not yet been run.

```
int denominator1 = 3 + 4;    // do some math
int denominator2 = 7;

System.out.println ("variables initialized");   // tracing statement

// result is "numerator divided by (denominator1 minus denominator2)"
int result = numerator / (denominator1 - denominator2);    // ERROR
System.out.println("result is: " + result);
```

While in break you can execute a *debugging command* to advance the execution of your program.

Debugging Commands

Most debuggers, including the Eclipse Java debugger, will support the same general set of commands:

Run or Continue	If your program is not running, this command will start running your program in the debugger. If you are already debugging the program and are in break, this command will put the program back into the running state. The program will run until it reaches the end of the program or a breakpoint (see below).
Step Over	This command tells the debugger to execute the currently highlighted statement, including any functions without stepping into any function. Afterwards the program will remain in break at the next statement.
Step Into	This is similar to the "Step Over" command, but if the next statement is one of your functions, you will switch into the function, still in break mode, so you can examine the program execution within the function.
Step Out	If you are already stepped into a function, this command will finish executing the entire function and transfer control back to the point where the function was called. Afterwards the program will remain in break at the next statement after the function call. If you are not within any sub-function, "Step Out" will usually act as a "Continue" and finish executing your program.
Stop	The "Stop" command will end your program immediately; no more statements will be executed. You can then edit or modify your code, build, and run it again.

Breakpoints

With most of the small programs you have seen so far it would not take long to start at the top of the **main()** function and then step through each line of code until the end. For larger programs, however, it can take a long time manually step through to a code section of interest. This is where *breakpoints* come into play!

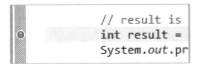

A breakpoint is a place in the code where you want the debugger to stop and put the program in a break state. When the program is paused, you can view the data in your variables at that precise point in the program.

You can set as many breakpoints in your program as you like. Usually your IDE will give you some visual signal, such as the little round circle to the left, to show you where your breakpoints have been set. Each of the debugging commands (Continue, Step Into, etc...) will automatically stop and put the program in break mode whenever a breakpoint is hit, regardless of what the command was originally going to do.

I Found the Error...Now What?

Once you have identified the statement(s) causing the runtime error, you need to *fix the bug* (change your code) to eliminate the problem. The solution to each problem depends on what the program is trying to do, and there may be many valid ways to prevent the runtime error. For instance, before doing any division you can check to see if the denominator will be zero, and if so avoid doing the calculation in the first place! For null pointer exceptions you might check your reference variable for **null** before using it, if you are unsure what the variable contains.

Lesson Three: The Eclipse Debugger

In this lesson, you are going to learn how to use the Eclipse debugger. We will be using the debugger to walk through the sample code discussed in this chapter. We have pre-written an Eclipse project named "RunTimeError" for you containing this code. All pre-written projects or Activity Starters are stored in a folder called "TeenCoder\Java Programming\Activity Starters". Let's quickly learn how to import a starter project into your Eclipse Workspace!

Importing an Existing Project to your Eclipse Workspace

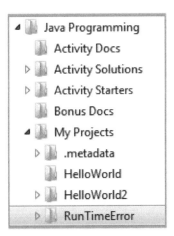

To use our activity starter projects you will want to *import* them into your "My Projects" Eclipse workspace. The first step is to copy the entire starter project directory ("RunTimeError" in this case) from "Activity Starters" into your "My Projects" directory. Making a copy of the project into your working area will preserve the original activity starter in case you need to start over with a fresh copy. Go ahead and do this now using Windows Explorer (Windows) or Finder (Mac OS).

After you have your "My Projects\RunTimeError" directory in place, you need to add the existing project to your Eclipse workspace. This is a bit different than creating a brand new project, so let's see how it's done.

All of the projects in your Eclipse workspace are listed in the "Package Explorer" panel. To add an existing project, right-click on the white area in your Project Explorer and select "Import".

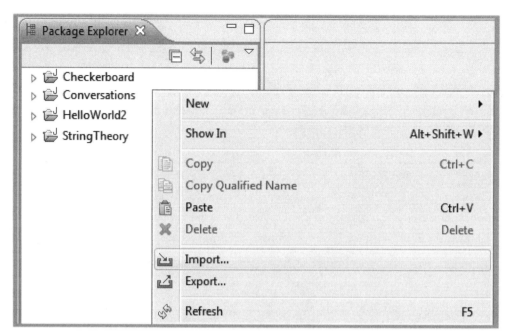

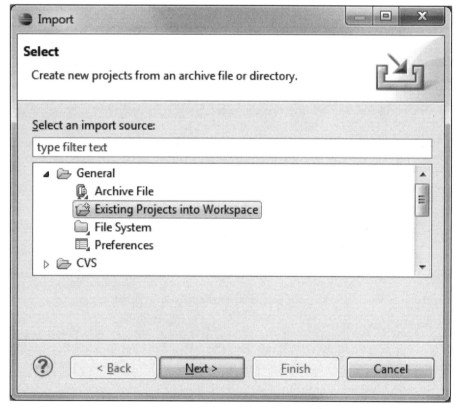

From the "Import" dialog, expand the top "General" node, select "Existing Projects into Workspace", and then click "Next".

You will then see the "Import Projects" dialog, which will allow you to select the target directory containing the project to import.

Leave the "Select root directory" radio button enabled and click the "Browse" button to the right of that text field. You will then see the "Browse For Folder" dialog shown below. Go to your "TeenCoder\Java Programming\My Projects" directory and select your "RunTimeError" folder, then click "OK".

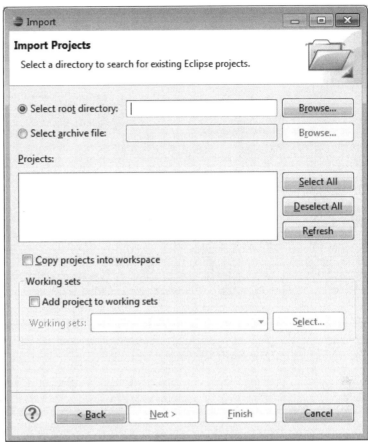

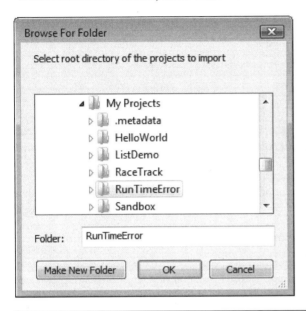

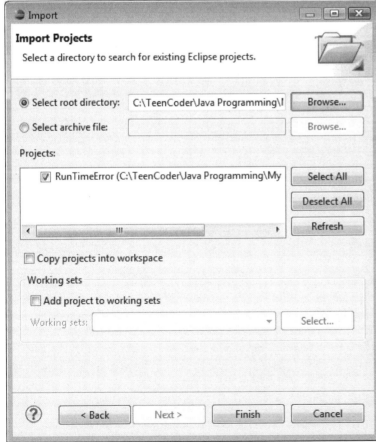

Finally, your Import dialog shows you have selected the correct root directory for your imported project, and you see "RunTimeError" listed in the Projects window with a checkbox. You are done, so click "Finish"!

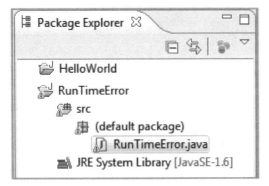

You should then see the "RunTimeError" project in your Package Explorer panel. You can drill down to the "RunTimeError.java" source file and double-click on it to bring up the source code in the IDE code editor.

 Each time you begin an activity for which we provide an "Activity Starter", you will need to follow this process! Copy the starter project directory from your "Activity Starters" folder to your "My Projects" folder, and then import the project into your Eclipse workspace.

The "RunTimeError.java" sample code demonstrates two different runtime errors. You already know the cause for each error, but we'll practice using the debugger to walk through the program line-by-line and watch it in action! As you find each error, change the code to fix the problem so we can continue further.

Starting In the Debugger

To run a program in the debugger, simply click on the debug button (which looks like a "bug") on the toolbar or select "Run → Debug" from the Eclipse menu.

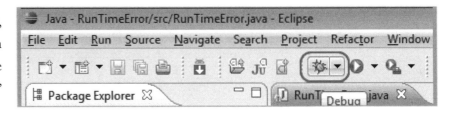

If you are prompted with a "Debug As" dialog asking you how to debug the program, select "Java Application" and click "OK".

The first time you run in the debugger, you may see a message asking if Eclipse can open the "Debug perspective". This means the IDE will change the visible windows to add useful display while you are debugging a program. If you see this message, just click on "Yes" to show the debugging perspective. You can also click "Remember my decision" so you don't get the prompt again.

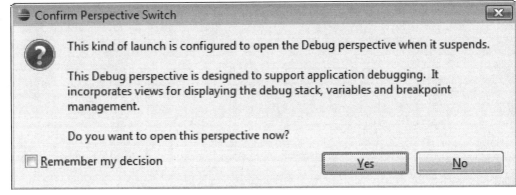

Now you should see a screen similar to the one shown below. If you do not see this Debug perspective, you can open it from the menu by selecting "Window → Open Perspective → Debug".

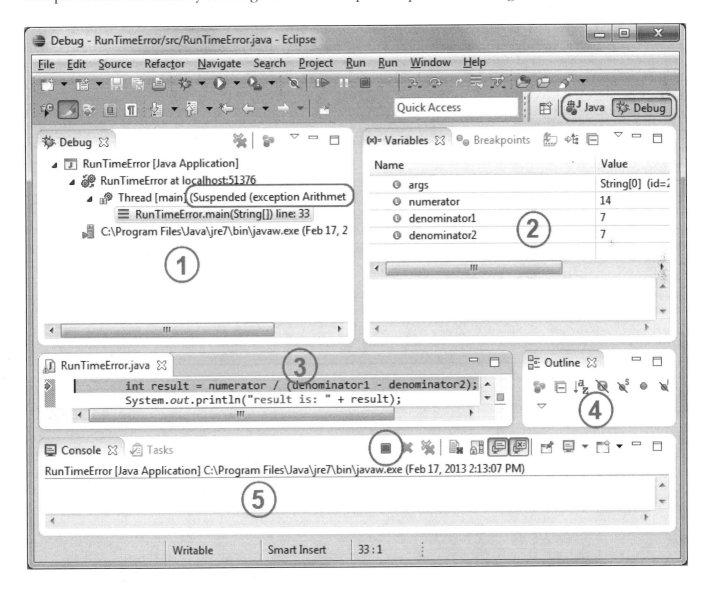

This is quite different than your normal Java perspective, so let's review each of the new windows.

The "Debug" tab (marked with circled "1") contains information about your running program. You can see in this example that the program is currently suspended (or in break) and has an "ArithmeticException" in your **main()** function on line 13. You may also see information about previous program runs, especially if you did not stop those programs and they are still running!

The "Variables" tab (marked with circled "2") shows each of your local variables and their contents. Right now you can see that **denominator1** and **denominator2** both equal 7. Just above this pane is a circled set of buttons labeled "Debug" and "Java". You can click on these buttons at any time to switch back and forth between the Debug and Java perspectives.

The code tab (marked with circled "3") shows your source code and the highlighted line where the program is in break. You can hover your mouse over any variable in this window and see the variable contents. If you have set any breakpoints you will also see those marked with a small circle to the left of the code line.

The "Outline" tab (marked with circled "4") shows your function calls that have been made to get you to this point in your code. Right now you are just sitting in the **main()** function because that's the only one we have! Finally, the "Console" tab (marked with circled "5") shows any output from your program, just like normal. Notice that the red box (circled) is a "Stop" command that will halt your program immediately.

You are free to close any of the window panes you don't want to see in order to get more room for the other windows. Should you change your mind you can restore any window from the menu by selecting "Window → Show View →" and then your window name.

When you run the program in the debugger, Eclipse will automatically switch to Debug perspective if it detects an exception or it hits a breakpoint. But if your program runs successfully with no errors or breakpoints you may not see the Debug perspective at all, because your program never goes into the break state!

When you first run our buggy program, the debugger will pause at the division statement. This indicates that an exception has been thrown by that line or that you have hit a *breakpoint* (which we'll talk about shortly)!

```
RunTimeError.java ✖

    int numerator = 14;
    int denominator1 = 3 + 4;    // do some math
    int denominator2 = 7;

    // result is "numerator divided by (denominator1 minus denominator2)"
    int result = numerator / (denominator1 - denominator2);    // ERROR
    System.out.println("result is: " + result);
```

Looking at Variable Contents

While in break mode you can do a variety of useful debugging tasks. For instance, just hover the mouse over a variable in your code, and a tool tip should show you the current contents of the variable. If you hover the mouse cursor over the **numerator** variable you'll see the current value is 14.

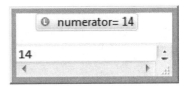

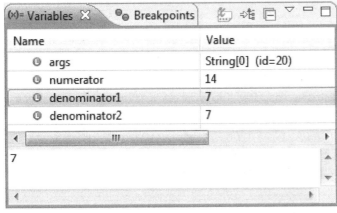

You can also view the contents of all the variables at this point in the program by taking a look at the "Variables" pane in the top-right corner.

You can actually modify the contents of a particular variable by hand, setting it to some new value. To modify the value, double-click on the Value field, type in the new data and then press "Enter". Your variable now has a new value!

By looking at **denominator1** and **denominator2** you see they are equal and of course will cause a divide-by-zero exception. The debugger is still running, so stop it by clicking on the Stop button, which looks like a red square ▣ or by choosing "Run → Terminate" from the menu.

To get back to your familiar Java perspective for writing code, click on the "Java" perspective button in the top-right corner of your screen. Go ahead and fix the code now so no exception is thrown. Use any technique you like, from commenting it out to changing the denominator variable contents or checking for a zero divisor with an **if()** statement.

Setting Breakpoints

At this point you're pretty confident that you fixed that first problem, right? So let's establish a breakpoint at the next interesting block of code, which will start with:

```
String myString = null;
```

To set a breakpoint, just double-click on the blue margin to the left of the code area. You should see a solid blue circle appear showing a breakpoint is now set on that line. You can remove a breakpoint by double-clicking on the same area. Practice this now, and leave the breakpoint enabled on that line when you are done. You can also right-click on the blue margin and selecting "Toggle Breakpoint" from the menu.

Now we want to run the program straight through until your breakpoint is reached. Just click on the debug button on the toolbar at the top of the screen or select "Run → Debug" from the menu to begin debugging

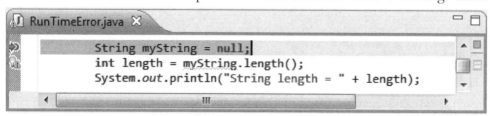

again. This time, the debugger should run past the error we just fixed and proceed down to our breakpoint. When it reaches

the breakpoint, the program will pause in break state. You can see the breakpoint line is again highlighted and you also have a little arrow on the left next to your breakpoint symbol showing you the current line.

Notice in your "Debug" window instead of an exception listed, we simply see "Suspended" indicting the program is in break state with no exceptions encountered yet.

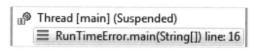

Now that you are a pro at starting in Debug mode and setting breakpoints, let's learn how to step through your program line-by-line using the debugger commands.

Stepping Through the Program

The Eclipse debugger has an easy way to step through the different lines of a Java program. The common debugging commands can be accessed through either the toolbar (shown below), or through the "Run" menu. You can also memorize a series of "shortcut" keys, like F6 and F11 to quickly perform debugging commands.

The three circled arrows above represent the "Step Into", "Step Over", and "Step Out" commands that were described in the last lesson. To execute the next line of code and remain in the break state, go ahead and execute the "Step Over" command now. You can do this by clicking this button on the toolbar, by selecting "Run → Step Over" from the menu.

Once you choose "Step Over", you will see how the highlight arrow moves down a single line and variables in the watch window gain a new entry – **myString**, with a value of **null**. Now the following line is highlighted; go ahead and try to "Step Over" this line as well!

```
int length = myString.length();
```

Whoops, your highlighted line in the source window didn't budge! Instead Eclipse noticed an exception was thrown, and shows you the "NullPointerException" details up in the Debug panel.

You can hold the mouse over the **myString** variable and view its contents to see the **null** value. The highlighted line definitely contains a null reference!

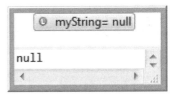

Now that you know what the error is, you should stop the debugger by clicking on the Stop button (red square) or by choosing "Run → Terminate" from the menu. Then you can fix the error by assigning some valid string to **myString** before trying to get the length.

Once you fix the code you can run your program again in the debugger. After you hit your breakpoint you can execute "Step Over" commands through the end of your program and you'll see your string length output to the console. Notice that if you continue to "Step Over" past the end of your **main()** function, you may get some odd displays as shown below:

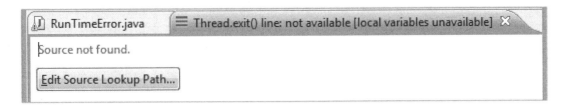

This merely shows that you have stepped completely out of your program and are now into core Java areas used to launch your program. Since you don't have any source code for this area there is nothing to display. At this point it's safe to just stop your program with the Stop (Terminate) command.

Do you want to learn more about testing your code and improving the quality if your work? Check out our bonus lesson "Testing Your Code" from your Student Menu! There we describe how write unit test code, check for boundary conditions, state pre- and post-conditions, and add assertion logic. The bonus material is not required to complete this course, but you may find it useful.

Activity: Bug Hunt

In this activity, you will be in charge of hunting and fixing for several bugs in a program!

Your activity requirements and instructions are found in the "Chapter_09_Activity.pdf" document located in your "TeenCoder\Java Programming\Activity Docs" folder. You can access this document through your Student Menu or by directly clicking on it from Windows Explorer (Windows) or Finder (Mac OS).

Complete this activity now and ensure your program meets the requirements before continuing!

Chapter Ten: Object-Oriented Java Programming

In this chapter you will learn about Object Oriented Programming (OOP). OOP is a programming technique that can be applied to many different languages, but we'll focus on how to implement your own objects in the Java language. This is a lengthy chapter that covers important topics, so plan some extra time!

Lesson One: Object-Oriented Concepts

Originally, most computer programs were written in a *structured* programming language like "C", "Pascal", or "FORTRAN". In structured languages, writing functions is supported and encouraged, but the orderly management of data is more difficult. Programmers may also find it difficult to re-use code across projects.

Re-Useable Code Objects

What is object-oriented programming? OOP revolves around the creation of re-usable code *objects*. In Java the terms *object* and *class* are used interchangeably. You have already created classes in your programs to hold your **main()** function. But classes can be much more powerful and complex than you have seen so far.

Some objects will be useful to many different programmers and can be shared by multiple projects. All of the objects in the Java Class Library such as **String** are frequently used by many programmers. Consider a **Button** object as another example. Creating a button on the screen for the user to click may involve quite a bit of work. The button may have properties like a text **Label**, methods such as **Paint()** to show the button on the screen, and other logic to handle communication of the user mouse clicks back to the application.

There would be a lot of wasted effort if every program needing to use a button on the screen had to create their own **Button** object from scratch. Instead, using OOP one person can make a **Button** object and share it with other projects. This is object-oriented programming!

Modeling Complex Systems

The OOP approach allows a programmer to break complicated systems down into smaller and simpler objects that work together. For example, let's say we needed to write a good representation of an airplane. Airplanes seem very complicated from the outside, but start to become more understandable when you break them down into smaller parts like a **Wing**, **Fuselage**, **Cockpit**, **Engine**, etc. You can even go further and define smaller objects that work together to form a **Cockpit** such as **Windshield**, **InstrumentPanel**, and maybe even **EjectorSeat**. You can keep going until the original **Airplane** object is entirely defined by very

159

small, easy-to-understand objects. A good rule of thumb when modeling real-world systems is to make the individual code objects match their real-world counterparts.

Inheriting Traits

Another great benefit of OOP is a concept called *inheritance*. Inheritance allows similar objects to share common details or traits. A car and a moving van may have many physical differences, but they are both vehicles that have wheels, seats, and other common properties. They also have behavioral similarities like accelerating and braking. Of course there may be behavioral differences too, like how you load cargo.

We could use object-oriented programming techniques to define a general **Vehicle** object that contains common properties and behaviors of all vehicles. Then we can define another object or *sub-class* which *inherits* from the **Vehicle** class to create more specialized objects like **Car** and **MovingTruck**. These sub-classes would re-use the common functionality of **Vehicle** and then add their own special properties and behaviors.

Data Encapsulation

Another great aspect of OOP is the ability of objects to hide their internal or "private" implementation details. Some objects are often referred to as "black boxes", meaning you can't see inside them. A programmer just interacts with the "public" parts of the object. The object's internal workings can be changed completely without breaking the programs that are currently using the object, so long as the public methods are the same. Hiding or restricting access to your internal data is also called *data encapsulation*. Allowing other objects to access data or behavior through public methods is called *procedural abstraction*. "Procedure" is another word for a function or method, so "procedural abstraction" in this context just means that the public user has no idea how the method is actually implemented to perform the action.

Let's say we created a "black box" **Calculator** object. A programmer can call the method (or function) **IsPrimeNumber()** to determine if an input X is a prime number. Your first version of **Calculator** might use one algorithm to check for prime that is quick and easy to implement. Later on you could release an improved **Calculator** object and completely re-write the internal implementation of **IsPrimeNumber()** so it runs faster and takes less computer memory. Your **Caclulator** is now much improved, but programs using the object would still call the same **IsPrimeNumber()** function without knowing the difference. Only the code inside in the "black box" would change, while the public interface remains the same.

In computing, a "black box" has nothing to do with plane crashes. A black box is any piece of code that a programmer can use without having to know how that code works.

It's certainly possible to write bad programs using OOP techniques. However well-written OOP code has a number of advantages over structured programming.

Lesson Two: Defining a Class

In the Java language (and in most languages), an object is referred to as a *class*. When we use the term **class**, you will know that we are talking about an object in a Java program. From your previous activities, you know you can create a new Java class through the Eclipse IDE by right-clicking on your project in the workspace and selecting "New → Class".

Every class in Java has its own "*.java" source file where "*" must match exactly with the name of the class. Recall that we discussed Java *package* concepts in Chapter Two. You should be familiar with package naming concepts and using the **import** statement to easily access objects in a different package. You should also understand that your "*.java" source files must be located in a directory structure that matches your package name, if any. For the objects in this course we are simply using the default (empty) package.

Within your source file, classes are defined with the keyword **class**, followed by the name of the class.

```
class Car
{
}
```

We have now defined a class named **Car**. The curly braces that follow the class name will enclose the entire implementation of the class. In order to create and use a class, you would declare a variable of the class type and use the **new** keyword to create an instance of the class.

```
Car myCar = new Car();
```

It's important to remember that class variables are *reference* data types. This means that the variable does not contain any data itself, it just refers to a location in memory where the class is stored. If you assign one class variable to another, you will end up with two variables that refer to the same object.

```
Car myCar1 = new Car();
Car myCar2 = myCar1;    // myCar2 and myCar1 now refer to the same Car object!
```

When defining a class, there are generally three main points to consider:

Properties	What variables or other objects does this class need to perform its tasks?
Methods	What methods (functions) are defined on the class for public or internal use?
Relationships	How does this class interact with other objects? Is it similar enough in nature to other objects that they should inherit traits from each other?

The first step to defining any class is to understand what the object needs to represent and what it will do within your program. This can be a bit of an art form where there is no one right answer. We have already created a **Car** object, so let's begin filling out the object's data, methods, and relationships.

Object Properties

Most objects own some sort of internal data. This data is represented by *properties* or *member variables* which are variables declared at the **class** level, and not locally within a function. For instance, our **Car** object might have the properties: **color** (a string), **year** (an integer), and **myEngine** (an **Engine** object reference). We can declare and optionally initialize those variables within the curly braces of the overall **class** just like you would normally declare local variables within a function:

```
class Car
{
    String color = "Blue";
    int year = 2012;
    Engine myEngine = new Engine();
}
```

Variables declared at the class level are visible to all functions or methods within the class. Each time you create a new instance of a class you get a new copy of all the variables to go along with it. The member variables "live" and "die" with the class instance, so they will be around as long as you are using the object. When the parent **Car** object instance goes away (meaning you no longer have any variable references to it in your program), all of the properties associated with the object instance are also deleted.

```
Car car1 = new Car();   // car1 now has it's own copy of all 3 properties
Car car2 = new Car();   // car2 now has it's own copy of all 3 properties
car1 = null; // remove all references to car1; the object will be deleted
```

Notice that while the reference variables belonging to a class are discarded when the class is deleted, the objects they refer to in memory may live on if they have been shared with someone else. For instance, we could have taken the **Engine** from **car1** and placed it into **car2** like this:

```
Car car1 = new Car();   // car1 now has an engine
Car car2 = new Car();   // car2 now has another engine
car2.myEngine = car1.myEngine;    // car2 now shares car1's engine!
car1.myEngine = null;             // now car1 has no engine!
```

In the example above, the original **Engine** object belonging to **car2** is discarded because there are no longer any reference variables pointing to it.

Object Methods

Class *methods* are functions defined within a class; you will see the terms *method* and *function* used interchangeably. You have been calling methods on objects in the Java Class Library such as **println()** on the **System.out** object. You have also created a **main()** method on a class in each of your projects, and you can create other methods belonging to your class. Let's define some sample methods in our **Car** class:

```java
class Car
{
    void start()
    {
        // implement the Start method here
    }
    void stop()
    {
        // implement the Stop method here
    }
}
```

You can define any sort of method you like with different return types and input and output parameters. Your class methods are called or invoked by using the variable name containing the object, then a dot, and then the function name with opening and closing parentheses, as in this example:

```java
Car myCar = new Car();  // create a new instance of the Car object
myCar.start();          // call the start() method on this Car instance
```

"this" Keyword

Within a method definition for an object, it is possible to refer to the unique object instance on which the method is being run with the "**this**" keyword. If you wanted to pass a reference to the current object to some other method, use the **this** keyword. Here we pass **this** into the **wash()** method of the input **CarWash**:

```java
class Car
{
    void clean(CarWash sparklingWash)
    {
        // pass reference to this Car object to the wash() method
        sparklingWash.wash(this);
    }
}
```

Object Relationships

Objects don't usually exist all by themselves. They have to interact with other objects in the program. There are three main types of relationships that two objects can have with each other.

Uses-a	Object A may "use" Object B by calling the methods defined by Object B. But Object A does not "own" Object B or "inherit" from Object B. For example, a **Driver** object might call a **start()** method on a **Car** object. But the **Car** is not a part of the **Driver** object.
Has-a	Object A "has-an" instance of Object B as internal data. Object A owns object B by carrying it around in one of Object A's internal data variables. A **Car** object might "have-a" **Wheel** object. "Has-a", "has-an", "have-a", and "have-an" are all the same relationship.
Is-a	Object A "is-an" (or "is-a") instance of Object B, meaning Object A *inherits* from or *subclasses* Object B. For example, a **RaceCar** object "is-a" **Car** object. The more general class (Object A) is called a *base* class. The more specific class (Object B) is called a *derived class* or *sub-class*.

The definition of objects and relationships in a program is not an exact science. There are often several effective ways to accomplish the same goals. To demonstrate this, let's consider a few ways to represent a **King** and his fellow **Knights** as objects.

We might define a **King** object and a **Knight** object separately. The **King** may "use" a **Knight** object by giving the **Knight** a command.

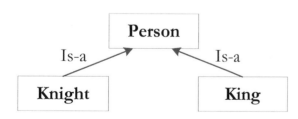

The **King** object may instead "have-a" **Knight** object since a knight belongs to one particular king.

Or, we could define a **Person** object that contains common properties like **Name** and **Age**. Then we can define a **Knight** object that inherits from a **Person** object (all knights are people) and adds some specific properties like **Armor** and methods like **joust()**. Finally, we define a **King** object that inherits from a **Knight** because a king is also the head knight and does everything a knight can do! But a **King** also has properties such as a **Crown** and abilities such as **offWithTheirHeads()**.

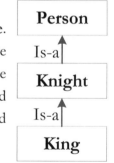

Of course we could decide that knights and kings do not have enough in common for kings to inherit from knights – maybe kings never learned how to ride. So we define a **Person** object but then both **King** and **Knight** objects can inherit directly from **Person**.

All of these approaches may be valid depending on the problem you are trying to solve. You will learn how to create your own class inheritance relationships later in the course.

Lesson Three: Public, Private and Protected Members

We have discussed the ability of objects to become a "black box" where some internal details are hidden from the outside world. Now it's time to find out how that works!

All properties and methods on an object can be marked as **public**, **private**, or **protected**. These keywords control how other objects can access the particular property or method.

public	Public properties and methods can be accessed by any other object.
private	Private properties and methods can only be accessed by the object that defines them.
protected	Protected properties and methods can only be accessed by the object that defines them, or by objects that inherit from or subclass from the first object with an "is-a" relationship.

Public properties and methods are essentially your object's "face" that it displays to the outside world. Once other objects start using your **public** methods and properties you cannot change how they are defined or how they behave without possibly breaking those other objects. A **public** method can internally call any other **public**, **protected**, or **private** method defined on the class.

Private properties and methods are things no other objects can see or use, so they are safely inside your "black box". You can freely change, add, or remove **private** properties and methods without worrying about whom might be using them (so long as those changes don't impact your **public** method behavior, of course). A **private** method can internally call any other methods defined on the class. Unless you specifically want to make something visible to the outside world, you should always use the **private** keyword when defining your methods and properties; that keeps your internal implementation safe from outside meddling!

Protected items act like items **private** in that external objects cannot see them. However if you have a derived class that inherits from a base class, then that derived class can also use any **protected** properties and methods from the base class.

Let's look at a **Knight** class that has a mixture of **public**, **private**, and **protected** attributes.

```java
public class Knight
{
    // everyone knows your name!
    public String myName = "Sir Jousts-a-Lot";

    // nobody else needs to know this
    private String horseNickname = "Stinker";

    // knights and anyone else inheriting from this class will have a skill level
    protected int skillLevel = 100;
    // anyone can wake you up, whether you like it or not!
```

```java
    public void wakeUp()
    {
    }


    // only you can tell if you are hungry!
    private boolean isHungry()
    {
        return true;      // jousting is hard work
    }


    // knights and anyone else inheriting from this class have the ability
    // to put on armor
    protected void donArmor()
    {
    }
}
```

Now let's review some code that uses the **Knight** class from a different, unrelated object:

```java
public class Camelot
{
    public static void main(String[] args)
    {
        Knight myKnight = new Knight();   // create a new Knight

        String yourName = myKnight.myName;  // OK!  name is a public property
        myKnight.horseNickname = "Pudgy"; // ERROR! Can't access private property
        int skill = myKnight.skillLevel;  // ERROR! Can't access protected property

        myKnight.wakeUp();       // OK!  wakeUp() is a public method.
        myKnight.donArmor();     // ERROR!  Can't access protected method
        if (myKnight.isHungry()) // ERROR!  Can't access private method
        {
        }
    }
}
```

You can see that any attempt to access a **private** property or method will result in a compile-time error. Only the **Knight** class can access these items from within other **Knight** methods. However, any program can call the **public wakeUp()** function or use the **public myName** property.

Wait! What's to keep someone from changing your public **myName** property? Nothing! Perhaps **myName** would be better coded as a **private** property, and then you can make others ask for the value instead. That will safely protect data that should not be changed and give **public** access to the value when needed.

```java
public class Knight
{
    // nobody can change your name but you
    private String myName = "Sir Jousts-a-Lot";

    // anyone can ask for your name
    public String askName()
    {
        return myName;  // yes I am friendly
    }

    // etc...
```

This example reinforces the practice that most properties and methods should be marked as **private** unless you have a really good reason to make them **public**.

Lesson Four: Constructors

A class *constructor* is a special method that is automatically called when the class is created with the **new** keyword. The constructor is commonly used to initialize the properties of a class. If you do not create this method yourself, the compiler will use a default constructor. But if there is anything special that you would like to do when your class is created, you should create your own constructor. The name of the constructor method is always the same as the class itself. Here is an example constructor for our **Knight** class:

```java
class Knight
{
    private String myName;

    public Knight()    // this is the constructor method
    {
        myName = "Unknown"; // set a property to some default value
    }
}
```

As you can see, we created a method inside our class definition with the same name as the class itself. Constructor methods should usually be defined as **public** and they have no return type (**void** or otherwise). Our **Knight**() constructor just sets the **myName** property to "Unknown". Now, every time a program creates a new **Knight** object the constructor will be called:

```
Knight myKnight = new Knight();    // Knight constructor automatically run
```

If you do not define a constructor, a default constructor with no parameters and no logic within the function is automatically created by the compiler. It is considered good programming practice to make sure all class member variables are initialized within your constructor or where they are declared! That way when any other method is called later, you know that all internal data has been initialized to some known starting point.

Constructors are particularly useful when you define parameters for the method. These parameters would be required by the program when calling the **new** keyword and are placed between the parentheses after the class name. Constructors with parameters ensure that no instance of your class is ever created without some required data. You can define any number of constructors to initialize your class in different ways, as long as they all take different combinations of parameters.

For example, if we wanted to ensure that no one ever created a **Knight** instance without providing a value for the **myName** property, we could create the following constructor:

```
public Knight(String name)
{
    myName = name;
}
```

With this constructor, you are required to provide a **String** parameter whenever a new **Knight** is created:

```
Knight myKnight1 = new Knight("Sir Gravy Train");
Knight myKnight2 = new Knight();  // ERROR!  No parameter provided
```

The compiler would show you an error on the second line because no constructor parameter was provided when trying to create that **Knight**.

Lesson Five: Object Interfaces

Often you might need to use a number of objects that all behave in a similar manner. For instance, consider the different cars that you can drive. Each car may have a different color, make, model, and fancy sound system. But, there are a few things you can count on!

You know for certain that every car has a steering wheel, a gas pedal, and a brake pedal. When you turn the wheel left, the car turns left. When you spin the wheel right, the car turns right. When you step on the gas, the car will speed up. When you step on the brake, the car will slow down. These behaviors are the same for any car you are likely to drive.

What did we just describe? An *interface*! An interface is a contract or guarantee of behavior that lets users interact with different objects in the same way. You don't know how the car will actually perform the steering – each car probably has a number of different parts and systems that combine to turn the car left and right. However, as a user, you don't really care. You can just use the interface promised in your owner's manual to drive around town.

Java classes can have interfaces too. A class interface contains a set of method declarations but no implementation or function body. Other objects will *implement* the interface and provide their own function body. When you are using an object that implements a certain interface, then you do not need to know any of the underlying details about the object – just use the interface. A car interface might define the methods **TurnLeft()**, **TurnRight()**, **SpeedUp()**, and **SlowDown()** to allow users to use the steering wheel, gas pedal, and brake.

Just like classes, interfaces are identified by a name and may be part of a particular package. It may not be easy to tell the difference between an interface and a full object just by looking at the name. Therefore in this course we will adopt a naming convention that all our interface names will start with a capital "I". For our car steering we might think **ICar** is a good interface name, but that could be too generic. There might be other aspects of a car that are defined by other interfaces such as turning the car on and off. So let's name our interface **IDriveable** instead to better reflect what the interface allows you to do.

To create an interface using the Eclipse IDE, right-click on your project in the Package Explorer and select "New → Interface" (this is very similar to creating a new class).

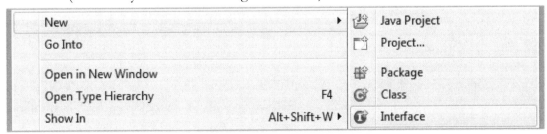

Now you can see the "New Java Interface" dialog, which should look like the new class dialog without some of the extra options such as creating a **main()** function.

Simply type in the name of your interface in the "Name" textbox, add in a "Package" if you are using any (we are leaving at the default package), and then click "Finish".

Eclipse will create a new project source file called <interface name>.java, or in this example "IDriveable.java".

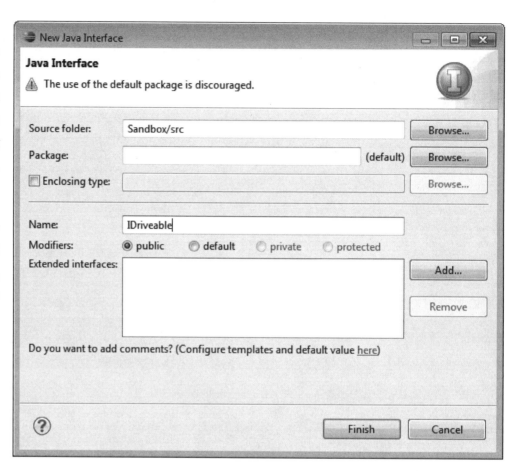

The new source file will contain an empty **interface** definition:

```java
public interface IDriveable
{
    // your interface definition will go here
}
```

Notice the **interface** keyword is used instead of **class** to define an interface instead of a full **class**. Once the interface is created you can then start adding method definitions that do not have any body or implementation. The interface should just specify which methods must be present by all other classes implementing the interface.

Let's add in the methods we described above for **IDriveable** now. Instead of curly braces after each method name that contain a body, just end each function declaration with a semicolon. There is no actual code for functions within the interface, just a definition of the methods that other classes implementing the interface will create.

```
public interface IDriveable
{
    // all classes implementing IDriveable must implement these methods!
    public void TurnLeft();
    public void TurnRight();
    public void SpeedUp();
    public void SlowDown();
}
```

If our **Car** object wanted to implement the **IDriveable** interface, it would use the keyword **implements** after the class name like this:

```
public class Car implements IDriveable
{
}
```

As soon as your **Car** class **implements** the **IDriveable** interface, Eclipse will show errors letting you know you have some work to do in order to finish your class:

```
- The type Car must implement the inherited abstract method IDriveable.TurnRight()
- The type Car must implement the inherited abstract method IDriveable.SlowDown()
- The type Car must implement the inherited abstract method IDriveable.SpeedUp()
- The type Car must implement the inherited abstract method IDriveable.TurnLeft()
```

The **Car** class has to implement the methods we defined in the **IDriveable** interface. Let's do that now:

```
public class Car implements IDriveable
{
    public void TurnLeft()   // Car's implementation of this method
    {
    }
    public void TurnRight()  // Car's implementation of this method
    {
    }
    public void SpeedUp()    // Car's implementation of this method
    {
    }
    public void SlowDown()   // Car's implementation of this method
    {
    }
}
```

Any other object such as **Truck** can also implement the **IDriveable** interface. Each class implementing an interface can internally accomplish the interface goals in different ways by using their own functions.

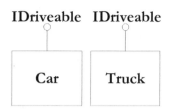

When drawing diagrams of objects, it is conventional to represent the interfaces an object implements with a "lollipop" coming from the object's box. In the example to the right you can see that both **Car** and **Truck** objects implement the **IDriveable** interface, so you can be confident that you can make them both move in the same way.

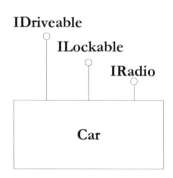

Keep in mind it's perfectly OK for one class to implement more than one interface! A **Car** object might predictably implement the **ILockable** and **IRadio** interfaces as well, since you can lock and unlock all cars and they all have at least a radio or some sort of audio system.

To implement multiple interfaces from your class, simply list each interface name separated by a comma after the **implements** keyword:

```
public class Car implements IDriveable, ILockable, IRadio
{
}
```

Lesson Six: Static Members

Most of the object properties and methods that we have used so far have belonged to specific instances of the class. In order to use any of these properties and methods, we had to use the **new** keyword. For example, in order to access a public **myName** property of our **Knight** class, we would create an instance of this class:

```
Knight myKnight = new Knight();
myKnight.myName = "Sir Gallop";    // this name belongs to myKnight only
```

Static Properties

It is possible, however, to define properties and methods that belong to *all* instances of the class simultaneously! That means there is only ever one copy of the property shared by all instances of the class. This is especially useful for any property that is intended to be a *global* setting, or a setting that is used throughout the program. These types of properties and methods are defined with the **static** keyword.

```java
class Knight
{
    static public String greeting = "Hail and well met, my name is ";
    private String myName;

    public String askName()
    {
        return Knight.greeting + myName;  // use static and non-static data!
    }
}
```

By adding the **static** keyword in front of the variable declaration, the **greeting** property is now accessible without creating an instance of the class. You can see above that other methods (static or non-static) on the **Knight** class can access that **static** property by using the class name **Knight** instead of a variable name. If your **static** property is **public**, then it can be accessed by code outside the object in the same way:

```java
String hello = Knight.greeting;
```

We can easily change the greeting for all **Knight** variables with just one statement, making them less friendly:

```java
Knight.greeting = "Who wants to know?  My name is ";
```

Static Methods

You can also define **static** methods for a class. However, there is one important thing to remember about **static** methods: these methods can only access other **static** methods and properties. In other words, static methods must work only with data that is not specific to any one instance of the class.

```java
class Knight
{
    static private King myKing;  // all Knights belong to this King

    // set a new King for all Knights!
    static public void setKing(King newKing)
    {
        // myKing is static, so OK to access from static method
        myKing = newKing;
    }
}
```

If we had tried to access any other non-static **Knight** property or method within the **static setKing()** method, we would receive a compiler error. A **static** method does not know anything about properties or methods that belong to a particular class instance.

Just as with **static** properties, you call **static** methods by using the class name itself:

```
King arthur = new King("Arthur Pendragon");
Knight.setKing(arthur);   // now all Knights belong to a this King
```

You may often find **static** methods on objects that perform some useful task or calculation based entirely on the parameters passed into the method. In that case there is no need to create an instance of the object because all of the required data is provided as method parameters, and no internal class variables are used. The **static String.format()** method you learned about earlier is one example.

Activity: Let's Go Racing!

In this activity, you will get to practice your new object-oriented Java skills by completing a racing program! To do this you will need to create a **RaceCar** class and an **IRacer** interface. You will integrate your new objects into the **RaceTrack** activity starter that we provide for you.

Your activity requirements and instructions are found in the "Chapter_10_Activity.pdf" document located in your "TeenCoder\Java Programming\Activity Docs" folder. You can access this document through your Student Menu or by directly clicking on it from Windows Explorer (Windows) or Finder (Mac OS).

Complete this activity now and ensure your program meets the requirements before continuing!

Chapter Eleven: Graphical Java Programs

In this chapter we're going to begin exploring a new way to interact with your programs – through a Graphical User Interface or GUI.

Lesson One: Java Swing

So far all of your Java programs have used the console for user input and output. The console was either embedded directly in your Eclipse IDE in the "Console" tab, or you ran the program manually from a command line from your operating system.

But how often have you used software that required you to interact with a command line? Probably never! Most computer programs today rely heavily on the use of graphicall user input and output. These programs have a *Graphical User Interface*, or GUI (pronounced "gooey").

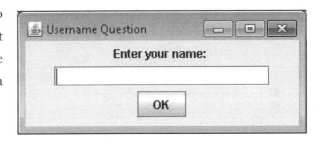

Java AWT and Swing

There are two main ways to add GUI elements to a Java program. The first and oldest method is to use a set of classes called the *Abstract Windowing Toolkit* or AWT. The AWT contains classes such as **Button** that correspond to the native operating system elements you normally see in a GUI. These Java classes under the covers would use the native operating system versions of each control, such as a button. So a Java AWT program would look like a native Windows application on a Windows OS, and it would look like a native Mac program when running on Mac OS.

There are two main problems with the AWT. First, the AWT is limited to using only the common controls that are shared among the major graphical operating systems. So if the Mac OS has a special useful control that no other operating system supported, it would not be available in the AWT. Second, the AWT program would have a different look and feel as it was run on each operating system, because it relied on the native OS controls to build the user interface. In practice this means that Java AWT programs need careful testing on each operating system to make sure the interfaces all work the same way.

Sun Microsystems, the creators of Java, came up with a new set of GUI classes in the late 1990s. This new set of tools was called "Swing". The Swing classes are written entirely in Java and implement their own version of all supported controls without relying on native operating system controls. This means that a GUI program written using the Swing classes look the same when run on different operating systems. It also means that the Swing classes can implement any controls without being limited to what the native operating system supports.

Both AWT and Swing classes are included today as part of the JDK. In fact, the Swing classes will use some of the objects from the AWT to perform certain tasks. However you do not want to mix AWT and Swing graphical objects at the same time. In this course we will use the Swing classes for your GUI programs.

Graphics programming in Swing is a very large topic. Since we can't fill an entire book with all the details, we are going to teach you enough to get started and handle most common user interface tasks. If you ever need more information on Swing, you can find an excellent Java Swing tutorial online, currently at this location:

http://docs.oracle.com/javase/tutorial/uiswing/TOC.html

You can find the tutorial if the location changes by searching for "Java Swing Tutorial" in a search engine.

Window Measurements

Today's GUI operating systems use the concept of "windows" that can be moved and resized on your computer screen. Each window generally contains all of the user interface elements (both input and output) for one program. You can run many programs at the same time, each with its own window. One program itself may also contain more than one window, either switching between different windows or displaying more than one window at the same time.

The size and position of all windows on your computer screen are specified by *pixel* values. A pixel is one tiny dot on your computer screen. Your entire screen is made up of thousands of pixels packed closely together in a large grid. Any one point on your screen is defined by a coordinate pair, which is simply a pair of numbers representing the column and row of the pixel measured from the upper-left corner. The pixel at the upper-left corner has column = 0 and row = 0, or (0, 0) as a coordinate pair. The column value increases by one each pixel you move to the right. The row value increases by one each pixel you move down the screen.

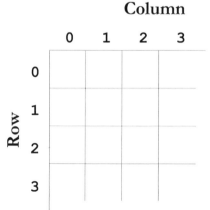

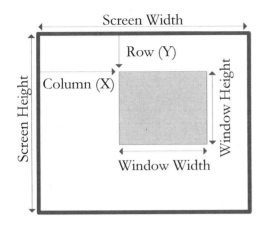

The position of a window on the screen is defined by the screen coordinates of the upper-left corner of the window, or (X, Y) in the diagram to the left. The width and height of a window and the width and height of the overall computer screen are also measured in pixels.

When creating your own windows on the computer screen you will be able to set the window size (width and height) as well as position in pixel coordinates.

Lesson Two: Creating a Simple Window

Now that you understand general window size and positioning, let's get started on our first window in Java! An application window is represented by a Swing object called **JFrame**. A **JFrame** is a top-level container object within which all other window components must be placed. Two other top-level container objects, **JDialog** and **JApplet**, serve more specialized purposes. We are going to focus on **JFrame**.

Creating an Empty Window

A **JFrame** represents one screen or window within the application. The **JFrame** object contains a window with a full border, a title bar, and controls for minimizing and maximizing the window. These surrounding elements use your native operating system look-and-feel native. Here are Windows and Mac OS examples:

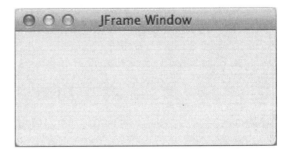

The interior gray part is your *client area*, which is where Swing places all of the other graphical elements using a common look-and-feel.

The first step when writing a GUI program is to import the Java Swing and AWT libraries:

```
import javax.swing.*;
import java.awt.*;
```

So far all of the console programs you have written start at the beginning of the **main()** function, do some work, and terminate when the **main()** function ends.

```
public static void main(String[] args)
{
    // Fun stuff happens here

    // Program ends
}
```

When writing a graphical Java program, your **main()** function is merely a launching point to create your **JFrame**. Once that **JFrame** is created, your **main()** function can end. But your program will live on so long as the **JFrame** window has not been destroyed! Here is a simple program that will create one of the **JFrame** windows we showed as examples above:

```
public static void main(String[] args)
{
    JFrame myFrame = new JFrame();
    myFrame.setTitle("JFrame Window");
    myFrame.setSize(400, 200);
    myFrame.setLocation(200, 300);
    myFrame.setDefaultCloseOperation(JFrame.EXIT_ON_CLOSE);
    myFrame.setVisible(true);
}
```

When your **main()** function ends the program will live on until the window is closed. You can probably guess what each line of code does, but let's take a closer look. First, to create a **JFrame**, you simply declare a **JFrame** variable and initialize it using the **new** keyword to create a new **JFrame** object.

```
JFrame myFrame = new JFrame();
```

Initially the **JFrame** window is hidden, so you have a chance to set some other properties before showing the window on the screen. The next line sets the title, which is displayed in the title bar at the top of the window.

```
myFrame.setTitle("JFrame Window");
```

The default **JFrame** window location is (0, 0) on the computer screen. The default window size has no client area either, so unless you change the default position and size you'll just get a tiny window in the upper-left corner.

You'll want to call the **JFrame** setSize() and **setLocation()** functions to set the window width and height and upper-left coordinates before displaying the window.

```
myFrame.setSize(400, 200);      // sets width = 400, height = 200
myFrame.setLocation(200, 300);  // sets upper left column = 200, row = 300
```

These two lines of code will change the size of the frame to 400 pixels wide and 200 pixels high. The window's upper-left corner will be located 200 pixels in from the left of the screen and 300 pixels down from the top of the screen. The next line is somewhat mysterious. What's going on here?

```
myFrame.setDefaultCloseOperation(JFrame.EXIT_ON_CLOSE);
```

By default, if you close a **JFrame** window using the operating system's controls on the title bar, the window is just hidden and not destroyed! This means your program does not end because the **JFrame** is still alive. The program will continue running in the background for some time.

Why doesn't closing the frame also close the program by default? This is so that you can perform any last-minute operations on the data in your program. If you have a program that needs to save user data before it truly exits, this is the time to do it. For now, however, our programs will be better off just exiting when the user closes the frame. To make this happen, call the **setDefaultCloseOperation()** method with the **JFrame.EXIT_ON_CLOSE** parameter as shown above.

The last method that we need to call on our frame is the **setVisible()** method. This method will show the frame with a **true** parameter, or hide the frame with a **false** parameter. Only call **setVisible(true)** after you have finished configuring the rest of the **JFrame** and any interior components.

```
myFrame.setVisible(true);
```

Ok, so we now have an empty window! But that's not very useful. You will want to add *controls*, or GUI elements, such as buttons, labels, text boxes, radio buttons, check boxes, and so on. These controls are what your user will interact with to provide input and receive output.

Adding a Layout Manager

Now that we have a frame on the screen, it's time to add some useful controls. But before we add our controls, we need to think about where the controls will be located within the window. In Swing, the placement of controls in the window client area is handled by an object called a *layout manager*. We will talk in depth about the different Swing layout managers in a later lesson. For now, we will use the simplest of layout managers called the **FlowLayout**.

The **FlowLayout** will place controls on the screen in the order they are added to the **JFrame**. If your controls will not fit on a single row, then they will automatically flow down to the next row. Later you will learn how fine-tune the display with alignment, spacing, and borders.

To use a layout manager, first create a new **FlowLayout** object, then use the **JFrame setLayout()** method to attach the layout manager to the window:

```
JFrame myFrame = new JFrame();
FlowLayout myLayout = new FlowLayout();
myFrame.setLayout(myLayout);
```

Now when we add our controls, they will be positioned in order from left-to-right, dropping down into a new row if necessary. As you resize the window on the screen the layout manager will automatically re-calculate the positions of each control within the window.

The JComponent Base Class

All Swing UI controls inherit either directly or indirectly from the **JComponent** base class. So the Swing classes representing a label, button, text box, radio button, check box, and so on all share this common base class. You will find many useful methods on **JComponent** that you can call from any of those derived classes. Also, making all UI elements inherit from one base class makes it easier for top-level containers such as a **JFrame** to handle all of the child controls in the same way.

Adding JLabels

The first control we will discuss is the *label*, which will display a line of text. This text cannot be edited by the user. Labels are most often used to describe other controls so that the user knows what information is needed. For example, if you have a text box on the screen, you can use a label control to tell the user to enter their name, address, or user ID.

In Swing, a label control is represented by the **JLabel** object. You can create a **JLabel** object like this:

```
JLabel myLabel = new JLabel("This is my label!");
```

Notice in the **JLabel** constructor we pass in the text that we want the label to display. Now, just creating the control does not mean it shows up in your window! You need to add the control to your **JFrame** with the **JFrame.add()** method:

```
myFrame.add(myLabel);
```

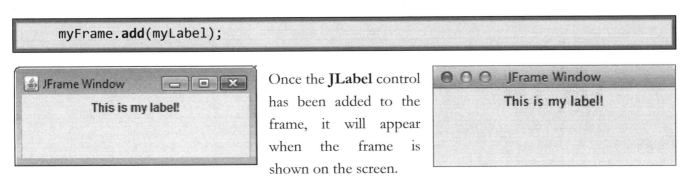

Once the **JLabel** control has been added to the frame, it will appear when the frame is shown on the screen.

Adding JButtons

A *button* control is one of the most recognizable controls in a graphical program. A button is a clickable box that allows a user to perform some sort of action. A button is represented by the Swing **JButton** object. Creating and displaying a **JButton** control is very similar to using a **JLabel**. You need to create new **JButton** object and then **add()** it to the **JFrame** object.

```
JButton myButton = new JButton("Click Here");
myFrame.add(myButton);
```

Just like the label, we also set the button's display text in the **JButton** constructor.

There are occasionally times when you will want to disable a button on the screen. For example, a "Login" button may be disabled until a user enters both a user name and a password. To disable a button, you can use the **JButton setEnabled()** method. Pass in **false** to disable the control or **true** to enable it.

```
myButton.setEnabled(false);  // disable control
myButton.setEnabled(true);   // enable control
```

Packing the Controls

Let's put all of our example code together to create a window with a label and button using the **FlowLayout**.

```java
JFrame myFrame = new JFrame();  // create the JFrame window

FlowLayout myLayout = new FlowLayout();   // create a layout manager
myFrame.setLayout(myLayout);              // attach layout manager to JFrame

// configure JFrame with basic settings
myFrame.setTitle("JFrame Window");
myFrame.setSize(400,200);
myFrame.setLocation(200, 300);
myFrame.setDefaultCloseOperation(JFrame.EXIT_ON_CLOSE);

JLabel myLabel = new JLabel("This is my label!");  // create a JLabel
myFrame.add(myLabel);                              // add JLabel to JFrame

JButton myButton = new JButton("Click Here");      // create a JButton
myFrame.add(myButton);                             // add JButton to JFrame

myFrame.setVisible(true);              // don't forget the last step!
```

Now our window contains both a label and button arranged on the same line, and it has lots of extra space in the client area since we set the initial size to 400 by 200 pixels.

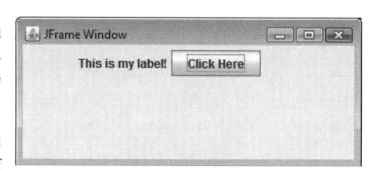

You can cause the **JFrame** to resize itself based on the layout manager and controls to get rid of extra space or enlarge the window if necessary.

Simply call the **JFrame pack()** method to resize the window to fit the controls exactly:

```java
myFrame.pack();
```

Now the size of your window will be adjusted so it is just large enough to hold your two controls!

Lesson Three: Event-Driven Programming

In console applications, the program flow starts at the beginning of the **main()** function and executes each statement in a predictable manner until the program ends. Graphical programs, however, work entirely differently. In graphical programming, a user is faced with a screen which has many different options on it.

There may be any combination of buttons, text boxes, list boxes, and other controls that the user can select at any time. There is no way to predict exactly which action the user will choose to perform. Instead of your program code executing start-to-finish in an orderly manner, your program must respond as the user executes actions. These actions are called *events*, so your GUI program is *event-driven*, meaning certain functions within your code will execute when specific events occur.

Some of the more common events in graphical programming occur when the user clicks a button, moves the mouse or types in a control on the screen. In our last lesson, you learned how to add a button to your window. In this lesson, you will see how to make your program respond to the user clicking on that button!

Organizing an Event-Driven Program

In the last lesson we created a **JFrame** in your program's **static main()** method. However because we were just using a **static** method, there was actually no instance of your program's class.

```
class MyProgram
{
    public static void main(String[] args)
    {
        // no instance of MyProgram was created here previously
    }
}
```

You can see the class **MyProgram** is never actually created with the **new** keyword; we are just running the **static main()** method. However, this approach will not let us respond to user events in a GUI application.

Events are sent to your program through Swing interfaces. This means you need an object to implement those interfaces in order to receive events! You also need to tie together your object that is capable of receiving events to the Swing components on your window that generate events.

One simple approach is to have your main class such as **MyProgram** implement an interface to receive events. Then you can tell your Swing components such as **JButton** to route any user event it generates to your instance of **MyProgram**. Here is our previous **static main()** example re-written by putting all of the **JFrame** logic into the **MyProgram** constructor. Then we simply create a **new MyProgram** from **main()**. We have skipped a few of the **JFrame** configuration details, and are just creating one **JButtton** control.

```
import javax.swing.*;
import java.awt.*;

class MyProgram
{
    public static void main(String[] args)
    {
        // create instance of MyProgram that will do all the work!
        new MyProgram();
    }

    public MyProgram()      // MyProgram constructor
    {
        JFrame myFrame = new JFrame();  // create the JFrame window
        myFrame.setLayout(new FlowLayout());      // attach layout manager

        myFrame.setDefaultCloseOperation(JFrame.EXIT_ON_CLOSE);

        JButton myButton = new JButton("Click Here");  // create a JButton
        myFrame.add(myButton);                          // add JButton to JFrame
        myFrame.pack();
        myFrame.setVisible(true);
    }
}
```

So far we haven't really changed much – the above code still cannot respond to user events. However, we now have the ability for **MyProgram** to implement an interface to receive events. Let's see how that is done!

The interface to receive a **JButton** event is called **ActionListener**. So we start by making **MyProgram** implement this interface. Notice we also need to **import java.awt.event**.* in addition to the other imports.

```
import java.awt.event.*;    // new import for event listeners

class MyProgram implements ActionListener
{
    // this method is required by the ActionListener interface!
    public void actionPerformed(ActionEvent event)
    {
        // handle actions performed here!
    }
}
```

Above we left out the rest of the **MyProgram** code and just focused on the new items. We added an **import** statement for **java.awt.event.***, we made **MyProgram implement** the **ActionListener** interface, and we added the **actionPerformed()** method required by the **ActionListener** interface.

Now we have successfully set up **MyProgram** to receive events, but we need to tell our **JButton** control where to send events. To do this, call the **addActionListener()** method on the **JButton** object, and pass in the object that implements the **ActionListener** interface. In our example the **MyProgram** object itself has implemented the interface, so we just pass in the keyword **this** to refer to the current object.

```
JButton myButton = new JButton("Click Here");  // create a JButton
myButton.addActionListener(this);              // connect button to listener
myFrame.add(myButton);                         // add JButton to JFrame
```

Now any time the **myButton** object is clicked by the user, the **actionPerformed()** method on the **MyProgram** object will automatically be called! Let's spice up our **actionPerformed()** method to display a message to the user when a button is clicked:

```
public void actionPerformed(ActionEvent event)
{
    JOptionPane.showMessageDialog(null,"Hey that tickles!");
}
```

What have we done here? The **JOptionPane** is a convenient Swing class that will display a simple message box pop-up to the user with the **showMessageDialog()** method. The pop-up will contain whatever text you specify and have an "OK" button to close the popup. Use **null** for the first parameter to center the dialog on the screen. You could instead use your **JFrame** reference to center the dialog on your window.

Now here is the full sample program that will display a single button that responds to a click event with a message pop-up.

```
import javax.swing.*;
import java.awt.*;
import java.awt.event.*;

class MyProgram implements ActionListener
{
    public static void main(String[] args)
    {
        // create instance of MyProgram that will do all the work!
        new MyProgram();
    }
```

```java
    public MyProgram()     // MyProgram constructor
    {
        JFrame myFrame = new JFrame();  // create the JFrame window
        myFrame.setLayout(new FlowLayout());      // attach layout manager

        myFrame.setDefaultCloseOperation(JFrame.EXIT_ON_CLOSE);

        JButton myButton = new JButton("Click Here");  // create a JButton
        myButton.addActionListener(this);              // connect button to listener
        myFrame.add(myButton);                         // add JButton to JFrame
        myFrame.pack();
        myFrame.setVisible(true);
    }

    public void actionPerformed(ActionEvent event)
    {
        JOptionPane.showMessageDialog(null,"Hey that tickles!");
    }
}
```

Here is the Windows-style frame shown when you run this program and the resulting message pop-up when the "Click Here" button is clicked:

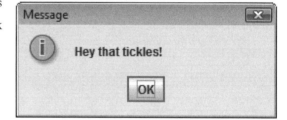

Of course it looks similar on a Mac OS:

Handling Multiple Controls

So what happens if we have more than one button on the screen? Or what if we have another control that sends action events? In this case, we need to check and see what control sent the message before we decide what to do about the event! Fortunately the **ActionEvent** parameter to the **actionPerformed()** interface contains information about the control that raised the event.

```
public void actionPerformed(ActionEvent event)
```

You can call the **getSource()** method on the **ActionEvent** parameter to get a reference to the control object that raised the event:

```
Object control = event.getSource();
```

The return data type is just a basic **Object**, because the control raising the event may be a **JButton** or some other type of object. Now that we have a reference to the control causing the event, how do we match that reference to the controls we added to the **JFrame**? We seem to have a bit of a problem, because the **JButton** we created was just added to the **JFrame** in the **MyProgram** constructor, and then we lost track of it!

```
JButton myButton = new JButton("Click Here");  // create a JButton
myFrame.add(myButton);                         // add JButton to JFrame
// Oops...we didn't store myButton anywhere to keep track if it!
```

In order to keep track of the buttons and other controls you add to your **JFrame**, you'll want to declare those variables at the **class** level instead of locally within a function. That way the variables will be available all the time for us to use from other functions in our class.

```
class MyProgram implements ActionListener
{
    JButton myButton1 = null;  // this variable is a member of the class
    JButton myButton2 = null;  // this variable is a member of the class
```

Now when you are creating and adding controls to the **JFrame**, you store the newly created controls in your member variables instead of a local function variable.

```
myButton1 = new JButton("Red");       // create a JButton
myButton1.addActionListener(this); // connect button to listener
myFrame.add(myButton1);               // add JButton to JFrame

myButton2 = new JButton("Blue");      // create a JButton
myButton2.addActionListener(this); // connect button to listener
myFrame.add(myButton2);               // add JButton to JFrame
```

You can then compare the object reference you get in your **actionPerformed()** method to your member variables to see which button was clicked.

```
public void actionPerformed(ActionEvent event)
{
    Object control = event.getSource();
    if (control == myButton1)  // if myButton1 was clicked
    {
        JOptionPane.showMessageDialog(null,"I like Red!");
    }
    else if (control == myButton2)  // else if myButton2 was clicked
    {
        JOptionPane.showMessageDialog(null,"I like Blue!");
    }
}
```

Any time you add a control to your **JFrame** that will generate an event you want to capture, make sure to save a reference to that control as a class member variable so you can find it later!

Other Listener Interfaces

So far we have only discussed the **ActionListener** interface, which handles very common events like button clicks or radio button selections or the "Enter" key getting pressed in a text box. There are many other kinds of listener interfaces that will let you capture events from different controls, the mouse, and the keyboard. Here is a list of the more common Swing listener interfaces and some brief comments on how they are used. You may wish to capture events in your own programs that we do not cover in this course.

Listener Interface	Methods	Comments
ItemListener	**itemStateChanged(ItemEvent)**	Method is called every time a check box, radio button, combo box, or similar widget is selected or de-selected.
KeyListener	**keyTyped(KeyEvent)** **keyPressed(KeyEvent)** **keyReleased(KeyEvent)**	Methods are called when the user presses a key, releases a key, and just after a full key press and release.
MouseListener	**mouseClicked(MouseEvent)** **mouseEntered(MouseEvent)** **mouseExited(MouseEvent)** **mousePressed(MouseEvent)** **mouseReleased(MouseEvent)**	Methods are called when the user moves the mouse into and out of a component area, when the user clicks on a component, etc.
WindowFocusListener	**windowGainedFocus(WindowEvent)** **windowLostFocus(WindowEvent)**	Methods are called whenever a window gains or loses focus

(Table continued on the next page.)

WindowListener	windowOpened(WindowEvent)	Methods are called before and after a window is closed, when a window has been minimized to a icon or returned to a full window, etc.
	windowClosing(WindowEvent)	
	windowClosed(WindowEvent)	
	windowIconified(WindowEvent)	
	windowDeiconified(WindowEvent)	
	windowActivated(WindowEvent)	
	windowDeactivated(WindowEvent)	

Since GUI programming is such a large subject area, we will not have time to cover these additional listeners individually. Now that you know how to use the **ActionListener**, however, you can refer to the Java API documentation and online tutorials for descriptions of how to use these other listeners should you need them in your program. As you might expect, the event parameters on each method will give you information about the control that raised the event and any other information related to the event.

Your class can implement more than one interface at a time. So if you need both an **ActionListener** and a **WindowListener**, for instance, simply list both in your class definition separated by commas:

```
class MyProgram implements ActionListener, WindowListener
```

Then make sure to implement all of the functions required by each interface in your class.

Lesson Four: Layout Managers

The arrangement of controls in a window is called a *layout*. Since users can often resize the window it is very helpful for the all of the controls to adapt to the current window width and height. Java uses the concept of a *layout manager* to place controls based on the current window size and control sizes. There are many different types of layout managers that arrange controls in different patterns depending on the program needs. In this lesson we will discuss some of the more popular layout managers that come with the Java class library.

JPanels

Before diving into the details of each layout manager, we should first talk about the object representing the client area in the window – the **JPanel**. A top-level container such as a **JFrame**

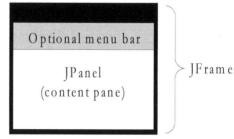

has a **JPanel** that actually holds the visible controls in the *content pane*. The content pane or client area is all the space inside the window frame, not including any optional menu bar.

When you call the **JFrame.add()** method to add a control, you are actually adding the control to the **JFrame**'s main **JPanel**. Similarly, when you call the **JFrame.setLayout()** to pick a layout manager, you are actually setting the layout manager for the **JPanel**. If you prefer to access the main **JPanel** directly you can get it with **JFrame.getContentPane()**. Notice you have to cast the result to a **JPanel** data type:

```
JFrame myFrame = new JFrame();          // create the JFrame window
JPanel contentPane = (JPanel)myFrame.getContentPane();
```

You can also swap out the default content pane with a new **JPanel** you create:

```
JFrame myFrame = new JFrame();          // create the JFrame window
JPanel contentPane = new JPanel();      // create new JPanel
myFrame.setContentPane(contentPane);    // replace default JPanel with ours!
```

Keep in mind that the layout manager we choose will belong to the **JPanel** content pane, and all controls we add to the **JFrame** actually belong to the **JPanel** as well. So these two groups of code are equivalent:

```
JFrame myFrame = new JFrame();          // create the JFrame window
myFrame.setLayout(new FlowLayout());// set layout manager to JPanel in JFrame
myFrame.add(new JButton("Red"));        // add JButton to JPanel within JFrame
```

Above we have simply added a layout manager and a button to the **JPanel** by calling functions on the **JFrame**. Below we get the content pane and then add the layout manager and a button to the **JPanel** directly.

```
JFrame myFrame = new JFrame();          // create the JFrame window
JPanel myPanel = (JPanel)myFrame.getContentPane(); // get the main JPanel
myPanel.setLayout(new FlowLayout()); // set layout manager to JPanel directly
myPanel.add(new JButton("Red"));        // add JButton to JPanel directly
```

Now, let's talk about the different kinds of layout managers!

Flow Layout

We've already used one simple layout manager in our earlier Swing examples: the **FlowLayout**. When you use the flow layout, all of your controls are added to the frame from left-to-right. If the window is not large enough to put all controls on the same row, the next control will drop down to start a new row.

A new **FlowLayout** manager is created with no parameters in the constructor, and then assigned to a **JPanel** using the **setLayout()** method.

```
FlowLayout layout = new FlowLayout();
myPanel.setLayout(layout);
```

Let's say we have a simple content panel with four buttons added in this order: "Apple", "Orange", "Pear" and "Banana". With the **FlowLayout**, our depending on the window size, our buttons might be arranged as shown to the right.

But if the user re-sizes the window the flow layout will adjust the buttons to fit as many as possible on the first row. This can result in a somewhat unpredictable design!

Grid Layout

The **GridLayout** is another popular Swing layout manager. When you create a **GridLayout**, you will need to tell the constructor how many rows and columns you want in your grid.

```
GridLayout layout = new GridLayout(3,2);
```

This code will create a grid that has 3 rows and 2 columns. Each space in the grid is referred to as a "cell" and each cell is the same height and width. Each control you add to a panel will land in one of the grid cells.

Controls added to a panel with grid layout will be assigned to cells from left-to-right starting at the top. When the last cell in the first row is occupied the next control will start on the left in the next row. If we construct a **GridLayout** with 3 rows and 2 columns, our four "Apple", "Orange", "Pear", and "Banana" buttons would be assigned to the first four cells, leaving the last two empty.

The **GridLayout** will automatically make each cell the same size and ensure they take up all space in the **JPanel**'s client area.

What happens if the text on the button is too long to display in a cell? The **GridLayout** will then add some dots (…) to the end of the text. In the example to the left we have changed "Banana" to "Watermelon". You should be aware of this possible design issue whenever you are using the grid layout in your programs.

How do you add some space between each of your cells so the controls don't all touch each other? You can set a buffer space measured in pixels for both the horizontal gap (between cells in the same row) and vertical gap (between cells in the same column). The gaps can be set when you construct the **GridLayout** object by adding the horizontal and vertical pixel values as parameters to the constructor:

```
GridLayout layout = new GridLayout(3,2,5,10);
```

This code will add 5 pixels of horizontal gap space between cells in a row and 10 pixels of vertical gap space between the cells in a column.

You can also get and set the horizontal and vertical gap functions after construction by calling the **GridLayout getHgap()**, **setHgap()**, **getVgap()**, and **setVgap()** methods.

Notice that the overall panel does not have any border space between the edges and the controls. We'll discuss how to add an overall border to your panel layout a bit later!

Border Layout

A **BorderLayout** will place the controls in five specific areas on the window: top (PAGE_START), bottom (PAGE_END), left (LINE_START), right (LINE_END), and middle (CENTER). The center is generally going to be the largest area. You can create a **BorderLayout** with no constructor parameters, or you can construct it with two parameters setting the horizontal and vertical gaps between areas, just like the **GridLayout**.

PAGE_START		
LINE_START	CENTER	LINE_END
PAGE_END		

```
BorderLayout layout1 = new BorderLayout();      // no spacing between areas
BorderLayout layout2 = new BorderLayout(5,10);  // set spacing between areas
```

When adding controls to a panel with this type of layout you need to give some extra information in the **add()** method. Each control must be placed in one of the five areas as shown below:

```
myPanel.setLayout(new BorderLayout()); // attach layout manager
myPanel.add(new JButton("Apple"),  BorderLayout.PAGE_START);
myPanel.add(new JButton("Orange"), BorderLayout.PAGE_END);
myPanel.add(new JButton("Pear"),   BorderLayout.LINE_START);
myPanel.add(new JButton("Banana"), BorderLayout.LINE_END);
```

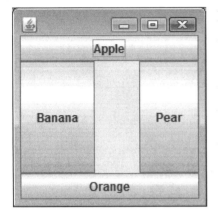

Notice that we do not have to add a control to every region. We did not put anything in **BorderLayout.CENTER** in this example. Any unused space on the screen is added to the center area.

The second example to the right uses horizontal and vertical gaps, and moves the "Banana" button to the center.

```
myPanel.setLayout(new BorderLayout(5,10));
myPanel.add(new JButton("Apple"),  BorderLayout.PAGE_START);
myPanel.add(new JButton("Orange"), BorderLayout.PAGE_END);
myPanel.add(new JButton("Pear"),   BorderLayout.LINE_START);
myPanel.add(new JButton("Banana"), BorderLayout.CENTER);
```

Note that the top, bottom, left, and right areas used to be called **NORTH, SOUTH, EAST**, and **WEST**. You may find some older code that still uses those terms. Also note that only one control can be added to each area. If you add a second control to the same area it will replace the first one.

Box Layout

The last layout that we will discuss is the **BoxLayout**. A box layout places all of the controls in a single column or row within the window. A simple value in the layout constructor will set the vertical or horizontal format. Controls are then added to the layout from left-to-right (in a horizontal orientation) or from top-to-bottom (in a vertical orientation).

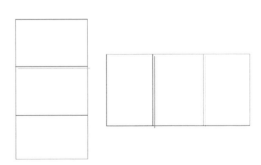

To build a new **BoxLayout**, you need to provide two parameters to the constructor. First you need to provide a reference to the parent container (**JPanel**), and second you need to specify **BoxLayout.X_AXIS** (for horizontal layouts) or **BoxLayout.Y_AXIS** (for vertical layouts).

```
myPanel.setLayout(new BoxLayout(myPanel, BoxLayout.X_AXIS));
myPanel.setLayout(new BoxLayout(myPanel, BoxLayout.Y_AXIS));
```

There are other ways to create a **BoxLayout** as well, but we'll stick with this approach. Once you've assigned your layout, simply add controls to your panel as usual:

```java
myPanel.add(new JButton("Apple"));

myPanel.add(new JButton("Orange"));

myPanel.add(new JButton("Pear"));

myPanel.add(new JButton("Banana"));
```

The resulting vertical and horizontal windows would look like the images shown to the left and right. Notice that each button control has a default alignment towards the left.

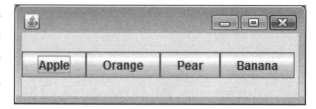

You can change the alignment on a control-by-control basis if you have a reference to the control.

Here we have changed a single "Apple" button to a center alignment:

```java
JButton apple = new JButton("Apple");
apple.setAlignmentX(Component.CENTER_ALIGNMENT);
myPanel.add(apple);
```

You can call **setAlignmentX()** on any **JComponent** control to specify a left, center, or right alignment. You can also call **setAlignmentY()** on any control to set a top, center, or bottom alignment.

JComponent Method	Possible Alignments
setAlignmentX()	Component.LEFT_ALIGNMENT
	Component.CENTER_ALIGNMENT
	Component.RIGHT_ALIGNMENT
setAlignmentY()	Component.TOP_ALIGNMENT
	Component.CENTER_ALIGNMENT
	Component.BOTTOM_ALIGNMENT

A **BoxLayout** has several more powerful features we don't have time to talk about now. For instance, you can create invisible fillers to add space in between individual controls. You can also create "glue" spacers that will expand to occupy all leftover space between controls. If you need these advanced features in your program, please refer to the online Java Swing documentation as described at the beginning of this chapter.

Adding JPanel Borders

A *border* refers to the area around the edge of any **JComponent** control or a **JPanel** client area. You can create borders that are decorative or that simply provide some extra space to make your layouts look better. The **Border** object represents this area. You first need to create **Border** that has the design you want, then assign it to your **JCompnent** or **JPanel** with the **setBorder()** method.

You don't create a **Border** with the **new** keyword! Instead Swing provides a **BorderFactory** object that will create borders for you. The **BorderFactory** contains over 20 methods for creating different kinds of Borders. We'll just describe a couple of common methods here.

First, to use border objects, you need to import an additional Java Swing package at the top of your code:

```
import javax.swing.border.*;
```

Now, you can create some empty space around the edges with **BorderFactory.createEmptyBorder()**. This example will create a border around the entire panel with pixel spacing of top = 5, left = 10, bottom = 15, and right = 20 pixels:

```
Border myBorder = BorderFactory.createEmptyBorder(5,10,15,20);
myPanel.setBorder(myBorder);
```

Let's return to our four-button **BorderLayout** example and add in an empty border with these dimensions.

```
JFrame myFrame = new JFrame();
myFrame.setDefaultCloseOperation(JFrame.EXIT_ON_CLOSE);

JPanel myPanel = (JPanel)myFrame.getContentPane();
myFrame.setSize(200,200);
myPanel.setLayout(new BorderLayout(5,10));

// create empty border with top, left, bottom, and right dimensions shown
Border myBorder = BorderFactory.createEmptyBorder(5,10,15,20);
myPanel.setBorder(myBorder);  // attach border to our panel

// add buttons to the panel using layout areas
myPanel.add(new JButton("Apple"),  BorderLayout.PAGE_START);
myPanel.add(new JButton("Orange"), BorderLayout.PAGE_END);
myPanel.add(new JButton("Pear"),   BorderLayout.LINE_START);
myPanel.add(new JButton("Banana"), BorderLayout.CENTER);
```

Now as you can see in the left image below, our resulting frame has an empty border of 5 pixels on the top, 10 on the left, 15 on the bottom, and 20 on the right!

Next let's look at creating a colored line border. The **BorderFactory** **createLineBorder()** method will make this type of border for you. The first parameter is a **Color** and the second is the thickness of the line, in pixels.

In the example to the right we have created a red border line with 4 pixels.

Here is the code to create a colored line border with the **BorderFactory**:

```
Border myBorder = BorderFactory.createLineBorder(Color.RED, 4);
```

You can use the **Color** object to select any of the other common colors as well.

Using Multiple JPanels

All of our previous examples used a single **JPanel** covering the entire **JFrame**. That **JPanel** can only have one layout manager for all of the controls in the panel. But what if we wanted to use different layouts for different groups of controls on the same screen? In this case, we can break the main **JPanel** area into multiple sections, each controlled by a child **JPanel**. The main **JPanel** will still have an overall layout manager that controls the location of the child **JPanels**, and each child **JPanel** can itself have a different layout that arranges controls within that panel.

We have shown a complicated example to the right. Here we have used a 2x2 **GridLayout** on the main panel to establish four child panel areas. The first cell we fill with a **JPanel** that has a horizontal **BoxLayout**. The second cell is filled with a **JPanel** and a vertical **BoxLayout**. The third cell has a **JPanel** with a **FlowLayout**. Finally we leave the fourth overall cell blank. You can imagine an endless variety of arrangements using combinations of child panels and layout managers!

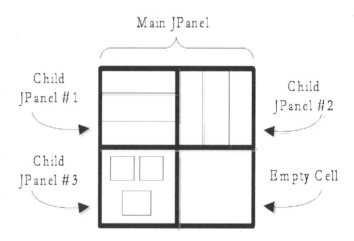

Let's look at a more concrete example. The **JFrame** to the left has two child **JPanels** in a vertical box layout, one on top and one on bottom. The top **JPanel** simply has a **FlowLayout** with a single label control and a thin black border. The bottom **JPanel** has a **GridLayout** with our four buttons and an empty space border around the edge.

Now let's explore the actual code that creates this example GUI. To begin we create the **JFrame** as usual, get the main **JPanel**, set the overall window size and install a vertical **BoxLayout** to stack the two child panels top-to-bottom.

```
JFrame myFrame = new JFrame();          // create the JFrame window
myFrame.setDefaultCloseOperation(JFrame.EXIT_ON_CLOSE);


// main JPanel and overall layout manager
JPanel myPanel = (JPanel)myFrame.getContentPane();
myFrame.setSize(200,200);
myPanel.setLayout(new BoxLayout(myPanel,BoxLayout.Y_AXIS));
```

Next we create our top child **JPanel** with a **FlowLayout** and black line **Border**. We then add a single **JLabel** control that asks the user our all-important question!

```
// child JPanel for the top area
JPanel topPanel = new JPanel();
topPanel.setLayout(new FlowLayout());
topPanel.setBorder(BorderFactory.createLineBorder(Color.BLACK,2));

// label that will go in the top child JPanel
JLabel myLabel = new JLabel("What is your favorite fruit?");
topPanel.add(myLabel);
```

Next we create our bottom child **JPanel** with a **GridLayout** giving a 2-pixel separation between the cells. We also add an empty **Border** with 5 pixels of space around the edges of the buttons. We then add each of the four buttons into the bottom panel.

```
// child JPanel for the bottom area
JPanel bottomPanel = new JPanel();
bottomPanel.setLayout(new GridLayout(2,2,2,2));
bottomPanel.setBorder(BorderFactory.createEmptyBorder(5,5,5,5));

// buttons that will go in the bottom child JPanel
bottomPanel.add(new JButton("Apple"));
bottomPanel.add(new JButton("Orange"));
bottomPanel.add(new JButton("Pear"));
bottomPanel.add(new JButton("Banana"));
```

Finally, we add the top panel and the bottom panel as child components to the main **JFrame** panel. The overall **BoxLayout** will stack them top and bottom.

```
// finally, add both child JPanels to the parent!
myPanel.add(topPanel);
myPanel.add(bottomPanel);

myFrame.setVisible(true);
```

You can see with a bit of creativity and straightforward code it is possible to create a very nice user interface using a hierarchy of Swing **JPanels** and layout managers.

Activity: Phone Dialer

In this activity, you will use your Java Swing skills to create a simple phone dialer program!

Your activity requirements and instructions are found in the "Chapter_11_Activity.pdf" document located in your "TeenCoder\Java Programming\Activity Docs" folder. You can access this document through your Student Menu or by directly clicking on it from Windows Explorer (Windows) or Finder (Mac OS).

Complete this activity now and ensure your program meets the requirements before continuing!

Chapter Twelve: Swing Input Controls

You now understand how to arrange controls in a window pane and process events from those controls. It's time to learn about some of the common user input controls you may want to use in your own programs!

Lesson One: Text and Numeric Input

In this chapter, we will take a look at the several ways to get input from a user. The first method we'll study uses the **JOptionPane** class. You may remember using a **JOptionPane** in the last chapter to show a simple pop-up message to the user. This handy class also contains a method which will allow you to easily get a single piece of information from a user.

Of course, with all Swing programs, you should import the main Swing package at the top of your code:

```
import javax.swing.*;
```

There are several versions of the **JOptionPane.showInputDialog()** method. The simplest takes a single **String** parameter containing a question you want to ask the user. This question is displayed in a simple pop-up dialog along with a text box where the user can enter their answer and "OK" and "Cancel" buttons. The method returns a **String** result containing the text the user entered in the text box. Here is an example:

```
String result = JOptionPane.showInputDialog("Enter your favorite color: ");
```

The above code will create a window that looks like this:

If the user clicks on "OK" the contents of the text box (including possibly an empty string) are returned as the **String** result. If the user clicks the "Cancel" button, the returned result will be **null**.

Note that this input window will only return text data. If you need the user to enter numeric data, you will need to parse the numeric data out of the **String** result.

Here is a slightly more complicated example where we provide a parent component such as our main frame; this will center the pop-up on our window instead of the center of the entire screen. We also specify the message, a title for the title bar, and a value selecting the type of icon to display.

```
String result = JOptionPane.showInputDialog(myFrame,
                                "Please enter your password",
                                "Security Alert",
                                JOptionPane.WARNING_MESSAGE);
```

Now our pop-up has a new title, icon, and would be centered on our **JFrame** object.

You can select different icons such as the warning exclamation point using these **JOptionPane** members:

ERROR_MESSAGE, **INFORMATION_MESSAGE**, **WARNING_MESSAGE**, **QUESTION_MESSAGE**, or **PLAIN_MESSAGE**.

JOptionPane has many more variants of the input dialog and other related pop-ups like a confirmation dialog. You can even change the buttons displayed, provide a selection of items to the user, and pre-select items. See the online Java API documentation for more details.

The JTextField Control

The **JOptionPane** input dialog is fast and simple, but what if you need to get more than one piece of data or create a more complicated input window? You can always put one or more **JComponent** controls on a **JPanel** within your **JFrame** and then read the contents of those controls directly.

The first input control we will discuss is the *text box*. A text box is simply a box where the user can type text. This is often used to retrieve a single line of text, like a name, address line, or password. In Swing we use a class called the **JTextField** to display a text box in a window. The **JTextField** is part of the **javax.swing** package and can be created with the **new** keyword like this:

```
JTextField userText = new JTextField(20);
```

Here, we have created a text box called **userText** that can take 20 characters of data. Typically, a **JTextField** control is paired on the screen with a **JLabel** telling the user information what type of data they should enter into the text field. Let's look at a complete example.

The code to produce our simple label and text box window is shown below.

```
JFrame myFrame = new JFrame();          // create the JFrame window
myFrame.setDefaultCloseOperation(JFrame.EXIT_ON_CLOSE);


// get the main content panel and set a flow layout
JPanel myPanel = (JPanel)myFrame.getContentPane();
myPanel.setLayout(new FlowLayout());


// add a descriptive label and new text field
myPanel.add(new JLabel("Enter your name:"));
myPanel.add(new JTextField(20));


// resize window to handle the controls and show window
myFrame.pack();
myFrame.setVisible(true);
```

So now that we can place a text field on the screen, how do we retrieve the text that the user enters back into our program? The **JTextField** has a method called **getText()** which can be used to get the current contents of the text field. But when do you call the **getText()** method? You will want to call this method when the user is finished entering data.

There are two easy ways for the user to signal "done" to your program. First, the "Enter" key on the **JTextField** box will trigger an **ActionEvent** in your program. If you have implemented the **ActionListener** interface you can capture this event in your **actionPerformed()** method. Notice, of course, that you will want to assign your new **JTextField** object to a member variable of your overall class so you can use it later.

```
class MyProgram implements ActionListener
{
    JTextField userText = null;
```

When you create your **JTextField** object, make sure to add the parent class (**this**) as an action listener:

```
userText = new JTextField(20);
userText.addActionListener(this);
```

Then in your **actionPerformed()** implementation, check to see if the control generating the event is equal to your text box. If so, you can call **getText()** to retrieve the current value and do something with it.

```
    public void actionPerformed(ActionEvent event)
    {
        Object control = event.getSource();
        if (control == userText)
        {
            String result = userText.getText();
            JOptionPane.showMessageDialog(null,"You entered: " + result);
        }
    }
```

Now when you enter some value and press "Enter", the **actionPerformed**() method will be called and your code can do something useful with the data.

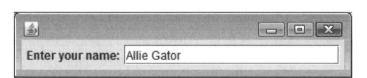

This would work well when there is a single text box in the window. However it gets more complicated when you have multiple text fields on the screen. In that case you may want to let the user click a button when they are done entering data in all the text fields.

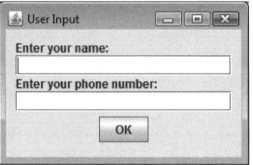

For example, consider this window that has two **JTextFields** stored in **userText** and **phoneText** class variables. We also created an **okButton** and added the main class as an action listener to that **JButton** object. Now in the **actionPerformed**() event handler method we can gather data from both text fields and do something with it!

```
    public void actionPerformed(ActionEvent event)
    {
        Object control = event.getSource();
        if (control == okButton)
        {
            String name = userText.getText();
            String phone = phoneText.getText();
            JOptionPane.showMessageDialog(null,name + "'s phone# is " + phone);
        }
    }
```

Now as soon as the user clicks the "OK" button, we will retrieve the contents of the user name box and the phone number box at the same time and display the results in a message box.

The JTextArea Control

The **JTextField** control is great when you want to retrieve a single line of information from your user, but what if you need them to enter more detailed information? How can we get multiple lines of text? To do this, we need to use a **JTextArea** control. First we'll declare our **JTextArea** variable as a class member:

```
class MyProgram implements ActionListener
{
    JTextArea myTextArea = null;
```

Then create a new **JTextArea** when building the frame. Notice the **JTextArea** constructor takes two parameters setting the number of rows and columns of text.

```
JPanel myPanel = (JPanel)myFrame.getContentPane();
myPanel.setLayout(new FlowLayout());
myPanel.setBorder(BorderFactory.createEmptyBorder(10,10,10,10));

myTextArea = new JTextArea(5,20);  // initialize class JTextArea member
myPanel.add(myTextArea);           // add JTextArea to the main panel

myFrame.pack();
myFrame.setVisible(true);
```

This code will create a text area that has 5 rows and 20 columns of text visible on the screen. So far so good, but see what happens if the user types in a single line of text greater than 20 columns wide? The **JTextArea** doesn't handle that very well unless you set the line wrap property of the control to **true**.

```
myTextArea.setLineWrap(true);
```

JScrollPane

It's quite possible that the user will enter more text than can be displayed on the visible rows and columns. In order for a **JTextArea** to handle more text than the visible number of rows and columns on the screen, we need to use a second class called a **JScrollPane**. The **JScrollPane** will allow the user to scroll around the text area to reach all of the text contents.

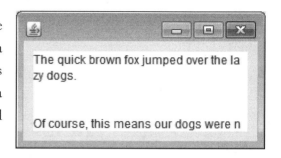

To create a **JScrollPane**, first create the **JTextArea** object and then pass that object into the **JScrollPane** constructor along with some flags to control when vertical and horizontal scroll bars are shown:

```
myTextArea = new JTextArea(5,20);
myTextArea.setLineWrap(true);
JScrollPane myScrollPane = new JScrollPane(myTextArea,
                        JScrollPane.VERTICAL_SCROLLBAR_ALWAYS,
                        JScrollPane.HORIZONTAL_SCROLLBAR_AS_NEEDED);
myPanel.add(myScrollPane,BorderLayout.CENTER);  // add JScrollPane to panel!
```

The particular parameters for vertical and horizontal scroll bars we chose above will always show the vertical scroll bar and only show a horizontal scroll bar if needed. Notice also that we add the **JScrollPane** object to the panel instead of the **JTextArea**. Now when the user types in more text than can be seen, the scroll bars will allow the user to see all the text.

Now that you know how to use a **JTextArea** control, how do you get the text the user has entered? You use the same procedure as we described for the **JTextField** control. You can wait for the user to click a button or press the "Enter" key to trigger an **actionPerformed()** event call, and then read the **String** from the control with the **getText()** method:

```
String userText = myTextArea.getText();
```

The JSpinner Control

The **JTextField** and **JTextArea** controls will both return **String** data. If you need to retrieve numeric data, you can either parse the text data into a numeric type or use a control that specifically handles numeric data. The **JSpinner** control can be used if you are sure the user will be entering numbers.

A **JSpinner** control is a number field with an up and down arrow next to it. The user can "spin" through the numbers by clicking the up or down arrow, or they can just type a number into the box.

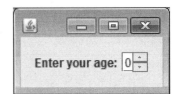

To create a **JSpinner** control you'll want to declare the **JSpinner** variable at your class level, just like any other data control that you'll need to reference later.

```
class MyProgram implements ActionListener
{
    JSpinner mySpinner = null;
```

Then assign a new **JSpinner** to the member variable when creating your screen.

```
JPanel myPanel = (JPanel)myFrame.getContentPane();
myPanel.setLayout(new FlowLayout());
myPanel.setBorder(BorderFactory.createEmptyBorder(10,10,10,10));

myPanel.add(new JLabel("Enter your age:"));
mySpinner = new JSpinner();  // create new JSpinner object
myPanel.add(mySpinner);        // add JSpinner object to JPanel

myFrame.pack();
myFrame.setVisible(true);
```

When using a **JSpinner** object you may want to set some parameters to control the minimum and maximum allowed values, the initial value, and the amount the value changes when an arrow is clicked. For instance, if you are asking the user to enter their age, you may want to limit the possible numbers to 1 through 99.

We can define these numeric parameters with a **SpinnerNumberModel** class. You will create an instance of this first, and then pass the model into your **JSpinner** constructor. The **SpinnerNumberModel** constructor will accept these parameters:

```
SpinnerNumberModel(<initial value>,<minimum value>,<maximum value>,<step>);
```

The first parameter will set the initial value for the **JSpinner** control. The next two parameters set the minimum and maximum possible values for the spinner. The final value sets the amount of increase or decrease every time the user clicks the up or down button. If the step value is 1, the number will increase or decrease by 1. If the step value is 5, the number will increase or decrease by 5 each time.

Here is an example that will create a **SpinnerNumberModel** and pass it to a **JSpinner** constructor:

TeenCoder™: Java Programming

```
mySpinner = new JSpinner(new SpinnerNumberModel(15,1,99,1));
```

Now the user can only choose numbers from 1 to 99, with a default value of 15. The value will increase and decrease by 1 on each arrow click.

The process of getting data from the **JSpinner** control is similar to pulling data from the **JTextField** and **JTextArea** controls. For the **JSpinner** control, use a method called **getValue**() to retrieve the user's number:

```
int userAge = (Integer)mySpinner.getValue();
```

Since you can put things other than basic numbers in a **JSpinner**, you will need to cast the result of **getValue**() to an **Integer** object. Note that pressing "Enter" in the spinner text area will not fire an **actionPerformed**() event! You can rely on user button clicks to signal when to read from the control.

Instead of using a button click you might also want to get an event each time the user clicks the up or down arrow buttons or changes the value. To do this, implement the **ChangeListener** interface on your class.

```
class MyProgram implements ActionListener, ChangeListener
```

The **ChangeListener** interface requires your main class to implement one method called **stateChanged**():

```
public void stateChanged(ChangeEvent e)
{
        if (e.getSource() == mySpinner)
        {
                int userAge = (Integer)mySpinner.getValue();
        }
}
```

Then call the **addChangeListener**() on your **JSpinner** object to set the main class as a listener.

```
mySpinner.addChangeListener(this);
```

Now your **stateChanged**() method will be called each time the user modifies the value, and you can read the current value each time.

Lesson Two: List Input

List box controls are useful for showing a user a group of items. A list box control is just a box that has one item per line. If there are more items than can be shown in the box, you can make a scroll bar appear. The user can then scroll up or down to see all of the list entries. A user can select one or more items at a time.

A Quick Introduction to Arrays

Controls that store groups of related information need you to provide this information in a special data structure called an *array*. You will learn all about arrays in the next chapter, but for now we'll introduce just enough array syntax to use them with GUI controls.

Arrays contain a group of individual *elements*, with each element having the same data type. You can make an array of any data type, including all of the primitive types like **integer** or **double** and any reference type like **String** or **Object**. Arrays are represented as variables just like any other single piece of data. To create an array variable, use the same syntax as a normal variable but add square brackets after the data type:

```
<data type> [] <variable name>;
```

So you could declare an array of **Strings** like this:

```
String[] dogBreeds = null;
```

All array variables are reference variables, regardless of what type of data (primitive or reference) is stored in the array! So the line above has just declared an array variable called **dogBreeds** that has a **null** value.

You can create an instance of the array with a number of elements at the same time you declare the variable:

```
String[] dogBreeds = {"Shepherd", "Retriever", "Beagle", "Poodle"};
```

This code will create an array of 4 **Strings** with each element initialized to the shown values.

Once you have created an array, or are given a reference to an existing array, you can figure out how many elements are in the array by reading the **length** property.

```
int numDogs = dogBreeds.length;
```

Finally, you can get or set individual elements in an array by using a numeric index that starts at 0 for the first element. The last valid index is the length of the array minus one.

```
String firstDog = dogBreeds[0];   // firstDog = "Shepherd"
String lastDog  = dogBreeds[3];   // lastDog  = "Poodle"
```

You'll learn more about arrays later, but this should be enough to get started with our GUI controls!

The JList Control

In Swing a list box is represented by the **JList** class. You can create a new **JList** object and pass in an array of **String** values in the constructor to populate the lines in the list box.

```
String[] dogBreeds = {"Shepherd", "Retriever", "Beagle", "Poodle"};
JList myList = new JList(dogBreeds);
```

Now once the list is created and displayed on the screen, the items in the list cannot be edited by the user. They can only select items from the list. You can decide if the user is able to select one item or multiple items at a time. The number of items that can be selected at one time is set by the *selection mode* of the list box. You pick the selection mode by calling the **JList.setSelectionMode()** method and pass in one of these values:

ListSelectionModel.SINGLE_SELECTION	This will allow the user to only choose one item from the list.
ListSelectionModel.SINGLE_INTERVAL_SELECTION	This will allow the user to choose multiple items if they are all next to each other.
ListSelectionModel.MULTIPLE_INTERVAL_SELECTION	This will allow the user to choose as many items as they want from the list, regardless of where they are in the list.

By default, the **JList** will allow a user to select multiple items from the list in any location. If you want to let a user select only one item, call **setSelectionMode()** like this:

```
myList.setSelectionMode(ListSelectionModel.SINGLE_SELECTION);
```

The **JList** control often has the same problem as the **JTextArea** control from the last lesson. If there are too many items in the list, the user may not be able to see all of the items at one time. You can wrap the **JList** in a **JScrollPane** in order to let the user scroll through the entire list in the list box. Creating a **JScrollPane** to use with a **JList** is identical to creating one to work with the **JTextArea** control.

```
JScrollPane myScroll = new JScrollPane(myList,
                          JScrollPane.VERTICAL_SCROLLBAR_ALWAYS,
                          JScrollPane.HORIZONTAL_SCROLLBAR_NEVER);
```

Make sure to pass in your **JList** object as the first parameter to the **JScrollPane** constructor, and also set the vertical and horizontal scroll bar options. Then, instead of adding the **JList** to the panel directly, add the **JScrollPane** instead:

```
myPanel.add(myScroll);
```

Now the user can easily scroll up and down through all the items in the list!

Once the user has selected items in the list, we need to figure out how to retrieve them. Remember to store your **JList** object as a class member variable, as usual, so you can get to it later. You can then wait for some other button click to trigger a listener event. Then the method you use to get these items depends on how many items the user is allowed to choose at a time. If the user is only allowed to choose one item in the list, the retrieval is very easy. You will simply call the **JList getSelectedValue()** method, like this:

```
String breedChoice = (String)myList.getSelectedValue();
```

Notice that we are casting the value returned by **getSelectedValue()** to a **String**. This is because **JLists** can actually hold other types of objects besides **Strings**. So when you pull an **Object** out of the list you need to cast it to the data type you know was inserted into the list initially. If the user has not selected any value in the list, the method will return a **null** value.

If your list box allows for multiple choices, the retrieval of these choices is slightly more involved. In this case, you will need to use the **JList.getSelectedValues()** method, which will return an array of **Objects**. You can then pull each **Object** out of the array and cast it to a **String** to do something useful with it.

A **for()** loop is a handy way to walk through each of the elements in an array. Start the loop index at a value of 0 (which is always the first numeric index in an array) and go up to (but not include) the array length.

```
Object[] breeds = myList.getSelectedValues(); // get array of selected values
String breedsChosen = "";    // initialize our summary string to empty
for (int i = 0; i< breeds.length; i++)  // loop over all elements in array
{
    // cast each element to a string and add it to the summary variable
    // with a newline character in-between each value
    breedsChosen = breedsChosen + (String) breeds[i] + "\n";
}
```

Once you have retrieved the user's selections from a list box, you may want to clear their selections and reset the list box. To do this, you can use the **JList.clearSelection()** method as shown below.

```
myList.clearSelection();  // remove any current user selections
```

This will clear any highlighted or selected items in the list. If you want to programmatically select a certain item in the list, you can use the **JList.setSelectedIndex()** method. Just pass in the number of the item that you want to highlight, like this:

```
myList.setSelectedIndex(2);   // select "Beagle" in our dogs list
```

Note that the items in the list are numbered from 0, not from 1. This means that the code listed above will highlight the third item in the list, not the second!

The JComboBox Control

The *combo box* control is a combination of a list box and a text box control. A user can type a new item into the box, or click on the arrow button on the right of the text box to show a list of available items. A combo box control will only take up one line of space on a window, which can be handy on a crowded area. The user must click on the arrow button to show the full list of items.

In Swing, the combo box is represented by the **JComboBox** class. You can create and initialize a **JComboBox** much like a **JList**, using an array of **String** values to set the initial items in the list:

```
String[] dogBreeds = {"Shepherd", "Retriever", "Beagle", "Poodle"};
JComboBox myCombo = new JComboBox(dogBreeds);
```

You could also choose to create a combo box that was initially empty, and then call **JComboBox.addItem()** once for each string you want to add:

```
JComboBox myCombo = new JComboBox();      // create empty JComboBox
myCombo.addItem("Shepherd");
myCombo.addItem("Retriever");
```

As usual, you will want to store your **JComboBox** object as a class member variable so you can access it later to pull data from the control.

By default a **JComboBox** will allow a user to choose an item from the existing list, but will not allow the user to add or edit the items in the list. You can add the ability to add and edit items in a combo box by calling the **setEditable**() method on the control with a **true** parameter.

```
myCombo.setEditable(true);
```

The combo box will now allow the user to type a new value into the text box area. This will give us the flexibility of the **JTextField** and the multiple item view of the **JList** control. This is why the combo box is called a "combo" box – it is a combination of these two controls!

The combo box will only allow the user to select one item at a time. To retrieve the currently selected item, we can use the **JComboBox.getSelectedItem**() method. Notice that the return value is actually an **Object** you'll need to cast to a **String**, because it is possible to store things other than **Strings** in the control.

```
String breedString = (String)myCombo.getSelectedItem();
```

You can also set the currently selected item by using the **JComboBox setSelectedIndex**() or **setSelectedItem**() methods. These methods will let you select an item by its numeric index or by its name:

```
myCombo.setSelectedIndex(1);       // select the second item in the list
myCombo.setSelectedItem("Poodle"); // select the "Poodle" item in the list
```

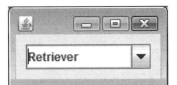

The first line will select the second item in the combo box list (remember that list items start at number 0, not number 1). The second line will select the item named "Poodle" in the list.

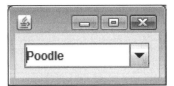

 The GUI code we describe works on older and newer versions of Java. Some Swing features have changed in Java 1.7 and later, so Eclipse may show warnings in your code regarding "raw types" or deprecated functions. These warnings may be safely ignored.

Lesson Three: Option Input

Option controls allow users to select one or more choices from a small group. There are two main types of options – radio buttons and checkboxes.

The JRadioButton Control

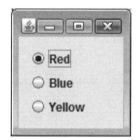

The *radio button* control is used when you want the user to select only one option from a small group of items. The user can only select one radio button option at a time. For instance, in this example screen, the user can select either "Red", "Blue" or "Yellow". Each radio button is represented by a **JRadioButton** object.

When you create a **JRadioButton** object, pass into the constructor the text you want displayed next to the selection circle. Don't forget to assign the object to a class-level member variable so you can access it later.

```java
JRadioButton redRadio = new JRadioButton("Red");
JRadioButton blueRadio = new JRadioButton("Blue");
JRadioButton yellowRadio = new JRadioButton("Yellow");
```

Radio button controls should work together in a group. When the user selects one button, the other buttons in the group are automatically de-selected. In order to organize a set of **JRadioButton** objects into a related group, you need to create a **ButtonGroup** container and then add each **JRadioButton** to the group.

```java
ButtonGroup myGroup = new ButtonGroup();
myGroup.add(redRadio);
myGroup.add(blueRadio);
myGroup.add(yellowRadio);
```

Finally, you need to add each **JRadioButton** object to your panel. Your layout manager will determine how the buttons are arranged on the screen. In the example above we have used a vertical box layout.

```java
myPanel.add(redRadio);
myPanel.add(blueRadio);
myPanel.add(yellowRadio);
```

If you want to create multiple groups of radio buttons on the same screen, create one **ButtonGroup** object for each set of radio buttons. The radio buttons within a specific **ButtonGroup** will work as a team, independent of any other radio buttons on the screen.

To figure out which radio button in a group is currently selected, you can call the **isSelected**() method on each control. If method returns **true**, the button is selected. If it returns **false**, the button is not selected.

```
if (redRadio.isSelected() == true)
{
    // the user selected the red radio button
}
```

Your best chance to call **isSelected**() is when some other event happens, such as a button press. Also, each time the user clicks on a radio button, an action event will be sent to an **ActionListener**. To demonstrate, we first implement the **ActionListener** interface and make each **JRadioButton** a class member variable:

```
class MyProgram implements ActionListener
{
    JRadioButton blueRadio = null;
    JRadioButton redRadio = null;
    JRadioButton yellowRadio = null;
```

Then, after each variable has been initialized, call the **addActionListener**() method with **this** as a parameter:

```
redRadio.addActionListener(this);
blueRadio.addActionListener(this);
yellowRadio.addActionListener(this);
```

Now in the **actionPerformed**() method you can check the event source to find which button was clicked:

```
public void actionPerformed(ActionEvent event)
{
    Object control = event.getSource();
    if (control == redRadio)
    {
        // red radio button was selected
    }
    else if (control == blueRadio)
    {
        // blue radio button was selected
    }
    else if (control == yellowRadio)
    {
        // yellow radio button was selected
    }
}
```

You can programmatically set the currently selected radio button in any group by using the **JRadioButton** **setSelected**() method with a **true** parameter:

```
blueRadio.setSelected(true);
```

You can also use this same method to clear a selected radio button with a **false** parameter:

```
blueRadio.setSelected(false);
```

The JCheckBox Control

The *check box* control is very similar to the radio button control. Check boxes are typically grouped together and offer the user a small selection of options. The biggest difference is that a user can select more than one check box at a time (or no check boxes at all)! The check box controls are independent and do not work as a group, even though they are usually arranged in visual groups on the screen.

In Swing, a check box is created with the **JCheckBox** class. Using **JCheckBox** is almost identical to using a **JRadioButton**, except you never need to put **JCheckBoxes** in a **ButtonGroup**. You can construct a **JCheckBox** with the text to display next to the text box. You can call the **isSelected**() and **setSelected**() methods to see if a check box is selected or programmatically set or clear a checkbox. You can also receive an action event through the **ActionListener** interface each time a checkbox is clicked

Using Borders

It's often a good idea to also include a visual border around groups of radio buttons and check boxes. You can do this with the same **Border** class we discussed earlier for **JPanels**. Remember the **BorderFactory** is used to create a **Border** object. You can get different kinds of borders by calling different methods on the **BorderFactory**. A handy type of border for radio buttons and check boxes is a "Titled" border, which is a simple frame with a text description at the top. Here is an example:

```
Border myBorder = BorderFactory.createTitledBorder("Shapes");
```

You still need to assign a border to a **JPanel**, so you would create a new **JPanel** for each group of radio buttons and check boxes. You can then assign a different **Border** to each **JPanel**. Here is an extended example showing two sets of controls on the screen at the same time. For simplicity we are not making class member variables or putting radio buttons into a **ButtonGroup** as you would normally! The code below will produce the example shown to the right.

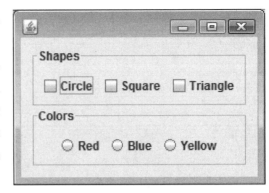

```java
JFrame myFrame = new JFrame();
myFrame.setDefaultCloseOperation(JFrame.EXIT_ON_CLOSE);

JPanel myPanel = (JPanel)myFrame.getContentPane();
myPanel.setLayout(new BoxLayout(myPanel,BoxLayout.Y_AXIS));
myPanel.setBorder(BorderFactory.createEmptyBorder(10,10,10,10));

JPanel shapePanel = new JPanel();  // create JPanel for check boxes

// add new check boxes to the shape panel
shapePanel.add(new JCheckBox("Circle"));
shapePanel.add(new JCheckBox("Square"));
shapePanel.add(new JCheckBox("Triangle"));

// create a titled border for the shape panel
shapePanel.setBorder(BorderFactory.createTitledBorder("Shapes"));
myPanel.add(shapePanel);  // add the color panel to the main content pane

JPanel colorPanel = new JPanel();  // create JPanel for check boxes

// add new radio buttons to the color panel
colorPanel.add(new JRadioButton("Red"));
colorPanel.add(new JRadioButton("Blue"));
colorPanel.add(new JRadioButton("Yellow"));

// create a titled border for the color panel
colorPanel.setBorder(BorderFactory.createTitledBorder("Colors"));
myPanel.add(colorPanel);  // add the color panel to the main content pane

myFrame.pack();            // pack all of the controls
myFrame.setVisible(true);  // finally, show the screen!
```

Activity: Pizza Place

In this activity, you will use different input controls to create a pizza ordering screen!

Your activity requirements and instructions are found in the "Chapter_12_Activity.pdf" document located in your "TeenCoder\Java Programming\Activity Docs" folder. You can access this document through your Student Menu or by directly clicking on it from Windows Explorer (Windows) or Finder (Mac OS).

Complete this activity now and ensure your program meets the requirements before continuing!

Chapter Thirteen: Arrays and Collections

In this chapter you will learn about data structures that will easily store groups or collections of data together under one variable name.

Lesson One: Arrays

You were introduced to *arrays* when learning how to use the list-based GUI controls. Now let's take a closer look at this important data structure!

Simple Arrays

A single piece of data such as a number or object may be very useful. However you may want to store many pieces of data together as a group. Let's think about how to track the number of hits a baseball player may get over an 8-game season. You could create 8 separate integer variables, one for each game, and store the number of hits in those variables. But it would be hard to manage all those variables, and think how hard it would be to track hits for an 80 game season! It would be much better to store this data as a group that we could reference by a single name. This type of data storage is called an *array*.

Arrays are data structures that contain a group of individual *elements* that have the same data type. You can create an array of any data type, including integers, floating point numbers, **Strings**, or any kind of **Object** or class reference. An array will allocate enough memory to hold all of the data together in a single area.

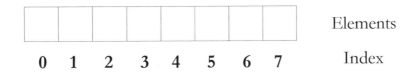

Each element in the array is uniquely identified by a numeric *index*. This integer starts at 0 for the first element in the array and increases by one as you move to the next element. The entire array is represented by one variable in your code. You can make the array any size you like, large enough to hold 8 or 80 or however many elements are required in your program.

Declaring Array Variables

To declare an array of a certain data type, the syntax is almost the same as a normal variable declaration. You only need to add a pair of square brackets after the data type to make it an array.

```
<data type>[] <variable name>;
```

So if we want to create an array of integers named **myIntArray**, this code would do it:

```
int[] myIntArray;
```

All array variables are reference variables! So the array variable may contain nothing (**null**) or some instance of an array. To create an array with a certain number of elements, use the **new** keyword, the data type, and square brackets containing the number of elements like this:

```
myIntArray = new int[5];
```

Now we have created an array with 5 integers, each of which will have a default value (0). Java has a handy shortcut for declaring and initializing an array of primitive data types with specific values in one step like this:

```
int[] myIntArray = {10,20,30,40,50};
```

In this format you don't specify the number of elements in the square brackets; instead just list each value inside the curly braces, separated by commas. Now we have an array with 5 elements, where the first value is 10, the second is 20, and so on. As you saw in the last chapter, this syntax also works for strings:

```
String[] dogBreeds = {"Shepherd", "Retriever", "Beagle", "Poodle"};
```

Accessing Array Elements

Array elements are accessed by an integer value called an *index*. The index represents the element's position in the array. In Java programming, arrays are *zero-based*. This means that the first element in any array is index 0. The second element is element 1, the third is element 2, and so on. The last valid index in an array is equal to the size (length) minus one.

 Forgetting that array indexes are zero-based is a common programming error! You must be careful to only use index values from "0" to the "length of the array minus 1", otherwise you will cause a runtime exception!

In order to get or set an element within the array, use the array name plus the index in brackets. For example:

```
int[] myArray = new int[3];    // declare a 3-element array

myArray[0] = 10;               // set first element equal to 10
myArray[1] = 20;               // set second element equal to 20
myArray[2] = myArray[1];       // set third element equal to second element

int anElement = myArray[2];    // get the third element value of 20
int oops = myArray[3];         // invalid index will cause a runtime exception!
```

In the example above, we begin by creating an array of 3 integers. We then set the first integer to 10, the second to 20, and the third equal to the second – 20 again! We next show how to get an element out of the array with a valid index 2, and then demonstrate code that will cause a runtime exception by using an index value of 3 that is too large. The maximum valid index value is equal to the size of the array (3) minus 1.

When you access an array with an index the Java language will check to make sure the index is valid. If the index is not valid then Java will throw an **ArrayIndexOutOfBoundsException**. So in our example above when the last line tries to execute with **myArray[3]**, an exception will be thrown.

Array Sizes

When you create an array, Java will set aside a block of memory just large enough to hold the array elements. The array therefore has a fixed size and you cannot add new elements or get rid of existing elements. You can only get and set the values of your original elements.

The number of elements in an array is called the array *size* or *length*. You can read the length of an array from the **length** property like this:

```
int numElements = myArray.length;
```

Of course, the **myArray** variable must reference a valid array and not **null**! If you try to get or set elements or read an array length on a **null** array variable, you will cause a **NullPointerException** to be thrown.

Walking an Array

You will often want to walk or *iterate* over each element in an array to do something useful with the data. Let's say we want to print out the value of each object to the console. A common approach is to create a **for()** loop where the loop's index variable runs from 0 to the size of the array minus 1. You can then use the loop's index variable to get or set each element in the array. Here is an example that creates a 100-element array and initializes each element with the values 0,1,2,3…99. Then a second loop will add up the values and print the total to the console.

```java
int[] myArray = new int[100];   // create 100-element array

for (int i=0; i<100; i++)       // loop over each element
{
    myArray[i] = i;             // set ith element to the value of i
}

int sum = 0;
for (int i=0; i<100; i++)       // loop over each element again
{
    sum += myArray[i];          // add the ith value to the sum
}
System.out.println("Sum is: " + sum);    // print the sum to the console
```

You would need to be very patient and have a calculator or lots of paper handy to find the answer by hand!

```
Sum is: 4950
```

Multi-Dimensional Arrays

Our simple arrays so far have all had one *dimension*. A single dimension array is like a list of items in a single row or column. However you can also create arrays with more than one dimension. A two-dimensional array is more like a table or a grid of information.

Each element in the array would be identified by two numeric index values… a column and a row. In the example to the right we have created an array with 4 columns and two rows. So the valid index values for columns are 0-3 and rows are 0-1.

Two-dimensional arrays can be very useful. For instance, returning to our baseball example, if you wanted to track the hits for an entire team across a season, you could use an array where the each column represented one game and the rows represented the 11 players on the team.

Java will let you create arrays with more than two dimensions. You can visualize a three-dimensional array as a cube. Higher dimensional arrays are conceptually more difficult to envision, so we are going to stick with just one or two dimensional arrays in our activities.

Creating Multi-Dimensional Arrays

In order to create a multi-dimensional array, you just add additional sets of square brackets for each dimension. For example, here we create a two-dimensional array with 2 rows and 4 columns:

```
int[][] my2DArray = new int[2][4];
```

You can use the same shortcut as a one-dimensional array to initialize the values of a multi-dimensional array when declaring the variable. Simply put the array values in curly braces separated by commas, separate rows of data by commas, and surround the entire set with outer curly braces.

```
int[][] my2DArray = {{1,2,3,4},
                     {5,6,7,8}};
```

Accessing Multi-Dimensional Array Elements

Multi-dimensional array elements are accessed just like one-dimensional arrays. The same rules and limitations for zero-based indexes and array bounds apply to each dimension. Specify one index for each dimension with a dedicated bracket pair like this:

```
int[][] my2DArray = {{1,2,3,4},
                     {5,6,7,8}};
int two   = my2DArray[0][1];   // get the value 2 out of the array
int seven = my2DArray[1][2];   // get the value 7 out of the array
my2DArray[1][3] = 0;           // replace the bottom-right value 8 with 0
```

You can read the number of rows in a 2D array by reading the **length** property. For any particular row you can get the number of columns by reading the **length** property of that row, identified by the row index in square braces.

```
int numRows = my2DArray.length;      // get the number of rows (2)
int numCols = my2DArray[0].length;   // get the number of columns in row 0 (4)
```

In order to walk or iterate over a multi-dimensional array, you could use nested **for()** loops to handle each index variable. In this next example we are going to walk our example 2D array left to right, top to bottom and print out the value in each cell.

```
    // create 2D array with 2 rows and 4 columns
    int[][] my2DArray = {{1,2,3,4},
                         {5,6,7,8}};


    // for each row
    for (int i=0; i<my2DArray.length; i++)
    {
        // for each column
        for (int j=0; j<my2DArray[i].length; j++)
        {
            // print the value in this cell
            System.out.print(my2DArray[i][j]);
        }
    }
```

If you follow along carefully, you will find the output of this code is simply:

```
12345678
```

Lesson Two: Java Lists

In the last lesson, we discussed storing information in arrays. Arrays are great ways to store groups of data, but they do have some limitations. For instance, let's say we create an array to hold the names of students in our programming class. We know on the first day of school that we have exactly 25 students, so we create an array that can hold 25 strings. Now on the second day of school, we welcome a transfer student into our class. How do we add the new student to the array? The simple answer is that we can't! In order to increase our array, we will need to create a new array of 26 strings, copy the original array to the new array and then add in our last student. This takes a lot of computing time and resources.

We would have a similar problem removing a student from the array. We can set student's element to **null**, but we cannot remove the element from the array without recreating a smaller array.

To solve these problems, Java has created a set of *collection* classes. These classes allow us to keep track of groups of objects in more flexible ways. In this lesson, we will take a look at two of the more popular collections: **ArrayList** and **LinkedList**. These classes both inherit from the Java **List** interface, so they have some methods in common. All collection classes and interfaces in this chapter belong to the **java.util** package, so make sure to **import java.util.*;** at the top of your program.

The Collection Interface

The simplest interface that all Java collection classes implement is called **Collection**. A **Collection** represents a group of individual elements but does not give any clues how the elements are stored within the class. The **Collection** also does not specify any order of the elements. All elements stored in any collection class must be an **Object** or some subclass of **Object**; they cannot be primitive data types like **int** or **double**. Since all primitive data types have corresponding object classes like **Integer** and **Double**, you can use those in a collection instead.

Collection

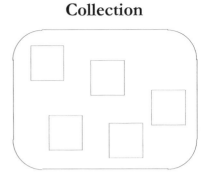

A **Collection** and related interfaces and classes can be used in "plain" form that simply store **Object** references, or they may be used in "generic" form that specifies a particular class type to be stored in the collection. In generic form the data type is specified in angle brackets after the **Collection** keyword like this:

```
Collection<Integer> myCollection1;    // "generic" form specifies a class type
Collection         myCollection2;    // "plain" form just holds Objects
```

In our generic example, you know that all objects in the **Collection** are **Integers**. If you did not specify a data type then everything in the collection is held as an **Object**, and you'd have to cast elements pulled from the collection to the correct data type. That could be a risky operation if you are not sure of the class type, so it's usually best to use the generic form and ensure no unexpected object types creep into your data set.

When you are given a **Collection** interface reference, you can perform several operations on the class without knowing any of the internal details. Some of the common **Collection** methods are shown in the table below.

Method	Description
boolean add(T obj)	Adds the object of type **T** to the collection.
void clear()	Removes all objects from the collection.
boolean isEmpty()	Returns **true** if the collection contains no elements, or **false** otherwise.
boolean remove(T obj)	Removes the specified object from the collection.
int size()	Returns the number of elements in the collection.

If you have a **Collection<Integer>** reference from somewhere, you can use these methods as follows:

```
Collection<Integer> myCollection =      // given to you from somewhere
Integer myInt = new Integer(3);
myCollection.add(myInt);                // collection contains myInt
int numElements = myCollection.size();  // numElements = 1 if empty at first
myCollection.clear();                   // collection is now empty
boolean empty = myCollection.isEmpty(); // empty = true
```

The List Interface

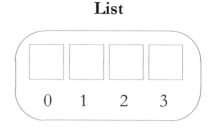

The **List** interface extends the **Collection** and adds a sense of order to the objects. All objects in a **List** are kept in a sequential order. Just like an array, objects in a **List** may be accessed by a numeric index starting at zero.

When you are using a **List** interface, you can use all of the **Collection** methods plus the following methods belonging to **List**:

Method	Description
void add(int index, **T** element)	Adds an object into the list, shifting all elements starting at **index** one space to the right to make room for the new object.
T get(int index)	Returns the object at the specified position in the list. Will throw **IndexOutOfBoundsException** if the index is not valid.
int indexOf(Object o)	Returns the index of the first value equal to the specified object in the list, or -1 if the object cannot be found.
int lastIndexOf(Object o)	Returns the index of the last value equal to the specified object in the list, or -1 if the object cannot be found.
T remove(int index)	Deletes the element at the specified index from the list, shifting higher elements one space to the left to fill up the space. Will throw **IndexOutOfBoundsException** if the index is not valid.
T set(int index, **T** element)	Replaces the object at the specified index with the new object. The old object is returned from the function. Will throw **IndexOutOfBoundsException** if the index is not valid.

Here are some examples using these methods in code, assuming you have a **List** reference of type **<Integer>** with a few existing elements already:

```java
List<Integer> myList =                       // given to you from somewhere
Integer myInt = new Integer(3);
myList.add(1,myInt);                          // insert myInt at index 1
Integer myInt2 = myList.get(1);              // myInt2 = myInt (from index 1)
int firstIndex = myList.indexOf(myInt);      // myInt will be found at index 1
int lastIndex  = myList.lastIndexOf(myInt);  // myInt found again at index 1
myList.remove(1);            // remove myInt reference from position 1
myList.set(0, myInt);        // replace whatever was at index 0 with myInt
```

We have not shown you how to create a **List** or **Collection** directly with the **new** keyword because they are interfaces and not classes. In your own code you might be given references to a **List** or **Collection** interface without really knowing what class is used under the covers to implement those interfaces. We are now going to study two common implementations of the **List** interface: the **ArrayList** and the **LinkedList**.

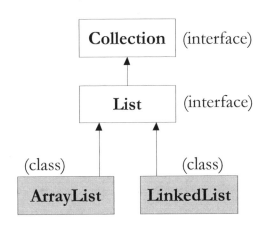

The ArrayList Class

An **ArrayList** implements the **List** interface using a simple array under the covers. Operations that get or set values by numeric index are very fast, just like an array. So if your program needs to do this very frequently, then **ArrayList** may be a good choice. If you add or remove elements from the **ArrayList**, the class will automatically create a new array internally using the new size and copy the elements into the new array. As you might guess, this resizing can be a resource-intensive process, so you wouldn't want to use an **ArrayList** if your program will be frequently adding or removing many items from the list.

You can create an **ArrayList** in your program with the **new** keyword. You should specify the data type that the list will hold in angle brackets. In this example we create an **ArrayList** holding **String** elements:

```
ArrayList<String> students = new ArrayList<String>();
```

Now you have a variable called **students** that holds an **ArrayList** of **Strings**. Because **ArrayList** implements the **List** interface, you can use all of the methods from the **List** and **Collection** interfaces.

For instance, if we wanted to add some strings to our list, we could use the **add**() method. The **ArrayList** implementation of the **add**() method will add items to the end of the list.

```
students.add("Sue");  // the list contains "Sue"
students.add("Joe");  // the list contains "Sue", "Joe"
```

The other **List** and **Collection** methods work as you would expect, for example:

```
int joeIndex = students.indexOf("Joe");  // joeIndex = 1
students.remove("Sue");                   // the list now contains "Joe"
```

The LinkedList Class

An **ArrayList** is a great data structure if your program needs to frequently access elements by index and does not have to grow or shrink the number of elements very often. But what if the reverse is true? If your program needs to add and remove elements frequently but doesn't care about accessing elements by index, there is a better collection class to use!

A **LinkedList** class implements the **List** interface using an internal data structure called, unsurprisingly, a *linked list!* A linked list can be visualized as a series of elements, called *nodes*, which are connected to each other like a string of beads. There are two main types of linked lists: singly-linked lists and doubly-linked lists.

In a singly-linked list, each node only knows how to reach the next node in the chain:

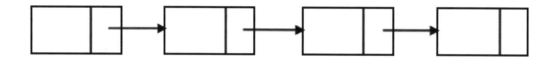

In a doubly-linked list, each node knows how to reach both the next and previous nodes:

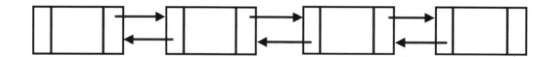

In order to "walk" through the elements in a linked list, you start with the first node in the list and then follow the *next* links until you reach the end of the list. In a doubly-linked list, you can also start your "walk" from the last node and walk backwards following the *previous* links. You know you have reached the beginning or end of a list when the next or previous reference is **null**.

A linked list can easily grow over time by adding new nodes to the list to hold new values. You don't need to recreate the entire list. With a linked list, you can just insert or clip nodes out of the list as you need. Here is what it would look like (conceptually) to add a node to a doubly-linked list:

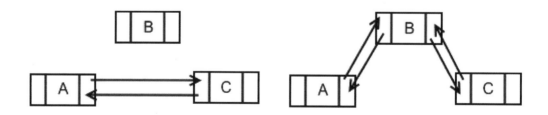

In our first image, we see the existing linked list with two items: item A and item C. We want to place item B in between A and C. To do this, we would need to set the "next" arrow on node A to point to node B, and the "previous" arrow on node B to point to node A. Then we need to set the "next" arrow from node B to node C and the "previous" arrow on node C to point to node B. Now we have a three-node list! If we wanted to remove node B, we would just do the opposite. Clip out node B by setting the next arrow on node A to point to node C and the "previous" arrow on node C to point to node A.

Sometimes a linked list is not as effective as an array. What if you need to frequently access the nodes in the middle of a list? An array can access these items directly by using the specific index number into the array. A linked list, however, would have to "walk" the entire list until the desired node is reached. This will typically take more time than directly accessing a specific element by index.

Creating and using a **LinkedList** in Java is similar to using the **ArrayList** class since they both implement the same **List** interface. To create a **LinkedList**, use the **new** keyword and the data type in angle brackets:

```
LinkedList<String> myClasses = new LinkedList<String>();
```

Now we have a linked list of **Strings** to work with. We can use the **List add()** method just like **ArrayList**:

```
myClasses.add("Geometry"); // the list contains "Geometry"
myClasses.add("History");  // the list contains "Geometry", "History"
```

In addition to the standard **List** and **Collection** methods, the **LinkedList** class adds a few more handy functions to let you get and add elements to the beginning and end of the list.

Method	Description
void addFirst(T obj)	Add the object to the beginning of the list.
void addLast(T obj)	Add the object to the end of the list
T getFirst()	Returns a reference to the first element in the list. Will throw a **NoSuchElementException** if the list is empty.
T getLast()	Returns a reference to the last element in the list. Will throw a **NoSuchElementException** if the list is empty.

Let's use these new methods in some example code:

```
LinkedList<String> myClasses = new LinkedList<String>();
myClasses.add("Math");         // "Math"
myClasses.add("History");      // "Math","History"
myClasses.addFirst("English"); // "English","Math","History"
myClasses.addLast("Health");   // "English","Math","History","Health"
myClasses.addLast("Gym");      // "English","Math","History","Health","Gym"
```

Now our list has five items: "English", "Math", "History", "Health", and "Gym".

Let's remove some items from the front and rear of the list, and then get the remaining items at the beginning and end of the list:

```
myClasses.removeFirst();           // "Math","History","Health","Gym"
myClasses.removeLast();            // "Math","History","Health"
String first = myClasses.getFirst(); // first = "Math"
String last = myClasses.getLast();   // last  = "Health"
```

All of the other **Collection** and **List** interface methods work exactly as you would expect.

Lesson Three: Iterators

Often you will want to process all of the items in a **Collection**. The process of accessing each item in turn is called *iterating* or *traversing* the list. Any class derived from a **Collection** interface can be traversed with an **Iterator** interface. An object implementing the **Iterator** interface knows how to access each element of the underlying data structure. So you can get an **Iterator** from an **ArrayList** that knows how to traverse the internal array. You can get an **Iterator** from a **LinkedList** class that knows how to traverse the underlying linked list.

The great thing about using **Iterators** is that you as a programmer don't need to know anything about the underlying data structure at all; the **Iterator** implementation takes care of that! In order to get an **Iterator** for one of your collection objects, you can call the **iterator()** method from the **Collection** interface:

Method	Description
Iterator<T> iterator()	Returns an **Iterator** that can traverse the **Collection** with a specific data type.

Once you have an **Iterator**, what can you do with it? There are only three simple **Iterator** methods:

Method	Description
boolean hasNext()	Returns **true** if there are any more elements to traverse, or **false** otherwise.
T next()	Returns a reference to the next element in the collection. Will throw a **NoSuchElementException** if there are no more elements in the collection.
void remove()	Will remove the element from the collection that was last returned by the **next()** method. You can call this method once and only once for each call to **next()**.

Traversing with an Iterator

To walk an entire list, the first step is to create an **Iterator** from the list. For these examples, let's continue using the **LinkedList**<String> `myClasses` object from the previous lesson. `myClasses` will start out with five items: "English", "Math", "History", "Health", and "Gym".

```
Iterator<String> myIterator = myClasses.iterator();
```

This line of code will create and initialize an **Iterator** from the list with type **String**. Now we can use this **Iterator** to loop through each of the items in the list. There are three common ways to loop over all list items.

First, you can use a standard **for()** loop to walk through the elements. In this technique, we will use the iterator itself as the loop index variable. The middle test expression will check the result of **hasNext()** to see if any more items remain, and **hasNext()** will return **false** when the iterator has finished. There does not need to be any assignment statement because the iterator will be modified inside the loop by calling **next()**.

```java
// get iterator from myClasses and loop until hasNext() returns false
for (Iterator<String> myIterator=myClasses.iterator(); myIterator.hasNext();)
{
    // use next() to get the next string from the list and print to console
    String className = myIterator.next();
    System.out.println(className);
}
```

Another method of traversing the list is to use the **Iterator** with a **while()** loop. The logical expression in the **while()** loop is simply the result of calling **hasNext()** on the iterator:

```java
// get iterator from myClasses and loop until hasNext() returns false
Iterator<String> myIterator = myClasses.iterator();
While (myIterator.hasNext())
{
    // use next() to get the next string from the list and print to console
    String className = myIterator.next();
    System.out.println(className);
}
```

Enhanced for() Loops

The last method of list traversal is very convenient; it hides the **Iterator** completely! A special kind of enhanced **for()** loop called a **for** "each" loop will automatically iterate over any collection that implements the **Iterable** interface to return an **Iterator**. The loop syntax is a bit different than a standard **for()** loop:

```
for (<data type> <loop variable name> : <Collection variable>)
{
    // body of the loop
}
```

The first part to the left of the colon declares a local variable name of the data type that will be used in the loop. The second part to the right of the colon specifies a collection object you want to traverse. Here is an example using our **myClasses** variable that holds a **LinkedList**<String>.

```
for (String className : myClasses)  // iterate over each element in the list
{
    System.out.println(className);  // use the local variable "className"
}
```

Inside the loop, we can just print out the current value of **className**. This value will automatically change to the next **String** in the **myClasses** list with each iteration of the **for()** loop. Here is the output:

```
English
Math
History
Health
Gym
```

You can also use the **for** "each" loop to iterate over simple arrays using the same syntax.

```
int[] myArray = {1,2,3,4};
for (int value : myArray)              // iterate over each element in the array
{
    System.out.println(value);  // use the local variable "value"
}
```

The resulting output is exactly what you expect:

```
1
2
3
4
```

One important restriction to remember when using the **for** "each" loop: you can only read (copy) individual values out of the collection. You cannot update values in the collection by setting the local variable. Let's say we wanted to create an array with 3 **JPanel** objects, each of which must be created with the **new** keyword. Using the **for** "each" loop would not work as you expected!

```
JPanel[] myPanels = new JPanel[3];
for (JPanel panel : myPanels)      // iterate over each element in the array
{
    // this statement will update the local panel variable,
    // but will not update the value in the array!
    panel = new JPanel();
}
```

Instead, use a regular **for()** loop that will allow you to get or set individual values in the array or collection:

```
JPanel[] myPanels = new JPanel[3];
for (int i=0; i<myPanels.length; i++) // iterate over each array element
{
    myPanels[i] = new JPanel();  // store new JPanel in the array element
}
```

Now that you know about arrays, lists, and iterators, it's time for a programming activity that uses all of these concepts!

Activity: Baseball Stats

In this activity, you are going to use arrays and **ArrayLists** to create an application that will track batting averages for players on a baseball team.

Your activity requirements and instructions are found in the "Chapter_13_Activity.pdf" document located in your "TeenCoder\Java Programming\Activity Docs" folder. You can access this document through your Student Menu or by directly clicking on it from Windows Explorer (Windows) or Finder (Mac OS).

Complete this activity now and ensure your program meets the requirements before continuing!

Chapter Fourteen: Recursion, Sorting, and Searching

In this chapter you are going to learn about a powerful programming technique called *recursion*. You will also learn how to sort and search lists of values using several different algorithms.

Lesson One: Recursion

By now you are comfortable writing your own methods and calling those methods from other places in your code. For instance you might receive a button click event in your **actionPerformed()** method and then call another function to perform some work.

```
public void actionPerformed(ActionEvent event)
{
    if (event.getSource() == myButton)
    {
        doSomething();
    }
}


private void doSomething()
{
    // do something useful
}
```

There are many interesting programming challenges (including sorting) that can be handled by having a function call *itself* from within the function body. This technique is called *recursion*. Here is a simple example:

```
private void doSomething()
{
    // some logic, including a recursive call to doSomething()!
    doSomething();
}
```

Clearly the **doSomething()** method shown above will have big problems because there is no way for **doSomething()** to ever stop calling itself. Once you enter this **doSomething()** method there is no way out!

All *recursive* functions will need to have some escape logic that will allow the recursive function calls to end (preferably before the computer runs out of memory). This means that the recursive function call should pass some data to itself as parameters that can eventually signal a stop to the recursion, or the recursive functions should modify some class member variables that can also signal a stop.

Envisioning what happens inside a recursive function call can sometimes be challenging. If you pictured each function call as a dinner plate, then making recursive function calls is like slipping a new dinner plate underneath all the rest, making the pile higher and higher as more recursive calls are made. Each call to the function has its own inputs and outputs. Once you stop making recursive function calls due to some logic in the bottom-most function (or dinner plate) then that bottom-most function will return. Each time a recursive function returns you can imagine the lowest dinner plate being removed from the stack. Eventually all recursive function calls return and your stack is empty, leaving some final result returned to the calling code.

Recursive Example: Reversing a String

Let's take a look at a more useful example that will reverse the order of characters in a string.

```java
private String reverseString(String input)
{
        // first check to see if the input is null or empty...if so that is
        // our signal to stop recursing and just return an empty string!
        if ((input == null) || (input.length() == 0))
        {
                return "";    // all done recursing!
        }

        // recursively call reverseString(), passing in all input
        // characters except the first one.  The resulting remainder
        // will be the reversal of what we pass in.
        String remainder = reverseString(input.substring(1));

        // now return the reversed remainder plus the very first character
        // in this input string in reverse order.
        return remainder + input.charAt(0);
}
```

The **reverseString()** function can be simply called with a starting string such as "Hello":

```java
String reverse = reverseString("Hello");   // recursive function call
System.out.println(reverse);   // let's see what we received!
```

The output printed to the console is indeed the reverse of the input "Hello":

```
olleH
```

How does the **reverseString()** method work? We can visualize a series of steps, where each step is either a method call or **return**. We have numbered the steps in the order that they occur in the program (down the first column then up the second one):

Step	Method call	Step	Return value
1	reverseString("Hello")	12	"olle" + "H" = "olleH"
2	reverseString("ello")	11	"oll" + "e" = "olle"
3	reverseString("llo")	10	"ol" + "l" = "oll"
4	reverseString("lo")	9	"o" + "l" = "ol"
5	reverseString("o")	8	"" + "o" = "o"
6	reverseString("")	7	""

As long as the input is not empty, the **reverseString()** function calls itself recursively, passing in a substring containing the input value without the first character. This continues until the input string is empty, which is our signal to stop making recursive function calls. The function then returns an empty string initially. That returned value is pre-pended to the first character of the previous input and again returned up the chain. When we return from the first call to **reverseString()** the output is the reverse of the input "Hello".

Each time a recursive function is called, the function body represents a new scope with its own copy of any local variables. When the recursive function returns, you go back to the previous scope where the recursive call was made and continue processing normally from that point.

Recursive Example: Raising a Number to a Power

Another common example uses a recursive function to raise a number to a power. In this function, the number "X" is raised to the "Y" power, or X^Y. If you know your algebra, you will recall that X^Y can also be written as $X * X^{Y-1}$ or $X * X * X^{Y-2}$, etc. This expansion works really well in a recursive function, like this:

```
public double power(double X, int Y)
{
    if (Y == 0)  // this is our recursion terminating condition
    {
        return 1.0;  // any number to the 0 power equals 1.0
    }
    // recursively call power() to get X to the Y-1 power
    return X * power(X, Y - 1);
}
```

Our **power()** function calls itself to calculate successively smaller values for X^{Y-1} until finally we reach X^0, which is just 1.0 in all cases (that's our loop termination condition). Consider the following calling code:

```
double result = power(3.0, 4);
System.out.println(result);
```

We will be raising the number 3.0 to the 4th power (or 3.0^4) which equals 81.0. How does the **power()** method work? Let's take a look at the individual steps:

Step	Method call	Step	Return value
1	**power**(3.0, 4)	10	3.0 * 27.0 = 81.0
2	**power**(3.0, 3)	9	3.0 * 9.0 = 27.0
3	**power**(3.0, 2)	8	3.0 * 3.0 = 9.0
4	**power**(3.0, 1)	7	3.0 * 1.0 = 3.0
5	**power**(3.0, 0)	6	1.0

You may be thinking "there are easier ways to reverse a string and calculate a power", and you are right! These simple examples are only meant to show how recursion works. There are many different valid uses for a recursive function. You could recursively walk through all the files and subdirectories on a hard drive. Imagine these files and directories as a giant tree where subdirectories are branches and files are the leaves. A recursive algorithm could follow the branches to the end, and then back up and search other branches. Recursive functions can also be used when writing an algorithm to find your way through a maze or sort data.

If recursion is so great, why isn't it used more often? Well, there are some drawbacks to consider:

- It can take quite a bit of computer memory to hold the nested recursive function calls.
- You need to be very careful to avoid an infinite recursion. You must always remember to include a termination condition in a recursive function. If you don't, your computer could run out of memory.
- Recursion can be difficult to visualize and implement correctly.

Still, recursion is a powerful tool when used properly, and certain categories of programming problems are easily attacked with a recursive solution.

Lesson Two: Sorting Algorithms

Sorting refers to putting un-ordered data into a sequence. Most often this involves numeric data in an array or list. Over time, many different sorting algorithms have been developed to arrange data. Each sorting algorithm can be measured in terms of its efficiency (or speed) and its computer resource requirements (e.g. memory consumption). The measurement of these factors is referred to in "Big O" notation.

 **The "O" in Big "O" notation is short for "order of" and is a rough approximation of the time and resources it would take to complete the sorting process.**

"Big O" notation is written as **O(f(n))**, where the "n" is the number of elements that need to be sorted, and "f(n)" is some function of that number. For instance, if "f(n) = n" then the Big O notation is simply **O(n)**. This is called a *linear* function, because there is a direct relationship between the number of elements and the time and resources it takes to sort the data. This means the more elements you have, the more time it takes! A "Big O" notation of **O(n²)** would mean that as the number of data elements increases, the time it takes to sort them increases exponentially by a factor of n-squared.

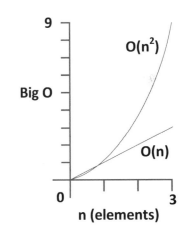

As you can see, for larger values of "n", the **O(n²)** algorithm would take much more time than the **O(n)** sorting algorithm. If you had 1000 data elements (n = 1000), then **O(n)** would equal 1000, but **O(n²)** would equal 1,000,000. That's a thousand times slower! This is why it's good to understand the time it takes to perform a sort using the "Big O" notation. Most sorting algorithms will have some "Big O" function that falls in between **O(n)** and **O(n²)**.

One good way to informally understand an algorithm's performance is to carefully count the number of iterative loops within the code. Your execution time will typically be proportional to the number of loops you have to make. How many times will the innermost useful logic be run in this example with 10 elements?

```
int numElements = 10;
for (int i=0; i<numElements; i++)
{
    for (int j=0; j<numElements; j++)
    {
        // do something useful here
    }
}
```

That's right, there are 100 iterations of the innermost logic and since $10^2 = 100$, you have **O(n²)** performance!

The Selection Sort Algorithm

One simple algorithm for sorting data is called the *selection sort*. In this algorithm, we start at the first element and search for the smallest value in the array. When this value is found somewhere other than the starting position, we swap it with the larger value at the starting position. Then we search the array again, starting at the second position. If we find a smaller value to the right of the second position, swap it with the value at the second position. Continue searching the array for smaller values starting at each position until the entire array is sorted. As the selection sort moves from left to right through the array, the sorted numbers are built up on the left and the unsorted numbers remain on the right side.

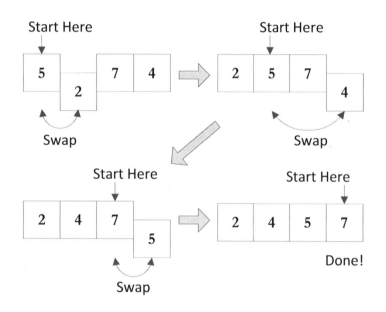

Here is an example of the selection sort in action. We start with an unsorted array containing the elements {5, 2, 7, 4}.

On the first pass starting at the 0ᵗʰ element (5), we find the smallest value is 2. So we swap the 5 and the 2 leaving us an array with {2, 5, 7, 4}.

On the next pass starting at the 1ˢᵗ element (5 again), we find the smallest value is 4. So we swap the 5 and the 4 leaving us with {2,4,7,5}.

On the third pass starting at the 2ⁿᵈ element (7), the smallest value is 5 so we swap the 7 and the 5 leaving us with {2,4,5,7}. The final pass starting at the last element can't do anything because there is only one value, so we're done! The final sorted array is {2,4,5,7}.

The selection sort algorithm is easily written as a Java function. We use a nested pair of **for()** loops to make multiple passes through the array, starting at each element in turn and scanning the remainder of the array for a smaller value to swap into the current location.

```java
public void selectionSort(int[] targetArray)
{
        // loop over the whole array
        for (int i = 0; i < targetArray.length; i++)
        {
                // start this search for smallest value at element i
                int minIndex = i;
```

```
        // check all elements from index i+1 to end of the array
        for (int j = i + 1; j < targetArray.length; j++)
        {
                // if the value at index j is smaller than
                // the value at the current minimum index
                if (targetArray[j] < targetArray[minIndex] )
                {
                        // remember the new index of the smallest value
                        minIndex = j;
                }
        }

        // if we found a smaller value anywhere other than
        // the beginning of this iteration
        if (minIndex != i)
        {
                // swap the minimum value into this first slot
                // and put the value from the first slot where
                // the minimum value was taken from
                int temp = targetArray[i];
                targetArray[i] = targetArray[minIndex];
                targetArray[minIndex] = temp;
        }
    }
}
```

The selection sort is very simple to visualize and implement in a program. However, it is not the most efficient algorithm. This sort has a "Big O" function of $O(n^2)$, which means as the number of elements gets larger, the time it takes to perform the search gets exponentially longer. So this algorithm will work fine for small lists but may become unrealistic for larger lists. Notice that we don't need any extra memory as all of the activity takes place within the original array, but the number of loop iterations increases exponentially.

The Insertion Sort Algorithm

Another simple type of sorting algorithm is the *insertion sort*. The insertion sort only requires one pass through the array, but it can spend a great deal of time moving elements around within the array. The "Big O" function on average is $O(n^2)$, though it may complete faster depending on how well the data was originally sorted before starting.

The insertion sort begins with the second element in the array (index 1). That value is removed from its original slot and "walked" backwards while the numbers to the left are greater. Each greater value is slid to the right into the empty array element vacated by its neighbor. When the removed value becomes less than the number that was slid to the right, it has found the right place in the sorted array. Then the insertion sort repeats starting with the third element (at index 2) and continues until all elements have been processed.

After you make one complete pass through the data you have a completely sorted set. Even though the list is sorted after only one pass, insertion sort is still not a very efficient sorting algorithm. This is mainly due to the number of times that you have to slide a bunch of elements down in the array. As you can imagine, a linked list would be a more efficient data structure for the insertion sort. You can easily remove and insert items within the list just by rearranging the **Previous** and **Next** links...no copying or sliding necessary!

Now let's watch a complete single-pass insertion sort in action against the original data set we used with the selection sort: {5,2,7,4}.

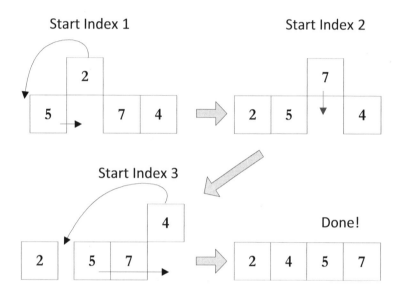

We begin at the 1st element and remove the 2 from the array. Comparing to the 0th element to the left we immediately find that 5 is greater than 2, so slide the 5 down to the empty slot and put 2 in the 0th slot Our array now contains {2,5,7,4}.

Then moving to the 2nd element we remove the 7 from the array. 7 is greater than the number to the immediate left, so simply drop the 7 back into the same position.

Finally we move to the 3rd and last element, removing the 4 from the array. Both 7 and 5 are greater than 4, so slide both of those elements to the right and insert the 4 into the 1st element. Our array is now completely sorted as {2,5,7,4} and we are done!

We can again write this algorithm in Java with a pair of nested loops. The outer **for()** loop will start at element 1 and iterate over the entire array. The inner **while()** loop will walk backwards from the starting point looking for the first smaller value, and sliding each larger element to the right.

```java
public void insertionSort(int[] targetArray)
{
        // loop over the array once starting at the 1st element
        for (int i = 1; i < targetArray.length; i++)
        {
                // temp holds the value pulled from the starting element
                int temp = targetArray[i];
                int j = i;   // walk backwards from the starting element
```

```
        // while we have not reached the beginning of the array
        // and the element to the left is greater than our temp value
        while ((j > 0) && (targetArray[j-1] > temp))
        {
                // slide the element to the left one space to the right
                targetArray[j] = targetArray[j-1];
                j--;  // move second index one slot to the left
        }
        // now the j index has found where we should store our temp value
        targetArray[j] = temp;
    }
}
```

An insertion sort, on average, has a complexity of $O(n^2)$. In special cases like a pre-sorted list the algorithm finishes in $O(n)$ time, but in general this algorithm is considered to have the same general computer resource requirements as the selection sort.

The Merge Sort Algorithm

The *merge sort* algorithm uses recursion to obtain a better "Big O" function. The merge sort function is usually $O(n * log(n))$. For larger values of "n", the function "n * log(n)" does not grow nearly as quickly as "n²", so the merge sort is better than the selection and insertion sorts on larger data sets. The merge sort method uses a "divide and conquer" approach to sorting data. This means that a large amount of data is progressively broken down into a series of smaller problems until the pieces are so small that they can be sorted very easily!

The first step in the merge sort function should check to see if the number of elements in the input list is zero or one. If so, there is nothing left to sort so the function can return right away. If there is more than one element, then the list is broken in half and each half is recursively sorted. After each half is sorted, then the two halves are merged together into a new list. The first element from each half is compared and the smaller one added to the new list first. This merge continues until all elements are added to the new list, and the resulting sorted list is returned to the calling function.

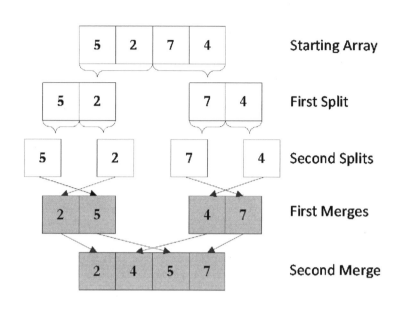

5 2 7 4	**Starting Array**
5 2	7 4	**First Split**
5	2	7	4	**Second Splits**
2 5	4 7	**First Merges**
2 4 5 7	**Second Merge**

Let's walk through this process with our familiar starting list, {5,2,7,4}. On the first recursive call, the list is split into two pieces {5,2} and {7,4}. Each piece is then passed to the recursive merge sort again.

The next level of recursion will split the two halves again into smaller lists {5}, {2}, {7}, and {4}. Since each list has one element, we are now ready to begin merging!

The first merge looks at the first (and only) element in the {5} and {2} lists. Since the 2 is smaller, it is added to the sorted array first. Then the 5 is added next as it's the only one left, resulting in {2,5}. Similarly, the recursive function merging the {7} and {4} lists builds a list with {4,7}.

Finally, the top-most merge function will merge the {2,5} and {4,7} lists. The first element in each list is compared, and the smaller 2 is added to the output first {2}. Next the 5 and 4 are compared and the smaller 4 is added {2,4}. Next the remaining 5 and 7 are compared and the 5 is chosen next {2,4,5}. Finally the 7 is added last, giving us the sorted list {2,4,5,7}.

Unlike the selection sort and insertion sort, the merge sort uses extra memory to hold the sorted output. It is possible to write a merge sort algorithm to swap all of the elements in-place with the original array, but that is more complicated. As you can tell, it may be difficult to visualize and write a recursive sorting algorithm. However the improved speed and efficiency are certainly worth it!

Exploring the SortDemo Program

Since the code for the merge sort is a bit longer, we have created a "SortDemo" example program for you to observe. Copy the "SortDemo" project from your "TeenCoder\Java Programming\Activity Starters" directory to your "My Projects" directory and import it into your Eclipse workspace. Then you can follow along in Eclipse and watch the algorithm at work.

The "SortDemo" program contains the full implementation of all three sorting algorithms: selection sort, insertion sort, and merge sort. In the **main()** method you can select which algorithm to run. Take some time now to run the merge sort algorithm and see the recursion in action. Our implementation will print some status lines to the console so you get a feel for the data each recursive function call receives. You can set breakpoints in the recursive function and step through the program line-by-line. You can also experiment with different input arrays with additional numbers to verify the sort works in other cases.

```java
public static void main(String[] args)
{
        // Declare the array we want to sort.
        // You can experiment with adding different numbers!
        int[] myNumbers = {5, 2, 7, 4};

        // Now call one of the 3 sorting algorithms to sort the array.
        // Un-comment the line for the sort you want to run, and ensure
        // the other two sort lines are commented out!
        mergeSort(myNumbers,0,myNumbers.length-1);      // run merge sort
        //selectionSort(myNumbers);                     // run selection sort
        //insertionSort(myNumbers);                     // run insertion sort

        // print the results to the console
        for (int num : myNumbers)
        {
                System.out.print(num + " ");
        }
}
```

Here is the console output for the merge sort using our {5,2,7,4} input array:

```
mergeSort from index 0 to index 3
mergeSort from index 0 to index 1
merging halves with lowIndex 0, middleIndex 0, highIndex 1
mergeSort from index 2 to index 3
merging halves with lowIndex 2, middleIndex 2, highIndex 3
merging halves with lowIndex 0, middleIndex 1, highIndex 3
2 4 5 7
```

Review the **mergeSort()**, **selectionSort()**, and **insertionSort()** functions on your own to see fully commented implementations of each sorting algorithm.

Lesson Three: Searching Algorithms

Now that you know how to sort data, let's turn our attention to finding values within an array or list. Many programs require *searching* through some kind of data. If the data is sorted (say, numerically or alphabetically) then we can apply a searching algorithm to find the value we want. We will discuss two different searching algorithms in this lesson.

Sequential Search

Let's consider an array with the following values: { 1, 3, 5, 6, 8, 9, 10, 12, 14, 15 }. Most searching algorithms require the data to be sorted first, and you can see this array has been pre-sorted in increasing order.

A *sequential search* is a very simple approach. Given a collection such as an array or list, you start at the beginning and compare every value one by one until you have found the element you are looking for or until you reach the end of the collection.

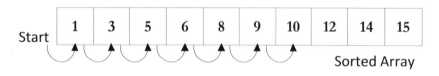

If we are searching for an element with the number "10", we would loop over the array, stopping when we reach the number "10". At that point, we have identified the element index containing our target value. In this example the 0-based index of the "10" value is 6. As you can see it took seven steps to compare every value from the beginning until we found the "10" at index 6.

The "Big O" rating of the sequential search algorithm is **O(n)**. This means that the average time it takes to find the value you're looking for depends directly on how many items are in the collection.

Here is a sequential search function written in Java:

```java
public int sequentialSearch(int[] targetArray, int targetValue)
{
    // start at the beginning and loop over the array
    for (int i=0; i<targetArray.length; i++)
    {
        // if this element contains the target value
        if (targetArray[i] == targetValue)
        {
            return i;   // return the resulting index!
        }
    }
    return -1;  // signal that the target value was not found
}
```

To run this search we just need to create a sorted array of numbers and call the **sequentialSearch()** function:

```java
int[] myNumbers = {1, 3, 5, 6, 8, 9, 10, 12, 14, 15};
int resultIndex = sequentialSearch(myNumbers,10);   // search for value 10
System.out.println("index " + resultIndex);        // will print "index 6"
```

This is a simple search process, but it can take a long time if you have a very large data set. You might get lucky if your target value is near the beginning, but the target value might be near the end of the list instead. Note that the sequential search algorithm actually does not require the data to be sorted… you'll still find the target value eventually because you check every element in the array!

Binary Search

A *binary search* is a popular and efficient search algorithm. The binary search will start by looking at the element in the middle of the collection. If the value there is higher than the target, then you can eliminate all of the elements to the right and only consider the remaining elements to the left. If the value in the middle is lower than the target, then you can eliminate all the elements to the left. Whichever half you choose, again sub-divide that smaller collection and look at the value in the middle. Continue eliminating half of the remaining collection until you land on your target value or run out of elements to compare. Because of how it operates, the binary search requires that the data is sorted in the collection in order to work properly.

Let's return to the same example we used for the sequential search and again try to find the "10" value. There are 10 elements in the collection ranging from a "low" index 0 to the "high" index 9. We calculate the middle index as "middleIndex = lowIndex + (highIndex – lowIndex) /2". So we start by subtracting the low index (0) from the high index (9) and then dividing the result by 2, yielding 4.5. Drop the remainder, add 4 to the low index (0) and we'll start at index 4: **0 + (9 – 0) / 2 = 4**. The value at index 4 is "8", which is too low, so that index and all elements to the left can be ignored.

For the next step our new "low" index is 5 and our "high" index is 9. We calculate the middle index again the same way: **5 + (9 – 5) / 2 = 7**. The value at index 7 is "12" which is too high, so we can eliminate that element and all others to the right.

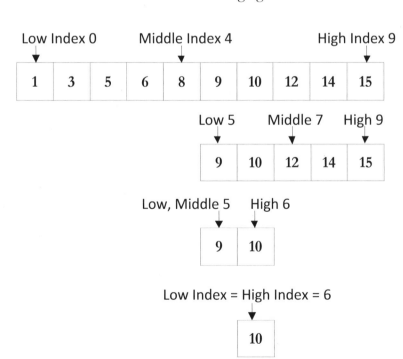

On the next step our low index is 5 and our high index is 6. There are only two elements remaining! Our middle index formula tells us to look at **5 + (6 − 5) / 2 = 5**. The value at index 5 is "9" which is too low, so discard that element. Our next low index is 6 and our high index is 6, so we know right away we've reached one remaining element. If we run our middle-index formula again (because sometimes programs aren't that smart) of course we'll just end up with **6 + (6 − 6) / 2 = 6**. We see the value at index 6 is "10" which matches our target value, so we are done. As you can see it only took 4 steps to search a 10-element array!

What happens if the value at the last element (where low index = high index) did not match the target value? That just means the target value is not present in the list at all. Your binary search function can return some index such as -1 to signal that the target value was not found.

The "Big O" rate of the binary search algorithm is **O(log (n))**. This means it is considerably more efficient than the sequential search for collections with many elements. We get this efficiency because we can toss out half of the remaining elements at each step in the search process.

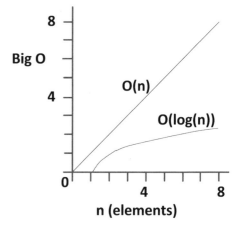

You are going to write a recursive binary search algorithm as part of your chapter activity, so start thinking about how you might implement this in Java code!

Activity: Recursive Binary Search

In this activity, you are going to write a binary search algorithm using recursion!

Your activity requirements and instructions are found in the "Chapter_14_Activity.pdf" document located in your "TeenCoder\Java Programming\Activity Docs" folder. You can access this document through your Student Menu or by directly clicking on it from Windows Explorer (Windows) or Finder (Mac OS).

Complete this activity now and ensure your program meets the requirements before continuing!

Chapter Fifteen: Inheritance and Polymorphism

The heart of object-oriented programming is the ability of one class to *inherit* shared behavior and data from another class. This powerful concept allows careful programmers to re-use code and simplify their logic. In this chapter you are going to learn to build your own class hierarchy and make use of OOP concepts.

Lesson One: Jail Break!

For your final project you will be writing a game called "Jail Break". Jail Break is based on old Viking board games called "Tablut" or "Hnefatafl". While similar games like chess and checkers have two sides with identical pieces, Tablut and related games are *asymmetrical*. Each side has different pieces and goals!

We are going to describe the rules for Jail Break in this lesson. Afterwards we'll then dive into some object-oriented programming techniques to let us easily implement this game.

The Jail Break Game Board

The Jail Break game board contains 81 squares arranged in a 9 x 9 grid. In code you can imagine a 2-dimensional array where the upper-left square is at [0][0] and the lower-right is at [8][8]. The center square at [4][4] is called the "Jail".

Around the edges are 4 groups of "Camp" squares arranged in a "T" shape, with the base of the "T" pointing towards the middle. Both the Jail and the Camp squares have some special rules that restrict certain game pieces from entering the square.

The Jail Break Teams

Jail Break is a two player game where each player controls a group of game pieces on the board. One player controls the "Outlaws" team. The Outlaws team contains one "Kingpin" piece and eight "Henchman" pieces. The Kingpin starts out in the Jail square and the Henchmen surround the Jail in a plus pattern. The second team is the "Posse" which contains 16 identical "Deputy" pieces that start out in Camp squares.

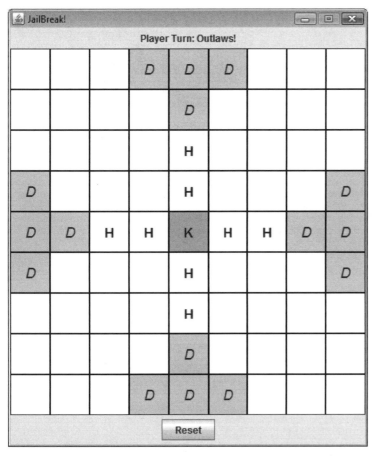

The picture to the left shows the starting game board, with the Camp squares shaded one color, the middle Jail another color, and all other squares in white. Each piece is shown by its first initial ("K" for Kingpin, "H" for Henchman, and "D" for deputy).

A label at the top shows which player has the current move, and a "Reset" button at the bottom will move all the pieces back to their starting location.

The goal for the Outlaws team is simply to get the Kingpin piece to any of the edge white squares to "escape". The Posse team is trying to capture the Kingpin before he escapes!

All pieces for both players move like a Rook in chess, which means they 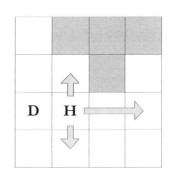 can move any number of squares in an up, down, left, or right direction. No piece can move through or hop over another piece, nor can any piece land on a square occupied by another piece. In addition, no Outlaw piece can ever land on or more through a Camp space. No piece (Kingpin, Henchman, or Deputy) may move into the Jail space once the Kingpin leaves it.

In the example above and to the right, the Henchman can move one square up before being blocked by the Camp. It can move more than one square to the right or down because there is no other piece or restricted square in the way. It is blocked from moving left entirely by the Deputy right next to it.

You can capture an opponent's piece and remove it from the game by sandwiching it between two of your own in a horizontal or vertical arrangement. The two examples to the right show a Henchman getting captured by two Deputies, first horizontally and second vertically. The Kingpin must be captured by getting surrounded on all four sides by Deputies.

					D	
D	H	D			H	
					D	

The game is over when the Kingpin either escapes or is captured. Now you know all about Jail Break!

Lesson Two: Base Classes and Derived Classes

Objects that *inherit* from one another use the "is-a" relationship we first described back in Chapter Ten during our introduction to object-oriented programming. First you need to define a *base* class, which is the class that has common methods and properties that other *derived* classes or *subclasses* will inherit. The derived classes will then expand on those common methods and properties with things that are unique to that specific class.

Creating a Base Class

If you think about our Jail Break game, you will probably see right away that all of the game pieces (Kingpin, Henchman, Deputy) share some things in common, yet have their own unique differences as well. So we have a good feeling that object-oriented programming can help us implement the game pieces.

It's possible to approach our object design in different ways; there is no one right answer. We will start simply with a base class called **GamePiece**. An object diagram is useful to visualize the object relationships as we build up our classes. Initially the diagram just contains one object named **GamePiece**!

GamePiece

We know that all game pieces on the board share certain common properties:

- Name
- One-letter abbreviation for display
- Team (Outlaws or Posse)
- Current location on the game board (column and row index values from 0-8)

In Java we could implement the **GamePiece** base class as follows:

```java
public class GamePiece
{
    // these values tell us which team the piece belongs to
    static public final int PLAYER_OUTLAWS = 0;
    static public final int PLAYER_POSSE = 1;

    public int myCol;  // column index 0 - 8
    public int myRow;  // row index 0 - 8

    public int myPlayerType;       // PLAYER_OUTLAWS or PLAYER_POSSE
    public String myAbbreviation;  // display character on board
    public String myName;          // full piece name
}
```

In this **GamePiece**, we have defined two **static** constants that tell us the possible teams the piece can belong to. We have also established **myCol** and **myRow** member variables so the piece knows where it is on the game board. We defined a class variable called **myPlayerType** that will hold one of the two team constants, and a couple of strings for the display character and full piece name. Again there is usually no one magical "correct" way to define an object, so we have just picked what feels like a good first try.

Within our Jail Break game we might then create an instance of a **GamePiece** like this:

```
GamePiece piece = new GamePiece();
```

Now, this is a nice starting point – our Jail Break game can manage all pieces in a common way by setting the **myCol**, **myRow**, **myPlayerType**, **myAbbreviation**, and **myName** properties.

Abstract Methods

We know that each piece moves in the same way, but has special restrictions on where they can move. When a player tries to move a piece, the game program will want to determine if it's valid move. So, let's add a method to our **GamePiece** class. This new method will tell us if a move to a target square is valid.

To complete this method, we will need to know some specific information about the piece type and where it can move on the board. Since movement logic will be slightly different for each piece, we are going to *define* this method in the **GamePiece** class, but *not actually implement it* yet.

```
abstract public boolean canMoveToLocation(int targetCol, int targetRow);
```

We use the keyword **abstract** in front of the method definition to show the method is defined in the base class but must be implemented by a derived class. Instead of curly braces and a method body after the parameter list, just end the method definition with a semicolon.

Once you declare any method in a class to be **abstract**, you must also mark the overall class as **abstract** by adding the **abstract** keyword in front of the class name. To make it clear that our class is now an **abstract** class, we will also change the name from **GamePiece** to **AbstractGamePiece**.

```
abstract public class AbstractGamePiece
{
    // This method is defined but not implemented by AbstractGamePiece.
    abstract public boolean canMoveToLocation(int targetCol, int targetRow);

    // plus the rest of the properties we already defined...
}
```

Abstract classes cannot be created with the **new** keyword, because they are not completely implemented! If you did try to create this **AbstractGamePiece** class directly, the compiler would generate an error:

```
// compile error because AbstractGamePiece is declared as abstract
AbstractGamePiece piece = new AbstractGamePiece();
```

Creating Derived Classes

So how do we use our **AbstractGamePiece** class? To use this class, you must *derive* a subclass from it. Let's define a new derived class called **Deputy** that inherits from **AbstractGamePiece**:

```
public class Deputy extends AbstractGamePiece
{
    // Implement the abstract method defined in the base class.
    public boolean canMoveToLocation(int targetCol, int targetRow)
    {
        // implementation details go here
    }
}
```

To create a derived class, place the keyword **extends** after the derived class name and then specify the base class name. We have now created an "is-a" relationship between **Deputy** and **AbstractGamePiece**.

To implement an **abstract** method in a derived class you need to repeat the method definition again without the **abstract** keyword. Then implement the method body normally. From a derived class method we are able to access any of the **public** or **protected** methods and properties of the base class as if they were declared in the derived class. However a derived class cannot access any **private** methods or properties on the base class.

Any derived class that fully implements all of the **abstract** methods from the base class is called *concrete*. A concrete derived class can now be created with the **new** keyword because all methods are implemented. Our **Deputy** class is ready to be used in a program.

```
Deputy piece = new Deputy();
piece.myPlayerType = AbstractGamePiece.PLAYER_POSSE;
piece.myName = "Deputy";
piece.myAbbreviation = "D";
piece.myCol = 3;
piece.myRow = 1;
```

By now, you are probably confident that our Jail Break game will define a class for each of the different pieces, all derived from the base class **AbstractGamePiece**.

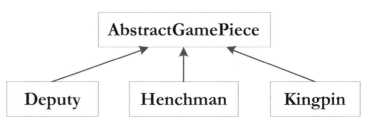

You can probably imagine other useful classes as well, such as **GameBoard** which might contain a 2-dimensional array of **GameSquare** objects.

Complex Class Hierarchies

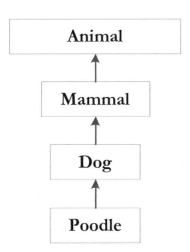

While we will stick to simple two-level class hierarchies for our final project, it is possible to create a deeply nested class structure. One class can derive from a parent and in turn serve as the base class for another more specialized object.

As you can see to the left, we have imagined a four-level class hierarchy with **Animal** as the most general base class. A **Mammal** is a kind of animal, a **Dog** is a kind of mammal, and a **Poodle** is a kind of dog. Each derived class would inherit all of the properties and behavior of the base class, plus add its own special code for the derived type.

You can find many examples of multi-level class hierarchies in the Java class library. For example, each time you use a **JButton** on your screen, that **JButton** is actually derived from a longer chain of objects starting with **java.lang.Object**:

```
java.lang.Object
    java.awt.Component
        java.awt.Container
            javax.swing.JComponent
                javax.swing.AbstractButton
                    javax.swing.JButton
```

The Java API documentation will show you the full class hierarchy of each object in the Java class library.

Lesson Three: Using References to Base and Derived Classes

When you create a variable of a class data type, you can of course assign an instance of that class to the variable. If your variable type happens to represent a base class, you can also assign an instance of any class *derived from* that base type to the variable.

```
Deputy piece1 = new Deputy();
AbstractGamePiece piece2 = new Deputy();
```

In the first line, we declare the variable **piece1** as a **Deputy** data type and initialize it with a new **Deputy** object. The variable **piece1** must always point to some instance of the **Deputy** (or some other class we might derive from it). In the second line we declare variable **piece2** as an **AbstractGamePiece**. We can then assign an instance of any class derived from **AbstractGamePiece** to this variable, including **Deputy**, **Kingpin**, or **Henchman**.

When to Use Derived Class References

If you want to use a method or property on a derived class that is not available on the base class, then you should declare your variable to be of the derived class type. That way Java knows how to use those items specific to the derived class. For instance, if there was something special on the **Kingpin** class that you want to use, you need to access that behavior through a **Kingpin** type variable and not **AbstractGamePiece**.

Let's consider an example. We know that **Kingpin** objects are trying to escape from the game board. We might define a method on the **Kingpin** class that will tell us if the **Kingpin** has escaped based on his current column and row.

```
public class Kingpin extends AbstractGamePiece
{
    // this special method is available only to Kingpins
    public boolean hasEscaped()
    {
        // implementation details go here based on myCol and myRow
    }
}
```

We have created a method called **hasEscaped()** which is defined only for a **Kingpin** object. This means that any **Kingpin** variable can use the method, but a variable of type **AbstractGamePiece** would have no knowledge of the method.

Now let's see what happens when we try to access that new method from variables of each data type.

```
      Kingpin piece1 = new Kingpin();
      AbstractGamePiece piece2 = new Kingpin();
      boolean hasEscaped1 = piece1.hasEscaped(); // OK!
      boolean hasEscaped2 = piece2.hasEscaped(); // ERROR!
```

As you can see, if we try to use the **hasEscaped()** method on the **piece2** variable, the compiler will generate an error because **AbstractGamePiece** doesn't know about the method. But what if we know for sure that **piece2** is really a **Kingpin**? In this case, we can temporarily treat it as a **Kingpin** and access the **hasEscaped()** method by using the *casting* technique previously described for the built-in data types.

Casting is a term which means changing a variable or reference to another data type. We can cast a class reference to another class type by putting the new class type in parentheses before the variable name like this:

```
      AbstractGamePiece piece = new Kingpin();  // upcast derived to base class
      Kingpin myKingpin = (Kingpin)piece; // downcast base to derived class (risky)
      boolean hasEscaped1 = myKingpin.hasEscaped();       // OK!
      boolean hasEscaped2 = ((Kingpin)piece).hasEscaped(); // also OK!
```

This would allow us to use the **hasEscaped()** method by temporarily converting the **piece** variable to a **Kingpin** reference, even though **piece** itself is not a **Kingpin** data type.

You can cast up an object hierarchy (*upcasting*) by casting a derived reference to a base data type. You can also cast down an object hierarchy (*downcasting*) by casting a base data type to a derived class. Notice that *upcasting* is guaranteed to work because the compiler knows in advance that a derived class inherits from the base class. Upcasting from a subclass (derived class) reference to a super-class (base class) reference does not require casting; you can simply make a direct assignment to the base class reference variable.

However, *downcasting* will cause an error if you attempt to cast a base class to a derived type, and the actual object is not of that derived type! For instance, you could always safely cast a **Deputy** reference to an **AbstractGamePiece**. But if you cast an **AbstractGamePiece** to a **Deputy**, and the object is actually a **Henchman**, you will cause an error at runtime!

When to Use Base Class References

So why would we want to declare a variable as the base class and not the specific derived class? By declaring a variable as an **AbstractGamePiece**, the variable is able to hold any sort of object that is derived from **AbstractGamePiece**. This variable can hold a **Deputy** object, or a **Kingpin**, or a **Henchman**. You can then use all of the public methods and properties on the **AbstractGamePiece** without really knowing about the derived type. If the user attempts to move a piece to a certain location, we don't actually need to know what the piece is. Simply call the **canMoveToLocation()** method, which we declared as **abstract**, and the correct method on the actual derived data type will be called automatically.

```
AbstractGamePiece piece = // some valid piece...Deputy, Kingpin, or Henchman
bool validMove = piece.canMoveToLocation(3,2);
```

We have just demonstrated the concept of *polymorphism*. Polymorphism means you can use an object as a *generic* type and it will actually behave differently, according to its *actual* type. Class hierarchies naturally implement polymorphism through the abstract methods defined in derived classes. This feature is one of the most powerful aspects of Java and other object-oriented programming languages! We will make good use of polymorphism in our final project.

Lesson Four: Overriding Base Methods

In previous lessons we discussed how to create base and derived classes and how to implement **abstract** methods in derived classes. But what if the base class implements a method that works for most derived classes, but not all? What if some of the derived classes want the method to work differently but others just want to use the base class implementation?

We can solve this problem by implementing the method on the base class first. Individual derived classes can then choose whether or not to override the base class implementation with another version. The overridden version in the derived class must match the base class method declaration exactly, including the same return data, function name, parameters, and **public/private/protected** scope. You may hear the term *virtual* used to describe methods that can be overridden by derived classes.

In Java all non-**private** methods are virtual by default, which means you don't have to do anything special for a derived class to override a base method with its own version. **Private** methods can never be overridden because derived classes have no access to them anyhow – they are only called internally by the base class. Java also allows you to block the override capability by marking a method with the **final** keyword. This means that no derived class can override that particular method.

For example, let's say we add a method called **isCaptured()** to our **AbstractGamePiece** base class. This method will return **true** if the piece is sandwiched by two opponents either horizontally or vertically.

```
abstract public class AbstractGamePiece
{
    // this method returns true if this piece is sandwiched by two opponents
    public boolean isCaptured()
    { /* implementation details go here */ }
}
```

Recall from the Jail Break game description that both **Deputy** and **Henchman** pieces can be captured if they are sandwiched between two opponents. So the base class implementation if **isCaptured()** works just fine for those two types of objects. However, **Kingpin** pieces are captured if they are surrounded by *four* opponents! So we would like the **Kingpin** class to override this method with its own implementation.

```java
public class Kingpin extends AbstractGamePiece
{
    // override the base method with our own version looking for
    // four surrounding opponents!
    public boolean isCaptured()
    {
        // alternate implementation details go here
    }
}
```

Now, consider the following code:

```java
    AbstractGamePiece piece1 = new Kingpin();
    AbstractGamePiece piece2 = new Deputy();

    // the overridden method will be called here for the Kingpin
    boolean isCaptured1 = piece1.isCaptured();

    // the original base method will be called for the Deputy, because
    // we didn't override the method for Deputy objects
    boolean isCaptured2 = piece2.isCaptured();
```

In both cases above our class variable was an **AbstractGamePiece** which could hold a **Deputy**, **Henchman**, or **Kingpin**. When you call a method through a base class reference, Java is smart enough to figure out which version to call based on the actual type of the object. In the case above, Java will select the overridden method **isCaptured()** for the **Kingpin** object stored in **piece1** and the base class method **isCaptured()** for the **Deputy** object in **piece2**.

Again this is a powerful example of polymorphism at work! Our program doesn't have to know about the kind of object it is using, we simply trust that each object will behave correctly according to its derived requirements when you call a method through the base class.

Lesson Five: The "Object" Base Class

In the Java language, all objects automatically inherit from a single root base class called **java.lang.Object**. This base class contains a small handful of common methods. The most interesting and useful of these are the **equals()** and the **toString()** methods.

Object Equality vs. Identity

The **Object.equals()** method will examine another **Object** and return **true** if the input is "equal" to the first:

```
boolean equals(Object obj)
```

You have already seen this method in action on the **String** object, which has a version of **equals()** that will check the characters in each string and return **true** if the strings have identical contents. More generally, any type of class can decide for itself what it means to be equal to another object by overriding the **equals()** method. Typically the **equals()** method will check all of the important characteristics of the two objects to figure out if they are close enough to be considered "equal". Exactly what "equal" means is up to the class!

An object's *identity* is sometimes confused with *equality*. A particular instance of an object in memory is unique even if it is "equal" to some other object containing the same data. For instance, two hammers are distinct, unique tools even though they may appear identical in every way. You test for equality with the **equals()** method, and you test to see if two variables refer to the same instance of an object with the == operator:

```
Deputy ref1 = new Deputy();
Deputy ref2 = new Deputy();
Deputy ref3 = ref1;
if (ref1 == ref3)    // true; ref1 and ref3 point to the same Deputy instance
if (ref1.equals(ref2)) // false, see below
```

In the example above the first expression "**ref1** == **ref3**" is **true** because they both point to the unique **Deputy** instance that was created on the first line. The second expression "**ref1**.equals(**ref2**)" would be **false** unless the **Deputy** object implements its own version of **equals()** and that method determines the first and second **Deputy** objects are equivalent enough to be considered "equal".

Using toString()

The **toString()** method returns a human-readable string representation of the object. Here is an example that calls this method on a simple **Object**:

```
Object o = new Object();
System.out.println( o.toString() );
```

This code creates a variable named "**o**", which contains an instance of the **java.lang.Object** class. When we display the results of the **toString()** method on the "**o**" variable, we get output similar to this:

```
java.lang.Object@7d8a992f
```

You can see the default output of **toString()** contains the full class name of the object, plus some other data that identifies the specific instance of that object we created with the **new** keyword.

It is a common practice to override the **toString()** method in derived objects to produce more descriptive data. For example, the primitive numeric data type wrappers such as **Integer** and **Double** have overridden the **toString()** to produce just the value of the number they contain instead of the object name:

```
Integer myInt = new Integer(3);
System.out.println( myInt.toString() );
```

The **toString()** output is just the number "3":

```
3
```

You may find it useful to override the **toString()** method on your own classes so they can produce some better human-readable descriptors. For instance, if we tried to use the default **toString()** method for the **Deputy** class, like this:

```
Deputy piece = new Deputy();
piece.myPlayerType = AbstractGamePiece.PLAYER_POSSE;
piece.myName = "Deputy";
piece.myAbbreviation = "D";
piece.myCol = 3;
piece.myRow = 1;

System.out.println( piece.toString() );
```

The resulting string is not very descriptive or informative at all!

```
Deputy@5f186fab
```

Let's override the **toString()** method in our **AbstractGamePiece** class to provide a better description.

```
abstract class AbstractGamePiece
{
    public String toString()
    {
        if (myPlayerType == PLAYER_OUTLAWS)
            return "Outlaw " + myName + " at (" + myCol + "," + myRow + ")";
        else
            return "Posse " + myName + " at (" + myCol + "," + myRow + ")";
    }
}
```

Now with the same **Deputy** object created as above, we get much better output.

```
Posse Deputy at (3,1)
```

It is often a good idea to override the **toString()** method on your classes to provide better information, especially if you want to use the method to create a description to show the user.

Lesson Six: Using Base Features from Derived Classes

In the last lesson we learned how to override the methods of a base class. However, there may be times when you will want to both override a base class method and yet still have access to that base method from the derived class. When this is the case, you can reference the base class version of a method by using the **super** keyword in front of the method call in your code (a base class is sometimes called a "super-class").

Let's use this feature in our **Deputy** class. We decide that the default **toString()** method on the **AbstractGamePiece** class needs a little sizzle! So on our **Deputy** class we'll override **toString()** again:

```
public class Deputy extends AbstractGamePiece
{
    public String toString()
    {
        // use the base class version of toString() and add extra text
        return super.toString() + " - Law man is coming!";
    }
}
```

Inside the **Deputy.toString()** implementation we still use the **AbstractGamePiece** method by calling **super.toString()** to get the results from the base class **toString()**. We just added another string to the end of the base results to give fair warning to anybody messing around with deputies.

```
Posse Deputy at (3,1) - Law man is coming!
```

So, remember, you can access base class methods from your derived class with the **super** keyword. Also remember to respect anyone with a badge riding a horse!

Calling Base Constructor Methods

Now you know how to call a normal base class *method* with the **super** keyword, but how would you call a particular version of a base class *constructor*? Let's say we decided not to allow an **AbstractGamePiece** to be created without specifying the piece's name and team right up front in the constructor. To do this, we would create a constructor for this **AbstractGamePiece** that demanded those two parameters:

```java
abstract public class AbstractGamePiece
{
    public int myPlayerType;      // PLAYER_OUTLAWS or PLAYER_POSSE
    public String myName;         // full piece name


    // plus the other member variables defined earlier...


    // here is the constructor for AbstractGamePiece
    public AbstractGamePiece(String name, int playerType)
    {
        myName = name;                // initialize member with passed-in data
        myPlayerType = playerType;    // initialize member with passed-in data
    }
}
```

Now, if we were to create a new instance of our **Deputy** class (which is derived from the **AbstractGamePiece**), we would have a problem. The constructor for the **Deputy** class does not give the **AbstractGamePiece** constructor any information. The following code would generate a compiler error:

```java
    // this calls the Deputy's default constructor, which doesn't help
    // call the AbstractGamePiece constructor with parameters!
Deputy piece = new Deputy();  // ERROR
```

When you create an object with the **new** keyword, that object's constructor will be called first. If the object is derived from a base class, you will want to call that base class constructor from within the derived class constructor to get the base class a chance to initialize too. If you have not defined any constructors for your objects, then a default constructor is automatically created for you, and that default constructor will call the default constructors of the base class also.

To fix this error we need to define a constructor for the **Deputy** class (and all other classes deriving from **AbstractGamePiece**) that will call the **AbstractGamePiece** constructor with the required parameters. To call the base class constructor, use the **super** keyword again as a function call on the first line in your derived class constructor.

```java
public class Deputy extends AbstractGamePiece
{
    // define a constructor that will call AbstractGamePiece constructor
    public Deputy()
    {
        // call the base constructor with the required parameters
        super("Deputy",AbstractGamePiece.PLAYER_POSSE);
    }
}
```

This will cause the **AbstractGamePiece** base constructor to be executed *before* any of the derived class constructor logic within the constructor function body. You want your base class to be initialized first prior to completing initialization of your derived class.

Now we can safely create a **Deputy** class again without any errors:

```java
Deputy piece = new Deputy();   // OK
```

Of course, we can demand parameters in our **Deputy** constructor also. Perhaps we want to ensure that a column and row is always specified for every **AbstractGamePiece** object. So the constructors for both **Deputy** and **AbstractGamePiece** might require an integer column and row value.

```java
public class Deputy extends AbstractGamePiece
{
    // define a constructor that will call AbstractGamePiece constructor
    public Deputy(int col, int row)
    {
        // call the base constructor with the required parameters
        super("Deputy",AbstractGamePiece.PLAYER_POSSE,col,row);
    }
}
```

Now when you try to create a **Deputy** object, you can't use the default constructor. You must provide a column and row value.

```
Deputy piece1 = new Deputy();     // ERROR - no column or row given
Deputy piece2 = new Deputy(3,2);  // OK - all required parameters given
```

As you might imagine, the constructors for **Henchman** and **Kingpin** would look similar, except they should substitute their own names and the correct player type when calling the **super()** constructor.

Looking Ahead to the Final Project

You now have the skills needed to complete the final project! Your actual implementation of the **AbstractGamePiece**, **Deputy**, **Henchman**, and **Kingpin** classes will be a little different than we described in the chapter as we shift focus from teaching concepts to making the game work. You are going to be responsible for writing these objects plus some of the main game logic.

For this chapter's activity you will get started writing the four game piece objects. We provide an activity starter that will ensure your classes and methods are defined as needed for the game. You will be defining the objects and methods first, but not providing the full implementation of each method. This is called *top-down development*, where you first paint a broad picture of how your objects will look, and then come back in later stages to fill in the details. Top-down development is a common programming practice that lets you establish all the major component definitions and how they relate to each other first instead of getting sidetracked in the detailed implementation of a single class.

 **Activity: Game Pieces**

In this activity, you are going to create the **Deputy, Henchman,** and **Kingpin** classes for your final project!

Your activity requirements and instructions are found in the "Chapter_15_Activity.pdf" document located in your "TeenCoder\Java Programming\Activity Docs" folder. You can access this document through your Student Menu or by directly clicking on it from Windows Explorer (Windows) or Finder (Mac OS).

Complete this activity now and ensure your program meets the requirements before continuing!

Chapter Sixteen: Final Project

It's time for your final project! You have learned about Java object-oriented programming and Java Swing user interface concepts. Let's put those skills to work. In this chapter you will complete the "Jail Break" game we described in the last chapter. The first lesson introduces the activity starter project, and then you will complete a series of activities to complete other parts of the Jail Break game.

Lesson One: The Jail Break Activity Starter

We have provided an activity starter for Jail Break that implements the GUI part of the program. Your responsibility will be to finish some of the main game logic and all of the game pieces. If you don't remember all of the rules to Jail Break, take some time to review that lesson in the last chapter now.

When we are finished, in our game GUI the current player turn (Outlaws or Posse) will be shown at the top. That player can select a piece on their team by clicking on it. A yellow rectangle will appear to show the piece is highlighted. The player can then click on a target square to move the piece there. If the player selects a target square that is not a valid move, then the piece will remain where it is. The user should get a descriptive message any time a piece is captured or one of the players wins the game.

Your final project will use your **AbstractGamePiece**, **Henchman**, **Kingpin**, and **Deputy** classes you wrote for the previous chapter activity, so make sure you have those ready before continuing.

Activity One: Exploring the Activity Starter

The goal of this activity is to establish a functional "JailBreak" project in your Eclipse workspace that builds and runs without any errors. The initial program will not do much, but will confirm that you have successfully integrated your **AbstractGamePiece** and other classes into the activity starter and are ready to begin adding new functionality to the game. We will then take some time to explore each of the activity starter classes.

Your activity requirements and instructions are found in the "Chapter_16_Activity1.pdf" document located in your "TeenCoder\Java Programming\Activity Docs" folder. You can access this document through your Student Menu or by directly clicking on it from Windows Explorer (Windows) or Finder (Mac OS).

Complete this activity now and ensure your program meets the checkpoint requirements before continuing!

The remainder of the chapter contains a series of additional activities that will add functionality to the game. After each activity is a checkpoint that you should confirm before continuing. Your game should behave as described at each checkpoint.

Activity Two: Completing JailBreak.reset()

Your first task will be to place all of the pieces on the board. You will do this by completing the **JailBreak.reset**() method. The **reset**() method is called when the game starts and each time someone clicks the "Reset" button in the GUI. The **reset**() method should take all steps necessary to initialize the game board to the initial configuration.

Your activity requirements and instructions are found in the "Chapter_16_Activity2.pdf" document located in your "TeenCoder\Java Programming\Activity Docs" folder. You can access this document through your Student Menu or by directly clicking on it from Windows Explorer (Windows) or Finder (Mac OS).

Complete this activity now and ensure your program meets the checkpoint requirements before continuing!

Activity Three: Selecting Game Pieces

The **handleClickedSquare**() method is called whenever a player clicks on a square in the game board. You will implement the full method logic in several stages. For this activity, our goal is to allow the user to select and then de-select a piece for the current player. When a player selects a piece, the game board will display a thick yellow border around the square. De-selecting a square will remove the yellow border.

Your activity requirements and instructions are found in the "Chapter_16_Activity3.pdf" document located in your "TeenCoder\Java Programming\Activity Docs" folder. You can access this document through your Student Menu or by directly clicking on it from Windows Explorer (Windows) or Finder (Mac OS).

Complete this activity now and ensure your program meets the checkpoint requirements before continuing!

Activity Four: Moving Game Pieces

Once a piece has been selected we need to allow it to move to a new square that the user clicks. This means you need to work on the third "else" case in the **handleClickedSquare**() method. You will also need to implement the movement logic in the **AbstractGamePiece**, **Deputy**, **Henchman**, and **Kingpin** classes. When you are finished each player should be able to move pieces around as allowed by the game rules.

Your activity requirements and instructions are found in the "Chapter_16_Activity4.pdf" document located in your "TeenCoder\Java Programming\Activity Docs" folder. You can access this document through your Student Menu or by directly clicking on it from Windows Explorer (Windows) or Finder (Mac OS).

Complete this activity now and ensure your program meets the checkpoint requirements before continuing!

Activity Five: Capturing Game Pieces

When a game piece moves, it may capture one or more opponents. In this activity you will implement the logic necessary to detect which opponent(s) have been captured and remove them from the game board!

Your activity requirements and instructions are found in the "Chapter_16_Activity5.pdf" document located in your "TeenCoder\Java Programming\Activity Docs" folder. You can access this document through your Student Menu or by directly clicking on it from Windows Explorer (Windows) or Finder (Mac OS).

Complete this activity now and ensure your program meets the checkpoint requirements before continuing!

Activity Six: Ending the Game

You have completed everything in the Jail Break game except finding the winner! In this final activity you will write the code to detect both end-of-game conditions. The game ends when either the **Kingpin** escapes to one of the edge squares or the **Kingpin** is captured.

Your activity requirements and instructions are found in the "Chapter_16_Activity6.pdf" document located in your "TeenCoder\Java Programming\Activity Docs" folder. You can access this document through your Student Menu or by directly clicking on it from Windows Explorer (Windows) or Finder (Mac OS).

Complete this activity now and ensure your program meets final checkpoint requirements!

Wrap-up and Extra Credit

Great job! You have now finished your final project. During this course you have learned many important Java skills and have demonstrated several of them while writing this object-oriented game.

The Jail Break game rules we defined are similar to the original Viking "Tablut" or "Hnefatafl" games, but there is no one true historical picture of how those games were played. If you search the Internet for information on those games you will find many rule variants. For extra credit you may wish to enhance or change the game as follows:

- After any "Outlaws" move, if the **Kingpin** has an open escape path then display a warning message box to the Posse player.
- If the game balance seems to favor the Posse team, consider some rule changes that would help the Outlaws such as preventing the **Deputy** pieces from re-entering Camp squares once they leave.
- Similarly, if the game balance seems to favor the Outlaws team, think of some rule changes that would help the Posse such as capturing the **Kingpin** with only two pieces, or allowing the **Kingpin** to move only one space at a time.

Have fun with your new programming abilities!

What's Next?

Congratulations, you have finished the *TeenCoder™: Java Programming* course! If you are interested in a career in computers, the concepts and skills you learned are a solid foundation for further study.

The next course in the TeenCoder Java series is *TeenCoder: Android Programming*. In this course you will build on your Java programming knowledge by writing applications for the **Android™** mobile operating system! No hardware is required for this course as you can complete all projects on software emulators on your Windows or Mac OS computer. You may also choose to pursue the "C#" programming language through our *TeenCoder: Windows Programming* and *TeenCoder: Game Programming* curriculum.

The KidCoder Visual Basic series covers graphical Windows and game programming in an easy-to-use language. The KidCoder Web Design series will teach you simple HTML, CSS, and JavaScript techniques so you can build your own websites.

We hope you have enjoyed this course produced by Homeschool Programming, Inc. We welcome student and teacher feedback on our website. You can also visit our website to request courses on other topics.

http://www.HomeschoolProgramming.com

Index

.java extension 31

abstract keyword 250

Abstract Windowing Toolkit (AWT) 175

ActionListener interface 184

    actionPerformed() function 185

    handling multiple controls 187

ArrayList object 225

arrays 207, 217

    declaring 218

    elements 217

    iterating (walking) 219

    length property 219

    multi-dimensional 220

    numeric index 218

    zero-based index 218

Association for Computing Machinery 16

base class 249

Big O notation 237

binary language 13

BorderFactory object 195, 214

    createEmptyBorder() function 195

    createTitledBorder() function 215

break keyword 124

breakpoints 148

    setting in Eclipse 155

bug 145

ButtonGroup object 212

bytecode 21

casting 74

    between base and derived types 254

ChangeListener interface 206

    stateChanged() function 206

class hierarchies 252

class keyword 34, 161

code review 145

Collection interface 223

    add() function 223

    clear() function 223

    isEmpty() function 223

    remove() function 223

    size() function 223

collections 222

command prompt 23, 37

command-line parameters 97

verifying 98

comments 32

common errors 39

compiler 14

compiling from command line 37

constructors 167

    calling base class 260

    parameters 168

course files 30

curly braces 34, 35

    aligning vertically 59

data types 19, 67

    boolean type 68

    byte type 68

    char type 68

    double type 68

    float type 68

    int type 68

    long type 68

    ranges 68

    reference 77

    short type 68

    String type 78

debugger 147

debugging commands 148

    run or continue 148

    step into 148

    step out 148

    step over 148

    stop 148

decrement operator (--) 74

default package 43

derived classes 251

directory slashes 12

do keyword 127

do-while() loop 127

downcasting 254

Eclipse 27, 47

    .classpath file 56

    .metadata directory 51

    .project file 56

    creating **main**() function 57

    debug perspective 60

    debugger 149

debugger walkthrough.................................152
getting help..62
IDE walkthrough..52
importing existing project 149
installation..49
new class...57
new project..54
Package Explorer..................................53, 55
perspectives, switching 61
running a program......................................60
src directory...56
versions...48
workspace 50
else if keyword 119
else keyword 106, 119
escape characters.......................................80
ethics in computers....................................16
event-driven programming 183
exceptions..143
stack trace...144
table of common exceptions....................143
extends keyword.....................................251
file extension 31
final keyword 69
flow control 109
for keyword..121
for() loop...121
body in curly braces................................123
change statement.....................................122
enhanced, for-each..................................229
initialization statement 122
test expression 122
functional decomposition 134
functions...19
calling..137
declaration...132
defined within a class..............................133
naming rules..132
overloading..136
parameter ordering..................................138
parameters...134
parameters by-value................................139
reference parameters 140
return value 135
HelloWorld...41
high-level languages...................................14
if keyword 99, 106, 117
curly braces...118
implements keyword.........................171, 172
import keyword 43, 161
increment operator (++) 123
infinite loop...126
inheritance...249

installation
course material...28
course shortcuts..29
JDK..30
Instructional Videos.....................................4
integers...67
Integrated Development Environment (IDE) 26
interface keyword.....................................170
interfaces..169
Iterator interface......................................228
hasNext() function..................................228
next() function...228
obtaining...228
remove() function....................................228
using with loops......................................229
Jail Break activity starter...........................263
Jail Break game rules.................................247
jar tool...23
java and **javax** packages.........................42
Java Class Library......................................22
Java Development Kit (JDK)........................22
java executable...39
Java history 14
Java language online reference....................64
Java language online tutorials.....................65
Java Platform.......................................21, 23
Java Runtime Environment (JRE)............21, 22
Java versions 15
identifying...23
Java Virtual Machine (JVM)........................21
Java, getting help.......................................63
java.lang.Object.....................................257
equals() function......................................257
toString() function...................................257
javac compiler......................................23, 37
JavaDoc..32
javadoc tool...23
JButton object..181
addActionListener() function.................185
setEnabled() function............................181
JCheckBox object....................................214
JComboBox object....................................210
addItem() function..................................210
getSelectedItem() function.....................211
setEditable() function.............................211
setSelectedIndex() function 211
setSelectedItem() function......................211
JComponent object..................................180
setAlignmentX(), **setAlignmentY**() functions.................194
setBorder() function...............................195
JFrame object...177
add() function...181
getContentPane() function 190

pack() function 182
    setContentPane() function....................................190
    setDefaultCloseOperation() function.....................179
    setLayout() function..180
    setLocation() object..179
    setSize() function..179
    setTitle() function...178
    setVisible() function...179
JLabel object...181
JList object..208
    clearSelection() function.....................................209
    getSelectedValue() function...................................209
    setSelectedIndex() function...................................210
    setSelectionMode() function...................................208
JOptionPane object...199
    showInputDialog() function....................................199
JPanel object..189
    setLayout() function..190
    using multiple panels..196
JRadioButton object..212
    addActionListener() function..................................213
    isSelected() function...212
    setSelected() function..214
JScrollPane object...204, 208
JSpinner object..204
    addChangeListener() function..................................206
    getValue() function...206
JTextArea object...203
    getText() function..204
JTextField object..200
    addActionListener() function..................................201
    getText() function..201
language
    core library..19
    implementation..20
    semantics...19
    syntax..18
layout managers..180, 189
    BorderLayout..192
    BoxLayout...193
    FlowLayout..180, 190
    GridLayout..191
LinkedList object..226
    addFirst() function...227
    adding and removing nodes..226
    addLast() function..227
    getFirst() function...227
    getLast() function..227
List interface...224
    add() function..224
    get() function..224
    indexOf() function..224
    lastIndexOf() function..224

    remove() function...
    set() function..
listener interfaces, table of...
logical expressions...
    short circuiting..11
logical operators AND (&&), OR (||), NOT (!).........................112
machine language..13
main() function...34
    args parameter..98
mathematical operators..73
methods .... *See* functions
multi-dimensional array..221
My Projects directory...36
native program..21
NetBeans..27
null keyword..78
numeric data..67
Object Oriented Programming (OOP)....................................159
objects..159
    base class references..253, 254
    black box..160
    constructors...167
    data encapsulation...160
    derived class references...253
    identity vs. equality..257
    inheritance..160
    methods...161, 163
    modeling...159
    procedural abstraction...160
    properties..161, 162
    relationships..161
    uses-a, has-a, is-a relationships................................164
open-source...27
operator precedence..114
overriding methods...255
package keyword...42
packages..41
    directory structure..44
parentheses..114, 115
perspectives, switching between Java and Debug.......................155
pixel screen coordinates...176
polymorphism...255, 256
private keyword..165
program states...147
    in break...148
    running..147
program tracing...14
protected keyword...
public keyword...34, 1
recursion...
    exit conditions..
relational operators..
    <, <=, >, >=...

......224

......224

188

19

....111

....120, 135

.ine.......................................40

....100

....101

..ons 105

...on 102

...e() function 100

..itive data **next**() functions................102

..ching algorithms

binary search 245

sequential search 244

shortcut operators

++, -- 74

+=, -=, *=, /=, %= 73

software piracy 17

sorting algorithms..237

insertion sort 239

merge sort 241

selection sort 238

SortDemo program.......................................242

source code 14, 31

SpinnerNumberModel object....................205

statements...33

static keyword..............................35, 132, 172

static methods...173

static properties 172

String...78

character index 85

charAt() function....................................85

concatenation (appending) 92

contains() function 86

converting to number 94

equals() function.......................................83

format conversion characters 90

format flags 91

format precision option 91

format specifiers..88

format width option...89

format() function..88

indexOf() function 86

lastIndexOf() function 86

length() function 86

replace() function 86

substring() function 86

toString() function 93

toUpperCase(), **toLowerCase**() functions.......87

sub-class 160

super keyword...259

Swing graphical objects 175

Swing online tutorials.......................................176

System.out.println() function 35, 79

Terminal window 37

testing your code 157

text editor 26, 36

this keyword 163

upcasting 254

variables 69

assigning values 71

declaration...69

default values 72

initialization 73

naming rules..69

void keyword 35, 132

while keyword 124

while()

logical expression..125

while() loop..124

body in curly braces 125

white-space..33

working directory 30, 36

wrapper classes..75

parse() functions.......................................94

165

165

233

234

109

110

273